shredded lamb and pumpkin soup (recipe page 32)

SHREDDED LAMB AND PUMPKIN SOUP

prep + cook time 6 hours 30 minutes **serves** 4

½ cup (100g) dried brown lentils

3 french-trimmed lamb shanks (600g)

2 tablespoons moroccan seasoning

500g (1 pound) pumpkin, chopped coarsely

1 litre (4 cups) chicken stock

400g (12½ ounces) canned diced tomatoes

400g (12½ ounces) canned chickpeas
  (garbanzo beans), drained, rinsed

½ cup finely chopped fresh flat-leaf parsley

1 Rinse lentils under cold water until water runs clear; drain.

2 Combine lamb, seasoning, pumpkin, stock, tomatoes, chickpeas and lentils in a 4.5-litre (18-cup) slow cooker. Cook, covered, on low, for 6 hours.

3 Remove lamb from cooker. When cool enough to handle, remove meat from bones; shred coarsely. Discard bones. Return meat to cooker; season to taste. Serve sprinkled with parsley.

(photograph page 31)

nutritional count per serving
10.6g total fat
4.3g saturated fat
1614kJ (386 cal)
34.7g carbohydrate
34.1g protein
10.3g fibre

serving suggestion
Serve with a dollop of thick yoghurt and crusty bread.

to freeze Complete the recipe to the end of step 3. Pack into freezer-proof containers, leaving a 2.5cm (1 inch) space to allow for expansion. Seal, label and freeze for up to 3 months. Thaw overnight in the fridge. Reheat in a saucepan or microwave on medium power (50%) until heated through.

SPICY LENTIL SOUP

prep + cook time 6 hours 30 minutes **serves** 4

½ cup (100g) dried red lentils

2 small carrots (240g), chopped coarsely

1 stick celery (150g), trimmed, sliced thinly

2 medium potatoes (400g), chopped coarsely

3 cloves garlic, crushed

400g (12½ ounces) canned diced tomatoes

⅓ cup (100g) mild indian curry paste

1 litre (4 cups) chicken stock

2 dried bay leaves

½ cup (140g) Greek-style yoghurt

½ cup finely chopped fresh coriander (cilantro)

1 Rinse lentils under cold water until water runs clear; drain.

2 Combine lentils, carrot, celery, potato, garlic, tomatoes, paste, stock and bay leaves in a 4.5-litre (18-cup) slow cooker. Cook, covered, on low, for 6 hours. Season to taste.

3 Serve soup topped with yoghurt and coriander.

nutritional count per serving
12.5g total fat
3.4g saturated fat
1421kJ (340 cal)
36.2g carbohydrate
15.8g protein
10.9g fibre

to freeze Complete the recipe to the end of step 2. Pack into freezer-proof containers, leaving a 2.5cm (1 inch) space to allow for expansion. Seal, label and freeze for up to 3 months. Thaw overnight in the fridge. Reheat in a saucepan or microwave on medium power (50%) until heated through.

spicy lentil soup

COOK IT
SLOW

THE AUSTRALIAN
Women's Weekly

COOK IT
SLOW

BAUER

CONTENTS

ABOUT SLOW COOKING 6

EVERYDAY WEEKNIGHTS 12

FOR THE SLOW COOKER 14

FOR THE STOVE 64

FOR THE OVEN 112

ACCOMPANIMENTS - POTATOES & MASHES 172

FREEZER FRIENDLY 176

FOR THE SLOW COOKER 178

FOR THE STOVE 228

FOR THE OVEN 278

ACCOMPANIMENTS - RICE, COUSCOUS, GRAINS & PULSES 312

SPECIAL OCCASION 316

FOR THE SLOW COOKER 318

FOR THE STOVE 356

FOR THE OVEN 400

ACCOMPANIMENTS - VEGETABLES 466

STOCKS 470

GLOSSARY 472 | CONVERSION CHART 486 | INDEX 487

ABOUT SLOW COOKING

Some of the best things in life take time.
Casseroles and other slow-cooked meals are among them,
providing us with hearty, heavenly meals infused with
flavour and melt-in-your-mouth tenderness.

Whether it's a casserole, braise, pot roast,
curry or stew, slow-cooked foods are luxurious, flavourful and
heart-warming – and relished equally at a special-occasion
dinner party or as weeknight family fare.
They also freeze beautifully, giving you a wonderful
comforting meal at the ready. Just reheat and eat.

Slow cooking can be done in an
electric slow cooker, on the stove or in the oven.
All with the same delicious result.

SLOW-COOKING CUTS

Long, slow cooking will tenderise even the toughest cut of meat. Stewing or braising cuts are the best choices. Tough cuts are usually inexpensive, but cutting the meat off the bone yourself can usually save you more money, as you're not paying for the convenience of pre-cut meat. In addition to saving money, cutting up the meat yourself gives you the opportunity to trim off visible fat and make the pieces a uniform size. The best cuts of meat to use are:

BEEF topside, oyster, blade, skirt, round, chuck, gravy beef.

VEAL osso buco, shanks, shoulder.

LAMB neck chops, boneless shoulder, shanks, boneless forequarter.

PORK forequarter chops, neck, belly, shoulder.

CHICKEN any pieces on the bone, such as drumsticks, thighs, marylands.

OTHER TYPES OF MEAT secondary cuts of goat, venison, rabbit, hare, kangaroo.

SEAFOOD is generally not suitable as it toughens quickly. However; there are many recipes for sauces that can be cooked in the slow cooker, then just before serving, add the seafood. Large octopus will cook and become tender in a slow cooker.

BROWN THE MEAT FIRST

As straightforward as most slow cooking recipes are, it is best not to just throw all your ingredients in. Browning the meat first enhances the flavour and gives the meat a beautiful rich colour. Do this in a heated, oiled, large frying pan, adding the meat in batches, and turning it so that it browns evenly. Make sure there is a sufficient amount of oil in the pan so that the meat caramelises rather than scorches. Be sure to have the pan heated before adding the meat – it's also important to maintain the pan heat during the browning process. If the pan is not hot enough the meat will stew rather than brown.

If you're pushed for time the meat and/or vegetables can be browned the night before. Once everything is browned, put it in a sealable container, along with any juices, and refrigerate until the next day.

THICKENING THE SAUCE

Coating the meat in flour before browning will result in a sauce that is thick enough to make a light coating gravy. If the recipe does not suggest coating the meat, then it is a good idea to thicken the sauce using plain flour or cornflour.

Blending the flour or cornflour with butter or a cold liquid such as water or some of the cooled juices from the cooker, will help it combine with the cooking juices when stirred into the pan at the end of the cooking time. Put the lid back on and leave the sauce to thicken while the slow cooker is on the highest setting – this will take 10–20 minutes.

Another trick to thicken the sauce is to blend some of the vegetables until smooth, and then stir them into the cooking juices.

SLOW COOKERS

Slow cookers are available in a range of shapes and sizes and come with a host of features. We tested the slow-cooker recipes in this cookbook using a 4.5-litre (18-cup) slow cooker. If you have a smaller or larger cooker you will have to decrease or increase the quantity of food, and almost certainly the liquid content, in the recipes.

The first step when using your slow cooker is to read the manufacturer's instructions as each cooker will differ depending on its features. It will also outline appropriate safety measures, such as not leaving the appliance unattended at any time.

Some cookers heat from the base and side, while others heat just from the base; some have timers that cut off after the cooking time has expired, while others have timers that will keep the food warm by reducing the temperature until you're ready to eat. It is about finding what works best for you and your slow cooking needs.

A general rule of thumb is that high heat settings on a slow cooker will cook twice as fast as the lower setting.

SLOW COOKER SETTINGS

The longer the meat takes to cook, the more tender and more intense the flavours will be; so if you have the time, set your cooker to a low setting. If you're pressed for time, setting the slow cooker on high will halve the cooking time. No matter which setting you use, the food will reach simmering point. Some slow cookers have a warm setting, this is not used for cooking, but is used to maintain the temperature of the food until you're ready to eat.

HANDY HINT The high setting comes in handy when you need to add ingredients or to thicken the sauce at the end of the cooking time. Remove the lid and add the ingredients, or the mixture you are using to thicken the sauce, replace the lid and leave it on high for 10–20 minutes.

SAFETY

Always read the instruction manual of the appliance carefully.

Make sure the slow cooker sits securely on a flat surface well away from water, any heat source, curtains, walls, children and pets.

Treat the slow cooker like any other electrical appliance. The cord should be well away from any water or heat source, and not hanging on the floor, as someone might trip over it.

The metal parts of a slow cooker get very hot, so make sure no one touches them when the cooker is in use.

Never submerge the base of the slow cooker in water or any other liquid.

CLEANING

The slow cooker insert can be washed in hot soapy water.

Soaking the insert in warm water and then scrubbing with a plastic or nylon brush will help remove cooked-on food.

Check the manual first, but most slow cooker inserts are dishwasher-proof.

To clean the outside of the appliance, simply wipe down with a damp cloth and dry.

Don't use abrasives, scourers or chemicals to clean the cooker, as these can damage the surface.

Never put a hot insert into cold water as this can cause the insert to break.

LIFTING THE LID

As tempting as it is to check on your meal while it's cooking, lifting the lid constantly causes heat to escape and can set the cooking time back by up to half an hour each time.

DID YOU KNOW? The condensation that you can see on the lid of your slow cooker is the evaporation of moisture from the meat, sauce and vegetables. As this liquid evaporates it hits the lid, gently drips down onto the food and slowly bastes the meat as it cooks, ensuring perfectly tender meat and a rich sauce.

USING YOUR FAVOURITE RECIPES

Most of your favourite soup, stew, tagine and curry recipes are suitable for use in a slow cooker. You may need to adjust the liquid content to accommodate the long, slow cooking times, but once you get to know the cooker, the possibilities are endless. For best results use recipes that you would normally slow-cook, well covered, in an oven set at a low temperature.

LIQUID CONTENT

CASSEROLES, STEWS, CURRIES AND TAGINES As a general rule a slow cooker should be at least half full when cooking these dishes. Place the vegetables into the cooker, put the meat on top of the vegetables and then add the liquid.

SOUP This is one of the easiest dishes to prepare in a slow cooker; just make sure the cooker is at least half full.

ROASTS Whole pieces of meat or poultry used for roasting are sometimes cooked with minimal liquid content, especially if the meat is being cooked on a bed of vegetables. Sometimes a small quantity of liquid is added to make a sauce or gravy.

CORNED MEATS These meats are delicious when prepared in a slow cooker and are usually cooked in just enough liquid to barely cover them.

THE FAT FACTS

When cooking meats over a long period of time they can often produce a lot of fat, which you will need to remove. The best method is to refrigerate the food first; the fat will set on top of the liquid, and then it can be lifted off and discarded. If you don't have time to refrigerate the food before serving, then there are gadgets available in kitchen/cookware shops for removing fat: one is a type of 'brush' that sweeps away the fat; the other is a type of jug that separates the fat from the liquid. One of the easiest ways to remove fat is to soak it up using sheets of absorbent paper, gently placed over the surface of the food.

A NOTE ON DRIED BEANS

Some dry beans need to be cooked before adding to a slow cooker because of a certain chemical they contain. Kidney-shaped beans of all colours and sizes are related to each other and MUST be washed, drained and boiled in fresh water until tender. Add the cooked beans to the slow-cooked dish, just like canned beans.

Dried, unsoaked chickpeas and soya beans are fine to use in the slow cooker, just rinse them well first; there's no need for overnight soaking before cooking.

FREEZING LEFTOVERS

One of the best assets of the slow cooker is its ability to cook a large amount of food at once. This allows you to feed large groups of people or, alternatively, have leftovers that you can freeze for another time. If frozen properly, slow-cooked meals will keep for up to three months. There is usually a large quantity of liquid, so transfer the meat and vegetables to appropriate-sized freezer-friendly containers, then pour in enough of the liquid to cover the meat etc. Leave a 2.5cm (1 inch) space between the food and the lid to allow for expansion, then seal the container. Label and date the container before placing in the freezer.

HANDY HINT Any sauce that is left over can be frozen separately and used as a base for another recipe such as a soup or a sauce.

EVERYDAY WEEKNIGHTS

FOR THE SLOW COOKER

Slow cookers are the perfect kitchen tool to help you get a nutritious meal on the table during the busy week. All you have to do is prepare the ingredients, throw them in the cooker and let the appliance do the work. Feed your family and friends with one of these mouth-watering dishes without wasting hours in the kitchen.

SIMPLE BEEF AND VEGETABLE CASSEROLE

prep + cook time 8 hours 30 minutes **serves** 6

1.2kg (2½ pounds) beef chuck steak, chopped coarsely

⅓ cup (50g) plain (all-purpose) flour

¼ cup (60ml) olive oil

2 medium brown onions (300g), cut into thick wedges

2 medium carrots (240g), chopped coarsely

2 sticks celery (300g), trimmed, chopped coarsely

1 medium parsnip (250g), chopped coarsely

1 medium swede (225g), chopped coarsely

3 cloves garlic, crushed

¼ cup (70g) tomato paste

400g (12½ ounces) canned crushed tomatoes

1 cup (250ml) beef stock

2 bay leaves

10 sprigs fresh thyme

1 Coat beef in flour; shake off excess. Heat 2 tablespoons of the oil in a large frying pan; cook beef, in batches, until browned all over. Transfer beef to a 4.5-litre (18-cup) slow cooker.

2 Heat remaining oil in same pan; cook onion, carrot, celery, parsnip, swede and garlic, stirring, until onion softens. Add paste; cook, stirring, for 1 minute. Remove from heat; stir in tomatoes and stock.

3 Stir vegetable mixture and bay leaves into cooker; add thyme. Cook, covered, on low, for 8 hours. Discard bay leaves and thyme; season to taste. Accompany with crusty bread, if you like.

nutritional count per serving
18.7g total fat
5.2g saturated fat
1827kJ (437 cal)
19.3g carbohydrate
44.9g protein
5.9g fibre

tips Gravy beef can be used instead of chuck steak. The swede and parsnip used in this stew give it a particularly thick, hearty quality. Use any vegetables you like – turnip, celeriac, jerusalem artichokes are all good choices.

to freeze Pack into freezer-proof containers, leaving a 2.5cm (1 inch) space to allow for expansion. Seal, label and freeze for up to 3 months. Thaw overnight in the fridge. Reheat in a saucepan or microwave on medium power (50%) until heated through.

CHILLI CON CARNE

prep + cook time 8 hours 45 minutes **serves** 6

1 tablespoon olive oil

1 large brown onion (200g), chopped finely

2 cloves garlic, crushed

750g (1½ pounds) minced (ground) beef

1 teaspoon ground cumin

1½ teaspoons dried chilli flakes

1 cup (250ml) beef stock

⅓ cup (95g) tomato paste

820g (1¾ pounds) canned crushed tomatoes

1 tablespoon finely chopped fresh oregano

800g (1½ pounds) canned kidney beans,
  drained, rinsed

½ cup loosely packed fresh coriander (cilantro) leaves

6 flour tortillas, warmed

1   Heat oil in a large frying pan; cook onion and garlic, stirring, until onion softens. Add beef, cumin and chilli; cook, stirring, until browned. Transfer to a 4.5-litre (18-cup) slow cooker. Stir in stock, paste, tomatoes and oregano. Cook, covered, on low, for 8 hours.

2   Add beans; cook, covered, on high, for 30 minutes or until hot. Season to taste.

3   Sprinkle chilli con carne with coriander leaves; serve with tortillas.

nutritional count per serving
14.8g total fat
5.4g saturated fat
1743kJ (417 cal)
30.9g carbohydrate
35.1g protein
9.5g fibre

serving suggestion
Serve topped with a dollop of sour cream; accompany with steamed rice and a green leafy salad.

to freeze Complete the recipe to the end of step 2. Pack into freezer-proof containers, leaving a 2.5cm (1 inch) space to allow for expansion. Seal, label and freeze for up to 3 months. Thaw overnight in the fridge. Reheat in a saucepan or microwave on medium power (50%) until heated through.

POACHED CHICKEN WITH SOY AND SESAME

prep + cook time 6 hours 30 minutes **serves** 4

1.6kg (3¼-pound) whole chicken

5cm (2-inch) piece fresh ginger (25g), sliced thinly

4 cloves garlic, halved

2 whole star anise

2 cinnamon sticks

1 cup (250ml) light soy sauce

1 cup (250ml) chinese cooking wine (shao hsing)

⅓ cup (75g) white (granulated) sugar

1 litre (4 cups) water

⅓ cup (80ml) light soy sauce, extra

2 teaspoons sesame oil

2.5cm (1-inch) piece fresh ginger (15g),
  cut into matchsticks

2 cloves garlic, cut into matchsticks

2 fresh long red chillies, sliced thinly

⅓ cup (80ml) peanut oil

4 green onions (scallions), sliced thinly

½ cup loosely packed fresh coriander (cilantro) leaves

1 Trim excess fat from chicken. Place chicken in a 4.5-litre (18-cup) slow cooker. Add sliced ginger, halved garlic, star anise, cinnamon, sauce, wine, sugar and the water to the cooker. Cook, covered, on low, for 6 hours. Remove chicken from cooker; discard poaching liquid.

2 Cut chicken into 12 pieces; place on a heatproof platter. Drizzle extra sauce and sesame oil over chicken; sprinkle with ginger and garlic matchsticks and chilli.

3 Heat peanut oil in a small saucepan, over medium heat, until very hot; carefully drizzle over chicken. Top with onion and coriander.

nutritional count per serving
52.9g total fat
13.7g saturated fat
3361kJ (804 cal)
22.7g carbohydrate
45.5g protein
1.5g fibre

serving suggestion
Serve with steamed rice
or noodles.

tip Chinese cooking wine
is also known as chinese
rice wine; dry sherry can be
used instead.

to freeze Complete the
recipe to the end of step 1.
Pack into freezer-proof
containers, leaving a 2.5cm
(1 inch) space to allow for
expansion. Seal, label and
freeze for up to 3 months.
Thaw overnight in the fridge.
Reheat in a saucepan or
microwave on medium power
(50%) until heated through.

SHREDDED BEEF TACOS

prep + cook time 6 hours 20 minutes **makes** 6

1kg (2-pound) piece beef chuck steak

¼ teaspoon chilli powder

1 teaspoon ground cumin

1 teaspoon ground coriander

1 teaspoon smoked paprika

1 cup (250ml) beef stock

2 tablespoons tomato paste

1 fresh long red chilli, sliced thinly

2 cloves garlic, crushed

6 large flour tortillas, warmed

1. Rub beef with combined spices; place in a 4.5-litre (18-cup) slow cooker. Pour over combined stock, paste, chilli and garlic. Cook, covered, on low, for 6 hours.

2. Remove beef from cooker. When cool enough to handle, shred meat coarsely using two forks. Discard half the liquid from slow cooker. Return meat to cooker; season to taste.

3. Serve shredded beef in tortillas.

nutritional count per serving
8.2g total fat
2.5g saturated fat
1354kJ (324 cal)
18.9g carbohydrate
42.4g protein
1.6g fibre

serving suggestion
Serve with guacamole, shredded lettuce, tomato salsa, grated cheese, sour cream and fresh coriander (cilantro) leaves.

to freeze Complete the recipe to the end of step 2. Pack into freezer-proof containers, leaving a 2.5cm (1 inch) space to allow for expansion. Seal, label and freeze for up to 3 months. Thaw overnight in the fridge. Reheat in a saucepan or microwave on medium power (50%) until heated through.

*As the temperature drops, our minds turn
to wintry comfort foods. The slow cooker comes out
of its summer hiding place in the back
of the cupboard and finds its new home on
the kitchen bench in preparation for
the cooler months ahead.*

MOROCCAN LAMB WITH KUMARA AND RAISINS

prep + cook time 6 hours 25 minutes **serves** 6

2 tablespoons olive oil

1.2kg (2½ pounds) boned lamb shoulder, chopped coarsely

1 large brown onion (200g), sliced thickly

4 cloves garlic, crushed

2 tablespoons ras el hanout

2 cups (500ml) chicken stock

½ cup (125ml) water

1 tablespoon honey

2 medium kumara (orange sweet potato) (800g), chopped coarsely

400g (12½ ounces) canned chickpeas (garbanzo beans), drained, rinsed

1 cinnamon stick

3 cardamom pods, bruised

⅓ cup (50g) raisins, halved

½ cup loosely packed fresh coriander (cilantro) leaves

⅓ cup (55g) coarsely chopped blanched almonds, roasted

1 Heat half the oil in a large frying pan; cook lamb, in batches, until browned all over. Remove from pan.

2 Heat remaining oil in same pan; cook onion and garlic, stirring, until onion is soft. Add ras el hanout; cook, stirring, until fragrant. Remove from heat; stir in stock, the water and honey.

3 Place kumara in a 4.5-litre (18-cup) slow cooker; stir in chickpeas, cinnamon, cardamom, lamb and onion mixture. Cook, covered, on low, for 6 hours.

4 Stir in raisins and coriander; season to taste. Serve sprinkled with nuts.

nutritional count per serving
30.5g total fat
9.7g saturated fat
2567kJ (614 cal)
34.9g carbohydrate
47.2g protein
6.3g fibre

serving suggestion
Serve with buttered couscous and steamed baby green beans.

tip Ras el hanout is a blend of Moroccan spices available in delis and specialist food stores. If you can't find it, use a moroccan seasoning available in supermarkets.

to freeze Complete the recipe to the end of step 3. Pack into freezer-proof containers, leaving a 2.5cm (1 inch) space to allow for expansion. Seal, label and freeze for up to 3 months. Thaw overnight in the fridge. Reheat in a saucepan or microwave on medium power (50%) until heated through.

lamb and potato stew with spinach

LAMB AND POTATO STEW WITH SPINACH

prep + cook time 6 hours 20 minutes **serves** 6

3 medium potatoes (600g), unpeeled,
  cut into thick wedges
2 large brown onions (400g), sliced thickly
2 large carrots (360g), sliced thickly
4 cloves garlic, sliced thinly
1.2kg (2½ pounds) boned lamb leg,
  chopped coarsely
1½ cups (375ml) chicken stock
1⅔ cups (410g) canned tomato puree
4 sprigs fresh thyme
60g (2 ounces) baby spinach leaves

1 Place potato, onion, carrot, garlic and lamb in a
   4.5-litre (18-cup) slow cooker; stir in stock, puree
   and thyme. Cook, covered, on low, for 6 hours.
2 Discard thyme. Stir in spinach leaves; season
   to taste.

nutritional count per serving
11.4g total fat
4.9g saturated fat
1676kJ (401 cal)
21.6g carbohydrate
49.6g protein
5.9g fibre

serving suggestion
Serve with steamed green
vegetables and crusty bread.

not suitable to freeze

PORTUGUESE CLADEIRADA

prep + cook time 4 hours 30 minutes **serves** 6

2 tablespoons olive oil
2 large brown onions (400g), sliced thickly
3 medium red capsicums (bell peppers) (600g),
  sliced thickly
1kg (2 pounds) potatoes, sliced thickly
1 cup (250ml) dry white wine
½ cup (125ml) water
800g (1½ pounds) thick white fish fillets,
  chopped coarsely
2 tablespoons olive oil, extra

1 Pour olive oil into a 4.5-litre (18-cup) slow cooker;
   layer onion, capsicum and potato in cooker,
   seasoning between each layer. Add wine and
   the water. Cook, covered, on high, for 3½ hours.
2 Add fish to cooker, season to taste; spoon
   vegetable mixture over fish. Cook, covered,
   on high, for 30 minutes.
3 Serve drizzled with extra oil; accompany with
   crusty bread, if you like.

(photograph page 30)

nutritional count per serving
15.4g total fat
2.6g saturated fat
1689kJ (404 cal)
24.6g carbohydrate
32.7g protein
3.9g fibre

tips Cladeirada is a
Portuguese fish stew. It
varies from region to region,
but usually contains a
variety of fish (and shellfish),
along with potato, onion
and tomato, or capsicum,
as we use here. It is similar
to the French seafood stew,
bouillabaisse.
You can use any firm white
fish you like; choose large
pieces. We used angel and
monk fish.

not suitable to freeze

portuguese cladeirada (recipe page 29)

OLD-FASHIONED CURRIED SAUSAGES

prep + cook time 8 hours 20 minutes **serves** 6

12 thick beef sausages (1.8kg)

1 tablespoon vegetable oil

2 medium brown onions (300g), sliced thinly

2 tablespoons mild curry powder

400g (12½ ounces) canned diced tomatoes

1 cup (250ml) beef stock

1 cup (250ml) water

4 medium potatoes (800g), unpeeled,
  cut into thick wedges

1 cup (120g) frozen peas, thawed

½ cup (80g) sultanas

1 Place sausages in a large saucepan, add enough cold water to cover sausages; bring to the boil. Boil, uncovered, for 2 minutes; drain.

2 Heat oil in same pan; cook onion, stirring, until softened. Add curry powder; cook, stirring, until fragrant. Remove from heat; stir in tomatoes, stock and the water.

3 Place potatoes in a 4.5-litre (18-cup) slow cooker; top with sausages and tomato mixture. Cook, covered, on low, for 8 hours.

4 Stir in peas and sultanas. Season to taste.

nutritional count per serving
79.8g total fat
37g saturated fat
4435kJ (1061 cal)
40g carbohydrate
41.3g protein
13.7g fibre

serving suggestion
Serve with steamed rice
or couscous.

not suitable to freeze

JERK-SPICED CHICKEN DRUMSTICKS

prep + cook time 4 hours 30 minutes **serves** 4

2 tablespoons olive oil

8 chicken drumsticks (1.2kg)

4 green onions (scallions), chopped coarsely

5cm (2-inch) piece fresh ginger (25g), grated

1½ teaspoons ground allspice

½ teaspoon ground cinnamon

2 fresh long green chillies, chopped coarsely

1 teaspoon cracked black pepper

2 cloves garlic, crushed

3 teaspoons finely chopped fresh thyme

2 tablespoons light brown sugar

1 tablespoon cider vinegar

2 tablespoons orange juice

1 Heat half the oil in a large frying pan; cook chicken, turning, until browned all over. Place chicken in a 4.5-litre (18-cup) slow cooker.

2 Meanwhile, process onion, ginger, spices, chilli, pepper, garlic, thyme and remaining oil until finely chopped. Add sugar, vinegar and juice; process until smooth. Pour paste over chicken. Cook, covered, on low, for 4 hours. Season to taste.

3 Serve chicken with sauce; sprinkle with extra thyme, if you like.

nutritional count per serving
30.1g total fat
7.6g saturated fat
1831kJ (438 cal)
8.2g carbohydrate
33.9g protein
0.9g fibre

serving suggestion
Serve with steamed green beans, rice and lime wedges.

to freeze Complete the recipe to the end of step 2. Pack into freezer-proof containers, leaving a 2.5cm (1 inch) space to allow for expansion. Seal, label and freeze for up to 3 months. Thaw overnight in the fridge. Reheat in a saucepan or microwave on medium power (50%) until heated through.

FRENCH ONION LAMB CHOPS

prep + cook time 6 hours 30 minutes **serves** 12

12 lamb forequarter chops (2.2kg)

2 tablespoons plain (all-purpose) flour

2 tablespoons olive oil

80g (2½ ounces) packaged french onion soup mix

2 medium leeks (700g), sliced thinly

3 sticks celery (450g), trimmed, chopped coarsely

2 cups (500ml) salt-reduced chicken stock

¼ cup coarsely chopped fresh flat-leaf parsley

1 Trim excess fat from lamb. Toss lamb in flour to coat, shake off excess. Heat oil in a large frying pan; cook lamb, in batches, until browned.

2 Place 4 lamb chops into a 4.5-litre (18-cup) slow cooker. Sprinkle one-third of the soup mix then one-third of the leek and celery over the chops. Repeat layering with remaining lamb, soup mix, leek and celery. Pour stock into cooker. Cook, covered, on low, for 6 hours.

3 Remove lamb from cooker; cover to keep warm. Skim fat from surface of sauce; season to taste. Serve lamb and sauce sprinkled with parsley.

nutritional count per serving
8.9g total fat
3.2g saturated fat
816kJ (195 cal)
5.8g carbohydrate
21.7g protein
2.2g fibre

serving suggestion
Serve with mashed potatoes and steamed green beans.

tip Lamb shoulder chops and chump chops are also suitable for this recipe.

to freeze Pack chops into freezer-proof containers; pour sauce over the chops, leaving a 2.5cm (1 inch) space to allow for expansion. Seal, label and freeze for up to 3 months. Thaw overnight in the fridge. Reheat in a saucepan or microwave on medium power (50%) until heated through.

PEA AND HAM SOUP

prep + cook time 8 hours 20 minutes **serves** 6

2½ cups (500g) green split peas

1 tablespoon olive oil

1 large brown onion (200g), chopped finely

3 cloves garlic, crushed

1 ham hock (1kg)

2 medium carrots (240g), chopped finely

2 sticks celery (300g), trimmed, chopped finely

4 fresh thyme sprigs

2 bay leaves

2 litres (8 cups) water

1   Rinse peas under cold water until water runs clear; drain.

2   Heat oil in large frying pan; cook onion and garlic, stirring, until onion softens. Place onion mixture into a 4.5-litre (18-cup) slow cooker; stir in peas and remaining ingredients. Cook, covered, on low, for 8 hours.

3   Remove ham from cooker. When cool enough to handle, remove meat from bone; shred coarsely, return meat to slow cooker. Discard skin, fat and bone. Season to taste.

nutritional count per serving
6.4g total fat
1.2g saturated fat
1517kJ (363 cal)
43g carbohydrate
27.3g protein
11g fibre

serving suggestion
Serve topped with Greek-style yoghurt, chopped fresh mint leaves and sliced green onions (scallions).

to freeze Complete the recipe to the end of step 2. Pack into freezer-proof containers, leaving a 2.5cm (1 inch) space to allow for expansion. Seal, label and freeze for up to 3 months. Thaw overnight in the fridge. Reheat in a saucepan or microwave on medium power (50%) until heated through.

LAMB BIRYANI-STYLE

prep + cook time 9 hours **serves** 8

40g (1½ ounces) ghee

½ cup (40g) flaked almonds

2 large brown onions (400g), sliced thinly

1 tablespoon vegetable oil

1.2kg (2½ pounds) boneless lamb shoulder,
  chopped coarsely

20g (¾ ounce) ghee, extra

4 cloves garlic, crushed

5cm (2-inch) piece fresh ginger (25g), grated

2 fresh long green chillies, sliced thinly

3 teaspoons garam masala

2 teaspoons ground cumin

2 teaspoons ground coriander

¾ cup (200g) Greek-style yoghurt

½ cup coarsely chopped fresh coriander (cilantro)

¼ cup coarsely chopped fresh mint

1 litre (4 cups) water

pinch saffron threads

2 tablespoons hot milk

2 cups (400g) basmati rice

1 lime, cut into wedges

½ cup loosely packed fresh coriander (cilantro) leaves

1   Heat half the ghee in a large frying pan; cook nuts, stirring, until browned lightly. Remove from pan. Heat remaining ghee in same pan; cook onion, stirring, for 10 minutes or until soft and browned lightly. Remove from pan.

2   Heat oil in same pan; cook lamb, in batches, until browned. Transfer to a 4.5-litre (18-cup) slow cooker. Heat extra ghee in same pan; cook garlic, ginger, chilli and spices, stirring, until fragrant. Remove from heat; stir in yoghurt, chopped herbs and half the onion mixture. Transfer to cooker with half the water. Cook, covered, on low, for 8 hours. Season to taste.

3   Meanwhile, sprinkle saffron over hot milk in a small bowl; stand for 15 minutes.

4   Wash rice under cold water until water runs clear; drain. Combine rice and the remaining water in a medium saucepan, cover; bring to the boil. Reduce heat; simmer, covered, for 8 minutes or until rice is tender. Season to taste.

5   Spoon rice over lamb in cooker; drizzle with milk mixture. Top with remaining onion mixture and nuts; cook, covered, for 30 minutes or until heated through.

6   Serve with lime wedges; top with coriander leaves.

nutritional count per serving
24.2g total fat
11.2g saturated fat
2307kJ (552 cal)
45.2g carbohydrate
36.8g protein
2.1g fibre

serving suggestion
Serve with raita (a minted yoghurt and cucumber dish).

note Biryani is a rice-based dish made with spices and meat, chicken, fish or vegetables. There are many versions available as this recipe is a favourite across the Middle-East and India.

not suitable to freeze

EGGPLANT PARMIGIANA

prep + cook time 6 hours 45 minutes **serves** 4

⅔ cup (160ml) olive oil

1 medium brown onion (150g), chopped finely

2 cloves garlic, crushed

400g (12½ ounces) canned diced tomatoes

1 cup (260g) bottled tomato pasta sauce

¼ teaspoon dried chilli flakes

2 medium eggplants (600g), sliced thickly

¼ cup (35g) plain (all-purpose) flour

⅓ cup loosely packed fresh basil leaves

200g (6½ ounces) bocconcini cheese, sliced thinly

⅔ cup (50g) finely grated parmesan cheese

½ teaspoon sweet paprika

1 Heat 1 tablespoon of the oil in a large frying pan; cook onion, stirring, until onion softens. Add garlic; cook, stirring, until fragrant. Stir in tomatoes, sauce and chilli. Transfer to medium jug.

2 Toss eggplant in flour to coat, dust off excess. Heat remaining oil in same pan; cook eggplant, in batches, until browned. Drain on absorbent paper.

3 Layer half the eggplant in a 4.5-litre (18-cup) slow cooker; season to taste. Top with half the tomato mixture, basil and bocconcini. Repeat layering, finishing with parmesan. Sprinkle with paprika. Cook, covered, on low, for 6 hours.

nutritional count per serving
49.9g total fat
12.8g saturated fat
2562kJ (613 cal)
20.6g carbohydrate
18.5g protein
7.2g fibre

serving suggestion
Serve with crusty bread and a rocket (arugula) salad.

to freeze Pack into freezer-proof containers, leaving a 2.5cm (1 inch) space to allow for expansion. Seal, label and freeze for up to 3 months. Thaw overnight in the fridge. Reheat in a saucepan or microwave on medium power (50%) until heated through.

BARBECUED AMERICAN-STYLE PORK RIBS

prep + cook time 4 hours 30 minutes (+ refrigeration) **serves** 4

2kg (4 pounds) american-style pork ribs

½ cup (140g) barbecue sauce

½ cup (140g) tomato sauce (ketchup)

½ cup (125ml) cider vinegar

¼ cup (85g) orange marmalade

3 cloves garlic, crushed

½ teaspoon chilli flakes

1 Cut pork into pieces to fit into a 4.5-litre (18-cup) slow cooker. Combine remaining ingredients in a large shallow dish; add pork, turn to coat in marinade. Cover; refrigerate mixture overnight.

2 Transfer pork and marinade to the slow cooker; cook, covered, on high, for 4 hours. Turn ribs twice during cooking time for even cooking.

3 Carefully remove ribs from cooker; cover to keep warm. Transfer sauce to a large frying pan; bring to the boil. Reduce heat; simmer, uncovered, skimming fat from surface, for 10 minutes or until sauce has reduced to about 1¾ cups. Season to taste. Serve pork drizzled with sauce.

nutritional count per serving
10.6g total fat
3.8g saturated fat
1860kJ (445 cal)
38.2g carbohydrate
48.6g protein
1.7g fibre

serving suggestion
Serve with steamed rice and lime wedges.

tip Ask the butcher to cut the ribs so that they will fit into your slow cooker.

to freeze Pack into freezer-proof containers, leaving a 2.5cm (1 inch) space to allow for expansion. Seal, label and freeze for up to 3 months. Thaw overnight in the fridge. Reheat in a saucepan or microwave on medium power (50%) until heated through.

CHICKEN, CELERIAC AND BROAD BEAN CASSEROLE

prep + cook time 4 hours **serves** 6

1.5kg (3 pounds) chicken thigh fillets

2 tablespoons plain (all-purpose) flour

2 tablespoons vegetable oil

20g (¾ ounce) butter

1 large brown onion (200g), chopped coarsely

2 medium carrots (240g), sliced thickly

2 stalks celery (300g), trimmed, chopped coarsely

2 cloves garlic, chopped finely

2 cups (500ml) chicken stock

2 tablespoons dijon mustard

1 medium celeriac (celery root) (750g), chopped coarsely

2 cups (300g) frozen broad beans (fava beans)

½ cup (50g) walnuts, roasted, chopped coarsely

¼ cup coarsely chopped pale celery leaves

1   Toss chicken in flour to coat, shake off excess. Reserve excess flour. Heat oil in a large frying pan; cook chicken, in batches, until browned. Remove from pan. Wipe pan with absorbent paper.

2   Heat butter in same pan; cook onion, carrot and celery, stirring, until softened. Add garlic; cook, stirring, until fragrant. Stir in reserved excess flour, then stock and mustard; stir over high heat until mixture boils and thickens.

3   Place celeriac in a 4.5-litre (18-cup) slow cooker; top with chicken then onion mixture. Cook, covered, on high, 3 hours.

4   Meanwhile, place broad beans in a medium heatproof bowl, cover with boiling water; stand 2 minutes, drain. Peel away grey skins.

5   Add broad beans to cooker; cook, covered, on high, 30 minutes. Season to taste.

6   Serve sprinkled with nuts and celery leaves.

nutritional count per serving
33.4g total fat
8.6g saturated fat
2504kJ (599 cal)
16.3g carbohydrate
54.6g protein
9.8g fibre

tip Roast the walnuts, in a preheated 180°C/350°F oven, for 5 minutes or until browned lightly.

to freeze Complete the recipe to the end of step 3. Pack into freezer-proof containers, leaving a 2.5cm (1 inch) space to allow for expansion. Seal, label and freeze for up to 3 months. Thaw overnight in the fridge. Reheat in a saucepan or microwave on medium power (50%) until heated through, then continue from step 4.

LEMON GRASS AND PORK CURRY

prep + cook time 6 hours 30 minutes **serves** 6

2 x 10cm (4-inch) sticks fresh lemon grass (40g), chopped coarsely

3 cloves garlic, quartered

4cm (1½-inch) piece fresh galangal (20g), sliced thinly

1 fresh small red thai (serrano) chilli, chopped coarsely

1 teaspoon ground turmeric

½ teaspoon ground cumin

¼ teaspoon ground cardamom

3 fresh kaffir lime leaves, shredded thinly

1 medium red onion (170g), chopped coarsely

½ cup (125ml) water

1 tablespoon peanut oil

1.2kg (2½ pounds) pork neck, chopped coarsely

800ml (3⅓ cups) canned coconut milk

3 baby eggplants (180g), sliced thickly

375g (12 ounces) baby carrots, halved lengthways

1 tablespoon fish sauce

2 tablespoons lime juice

½ cup loosely packed fresh coriander (cilantro) leaves

1   Blend or process lemon grass, garlic, galangal, chilli, spices, lime leaves, onion and the water until mixture is smooth.

2   Heat oil in a medium frying pan; cook lemon grass paste, stirring, for 5 minutes or until fragrant.

3   Transfer lemon grass paste to a 4.5-litre (18-cup) slow cooker; stir in pork, coconut milk and eggplant. Cook, covered, on low, for 4 hours.

4   Add carrots; cook, covered, on low, for 2 hours. Stir in sauce and juice; season to taste. Serve sprinkled with coriander.

nutritional count per serving
46.9g total fat
30.2g saturated fat
2759kJ (660 cal)
10.9g carbohydrate
46.6g protein
5.8g fibre

serving suggestion
Serve with steamed rice.

not suitable to freeze

ITALIAN CHICKEN SOUP

prep + cook time 9 hours **serves** 6

1.5kg (3-pound) whole chicken

3 large tomatoes (650g)

1 medium brown onion (150g), chopped coarsely

2 sticks celery (300g), trimmed, chopped coarsely

1 large carrot (180g), chopped coarsely

2 dried bay leaves

4 cloves garlic, halved

6 black peppercorns

2 litres (8 cups) water

¾ cup (155g) risoni pasta

½ cup coarsely chopped fresh flat-leaf parsley

½ cup coarsely chopped fresh basil

2 tablespoons finely chopped fresh oregano

¼ cup (60ml) fresh lemon juice

1 Remove then discard as much skin as possible from chicken. Chop 1 tomato coarsely. Chop remaining tomatoes finely; refrigerate, covered, until required.

2 Place chicken, coarsely chopped tomato, onion, celery, carrot, bay leaves, garlic, peppercorns and the water in a 4.5-litre (18-cup) slow cooker. Cook, covered, on low, for 8 hours.

3 Carefully remove chicken from cooker. Strain broth through a fine sieve into a large heatproof bowl; discard solids. Skim and discard any fat from broth. Return broth to cooker; add risoni and finely chopped tomatoes. Cook, covered, on high, for 30 minutes or until risoni is tender.

4 Meanwhile, when cool enough to handle, remove meat from bones; shred coarsely. Discard bones. Add chicken, herbs and juice to soup; cook, covered, on high, for 5 minutes. Season to taste.

nutritional count per serving
14.1g total fat
4.4g saturated fat
1555kJ (372 cal)
21.7g carbohydrate
37g protein
4.5g fibre

to freeze Complete the recipe to the end of step 2. Pack into freezer-proof containers, leaving a 2.5cm (1 inch) space to allow for expansion. Seal, label and freeze for up to 3 months. Thaw overnight in the fridge. Reheat in a saucepan or microwave on medium power (50%) until heated through, then continue from step 3.

SPICY TOMATO AND SAFFRON CHICKEN CASSEROLE

prep + cook time 6 hours 25 minutes **serves** 6

¼ cup (35g) plain (all-purpose) flour

2 tablespoons moroccan seasoning

6 chicken thigh cutlets (1.2kg)

1 tablespoon vegetable oil

1 large brown onion (200g), sliced thickly

2 cloves garlic, crushed

2.5cm (1-inch) piece fresh ginger (15g), grated

1 fresh long red chilli, sliced thinly

2 cups (500ml) chicken stock

400g (12½ ounces) canned diced tomatoes

¼ cup (70g) tomato paste

¼ teaspoon saffron threads

PRESERVED LEMON GREMOLATA

⅓ cup finely chopped fresh flat-leaf parsley

1 tablespoon thinly sliced preserved lemon rind

1 clove garlic, crushed

1 Combine flour and 1 tablespoon of the seasoning in a small shallow bowl; toss chicken in flour mixture to coat, shake off excess. Heat half the oil in a large frying pan; cook chicken, in batches, until browned. Transfer to a 4.5-litre (18-cup) slow cooker.

2 Heat remaining oil in same pan, add onion, garlic, ginger, chilli and remaining seasoning; cook, stirring, until onion softens. Add ½ cup of the stock; cook, stirring, until mixture boils.

3 Stir onion mixture into cooker with remaining stock, tomatoes, paste and saffron. Cook, covered, on low, for 6 hours. Season to taste.

4 Before serving, make preserved lemon gremolata.

5 Sprinkle casserole with gremolata.

PRESERVED LEMON GREMOLATA Combine ingredients in a small bowl.

nutritional count per serving
23.8g total fat
7.2g saturated fat
1522kJ (364 cal)
10.2g carbohydrate
26.5g protein
2.5g fibre

serving suggestion
Serve with steamed rice or couscous.

tip Preserved lemon is available at delicatessens and some supermarkets. Remove and discard the flesh, wash the rind, then use it as the recipe directs.

to freeze Complete the recipe to the end of step 3. Pack into freezer-proof containers, leaving a 2.5cm (1 inch) space to allow for expansion. Seal, label and freeze for up to 3 months. Thaw overnight in the fridge. Reheat in a saucepan or microwave on medium power (50%) until heated through, then continue from step 4.

CREAMY VEGETABLE AND ALMOND KORMA

prep + cook time 6 hours 45 minutes **serves** 6

½ cup (150g) korma paste

½ cup (60g) ground almonds

1 large brown onion (200g), sliced thinly

2 cloves garlic, crushed

½ cup (125ml) vegetable stock

½ cup (125ml) water

300ml (½ pint) pouring cream

375g (12 ounces) baby carrots

125g (4 ounces) baby corn

500g (1 pound) baby potatoes, halved

375g (12 ounces) pumpkin, chopped coarsely

315g (10 ounces) cauliflower, cut into florets

6 medium yellow patty-pan squash (180g), halved

½ cup (60g) frozen peas

½ cup (70g) roasted slivered almonds

2 teaspoons black sesame seeds

1 Combine paste, ground almonds, onion, garlic, stock, the water, cream, carrots, corn, potato, pumpkin and cauliflower in a 4.5-litre (18-cup) slow cooker. Cook, covered, on low, for 6 hours.

2 Add squash and peas; cook, covered, on high, for 20 minutes. Season to taste. Serve curry, sprinkled with slivered almonds and seeds.

nutritional count per serving
42.8g total fat
16.2g saturated fat
2429kJ (581 cal)
29.6g carbohydrate
14.4g protein
12.4g fibre

serving suggestion
Serve with steamed rice, naan and yoghurt.

tip This is a mild curry. For more heat, serve curry sprinkled with some sliced fresh red chilli.

to freeze Complete the recipe to the end of step 1. Pack into freezer-proof containers, leaving a 2.5cm (1 inch) space to allow for expansion. Seal, label and freeze for up to 3 months. Thaw overnight in the fridge. Reheat in a saucepan or microwave on medium power (50%) until heated through, then continue from step 2.

CREAMY TURKEY STEW WITH MUSTARD

prep + cook time 2 hours 30 minutes **serves** 8

4 turkey drumsticks (3kg), skin removed

2 tablespoons olive oil

375g (12 ounces) button mushrooms

2 medium leeks (700g), sliced thickly

4 rindless bacon slices (260g), chopped coarsely

2 cloves garlic, crushed

2 tablespoons plain (all-purpose) flour

1 cup (250ml) chicken stock

½ cup (125ml) dry white wine

2 tablespoons wholegrain mustard

6 sprigs fresh lemon thyme

½ cup (125ml) pouring cream

2 teaspoons fresh lemon thyme leaves

1 Using a sharp heavy knife, cut turkey meat from bones, chop meat coarsely; discard bones.

2 Heat oil in a large frying pan; cook turkey, in batches, until browned all over. Transfer turkey to a 4.5-litre (18-cup) slow cooker.

3 Cook mushrooms, leek, bacon and garlic in same frying pan, stirring, until leek softens. Add flour; cook, stirring, for 1 minute. Stir in stock, wine, mustard and thyme sprigs; bring to the boil. Boil, uncovered, for 2 minutes. Remove from heat; stir in cream. Transfer mushroom mixture to cooker. Cook, covered, on low, for 2 hours.

4 Season to taste; sprinkle with thyme leaves.

nutritional count per serving
23.2g total fat
8.8g saturated fat
1914kJ (458 cal)
5.3g carbohydrate
53.2g protein
3.1g fibre

serving suggestion
Serve with mashed potato and steamed green beans.

tip Use 3kg (6 pounds) turkey marylands if you can't get drumsticks.

not suitable to freeze

CROISSANT CUSTARD PUDDING WITH STRAWBERRIES

prep + cook time 3 hours 15 minutes (+ standing) **serves** 8

4 croissants (200g)

½ cup (160g) strawberry jam

80g (2½ ounces) white eating chocolate, chopped finely

2½ cups (625ml) milk

600ml (1 pint) pouring cream

½ cup (110g) caster (superfine) sugar

1 teaspoon vanilla extract

6 eggs

MACERATED STRAWBERRIES

250g (8 ounces) strawberries, halved

1 tablespoon orange-flavoured liqueur

1 tablespoon icing (confectioners') sugar

1 Grease a 4.5-litre (18-cup) slow cooker bowl.

2 Split croissants in half; spread cut-sides with jam. Sprinkle chocolate over half the croissants; sandwich croissants together. Arrange croissants in cooker.

3 Bring milk, cream, sugar and extract to the boil in a medium saucepan. Whisk eggs in a large bowl; gradually whisk in hot milk mixture. Pour custard over croissants; stand for 10 minutes.

4 Cook, covered, on low, for 2¾ hours, or until firm (do not lift the lid during the cooking process, see tip).

5 Meanwhile, make macerated strawberries.

6 Remove the bowl from the cooker. Stand pudding for 5 minutes before serving. Serve pudding with macerated strawberries and drizzled with a little extra cream.

MACERATED STRAWBERRIES Combine ingredients in a medium bowl; stand for 30 minutes.

nutritional count per serving
44.7g total fat
28.8g saturated fat
2658kJ (636 cal)
51.4g carbohydrate
7.9g protein
1.7g fibre

serving suggestion
Serve with ice-cream.

tip It's important not to lift the lid while the pudding is cooking, as the condensation will run down the side of the cooker and cause damp patches on the pudding.

not suitable to freeze

CHOCOLATE SELF-SAUCING PUDDING

prep + cook time 2 hours 50 minutes **serves** 6

90g (3 ounces) butter

¾ cup (180ml) milk

1 teaspoon vanilla extract

1 cup (220g) caster (superfine) sugar

1½ cups (225g) self-raising flour

2 tablespoons cocoa powder

1 egg, beaten lightly

1 cup (220g) firmly packed light brown sugar

2 tablespoons cocoa powder, extra

2½ cups (625ml) boiling water

1 Grease a 4.5-litre (18-cup) slow cooker bowl.

2 Melt butter in milk over low heat in a medium saucepan. Remove from heat; cool for 5 minutes. Stir in extract and caster sugar, then sifted flour and cocoa, and egg. Spread mixture into the cooker bowl.

3 Sift brown sugar and extra cocoa evenly over mixture; gently pour the boiling water evenly over mixture. Cook, covered, on high, for 2½ hours or until centre is firm.

4 Remove the bowl from the cooker. Stand pudding for 5 minutes before serving.

nutritional count per serving
15.5g total fat
9.6g saturated fat
2424kJ (580 cal)
101.3g carbohydrate
6.9g protein
1.6g fibre

serving suggestion
Serve hot or warm, dusted with a little sifted icing (confectioners') sugar, with cream and ice-cream.

not suitable to freeze

FOR THE STOVE

All these recipes are very simple, easy and perfect for feeding hungry mouths. Think mouth-watering casseroles, hearty soups and wholesome stews with meat so tender you will want more than one serve.

PROVENCALE BEEF CASSEROLE

prep + cook time 2 hours 30 minutes **serves** 4

2 tablespoons olive oil

1kg (2 pounds) gravy beef, cut into 2cm (¾-inch) pieces

2 rindless bacon slices (130g), chopped finely

1 medium leek (350g), sliced thinly

2 medium carrots (240g), chopped coarsely

1 stick celery (150g), trimmed, chopped coarsely

2 cloves garlic, crushed

410g (13 ounces) canned crushed tomatoes

1½ cups (375ml) beef stock

1 cup (250ml) dry red wine

2 bay leaves

4 sprigs fresh thyme

6 sprigs fresh flat-leaf parsley

2 medium zucchini (240g), sliced thickly

½ cup (75g) pitted black kalamata olives

1 Heat oil in a large saucepan; cook beef, in batches, until browned. Remove from pan.

2 Cook bacon, leek, carrot, celery and garlic in same pan, stirring, until leek softens.

3 Return beef to pan with tomatoes, stock, wine, bay leaves, thyme and parsley; bring to the boil. Reduce heat; simmer, covered, for 1 hour, stirring occasionally.

4 Add zucchini and olives; simmer, covered, for 30 minutes or until beef is tender. Season to taste. Discard bay leaves, thyme and parsley before serving.

nutritional count per serving
25.8g total fat
7.8g saturated fat
2458kJ (588 cal)
14.1g carbohydrate
61.4g protein
6.4g fibre

serving suggestion
Serve with crushed kipfler (fingerling) potatoes.

to freeze Complete the recipe to the end of step 3. Pack into freezer-proof containers, leaving a 2.5cm (1 inch) space to allow for expansion. Seal, label and freeze for up to 3 months. Thaw overnight in the fridge. Reheat in a saucepan or microwave on medium power (50%) until heated through.

COUNTRY-STYLE BEEF AND POTATO CASSEROLE

prep + cook time 2 hours 35 minutes **serves** 6

1kg (2 pounds) beef chuck steak

½ cup (75g) plain (all-purpose) flour, approximately

2 tablespoons olive oil

3 small brown onion (240g), halved

2 cloves garlic, crushed

2 rindless bacon slices (130g), chopped coarsely

2 tablespoons tomato paste

3 cups (750ml) beef stock

410g (13 ounces) canned crushed tomatoes

¼ cup (60ml) worcestershire sauce

2 medium potatoes (400g), chopped coarsely

1 medium kumara (orange sweet potato) (400g),
   chopped coarsely

1 large red capsicum (bell pepper) (350g),
   chopped coarsely

1 tablespoon coarsely chopped fresh thyme

1 Cut beef into 2cm (¾-inch) pieces. Coat beef in flour, shake away excess. Heat oil in a large saucepan; cook beef, in batches, until browned. Remove from pan.

2 Cook onion, garlic and bacon in same pan, stirring, until bacon crisps. Add paste; cook, stirring, for 1 minute.

3 Return beef to pan with stock, tomatoes and sauce; bring to the boil. Reduce heat; simmer, covered, for 1 hour, stirring occasionally.

4 Add potato, kumara and capsicum to pan; simmer, uncovered, stirring occasionally, for 30 minutes or until beef is tender. Season to taste. Serve sprinkled with thyme.

nutritional count per serving
21.3g total fat
5.9g saturated fat
2237kJ (534 cal)
34.1g carbohydrate
48.9g protein
4.8g fibre

serving suggestion
Serve with creamy polenta or crusty bread.

not suitable to freeze

INDIAN DRY BEEF CURRY

prep + cook time 1 hour 55 minutes **serves** 6

2 tablespoons peanut oil

2 medium brown onions (300g), chopped coarsely

4 cloves garlic, crushed

4cm (1½-inch) piece fresh ginger (20g), grated

2 teaspoons ground coriander

2 teaspoons ground cumin

2 teaspoons ground garam masala

1 teaspoon ground turmeric

1.5kg (3 pounds) beef chuck steak,
   cut into 2cm (¾-inch) pieces

1 cup (250ml) beef stock

½ cup (140g) yoghurt

¼ cup loosely packed fresh coriander (cilantro) leaves

1 Heat oil in a large saucepan; cook onion, garlic, ginger and spices, stirring occasionally, until onion softens. Add beef; cook, stirring, until beef is covered in spice mixture.

2 Add stock to pan; bring to the boil. Reduce heat; simmer, covered, for 1 hour, stirring occasionally.

3 Uncover; cook for 30 minutes or until liquid has almost evaporated and beef is tender, stirring occasionally. Season to taste.

4 Serve curry topped with yoghurt and coriander.

nutritional count per serving
18.3g total fat
6.4g saturated fat
1659kJ (397 cal)
4.5g carbohydrate
53g protein
1.1g fibre

serving suggestion
Serve with mango chutney and warm naan or steamed white rice.

note In Indian cooking terms, masala simply means ground or blended spices, so a masala can be whole spices, or a paste, or a powder. The garam masala used here is a North Indian blend of spices, and is based on varying proportions of cardamom, cinnamon, cloves, coriander, fennel and cumin, roasted and ground together.

to freeze Complete the recipe to the end of step 3. Pack into freezer-proof containers, leaving a 2.5cm (1 inch) space to allow for expansion. Seal, label and freeze for up to 3 months. Thaw overnight in the fridge. Reheat in a saucepan or microwave on medium power (50%) until heated through.

PUMPKIN AND EGGPLANT DHAL

prep + cook time 1 hour 30 minutes **serves** 4

2 tablespoons olive oil

1 medium brown onion (150g), sliced thinly

2 cloves garlic, crushed

4cm (1½-inch) piece fresh ginger (20g), grated

2 teaspoons ground coriander

2 teaspoons ground cumin

1 teaspoon ground turmeric

⅓ cup (65g) red lentils

⅓ cup (85g) yellow split peas

⅓ cup (85g) green split peas

410g (13 ounces) canned crushed tomatoes

1½ cups (375ml) vegetable stock

2 cups (500ml) water

300g (9½ ounces) pumpkin, chopped coarsely

1 medium eggplant (300g), chopped coarsely

400g (12½ ounces) canned chickpeas (garbanzo beans),
   drained, rinsed

1 Heat oil in a large saucepan; cook onion, garlic and ginger, stirring, until onion softens. Add spices; cook, stirring, until fragrant.

2 Add lentils and peas to pan. Stir in tomatoes, stock and the water; simmer, covered, stirring occasionally, for 30 minutes.

3 Add pumpkin and eggplant to pan; bring to the boil. Reduce heat; simmer, covered, for 20 minutes or until pumpkin is tender. Stir in chickpeas, simmer for 10 minutes. Season to taste.

nutritional count per serving   **not suitable to freeze**
12.9g total fat
2g saturated fat
1793kJ (429 cal)
48.1g carbohydrate
22.8g protein
14.4g fibre

CRISP HOT AND SWEET BEEF WITH NOODLES

prep + cook time 2 hours 5 minutes (+ standing) **serves** 4

750g (1½ pounds) piece corned silverside (beef)

1kg (2 pounds) fresh wide rice noodles

¼ cup (60ml) peanut oil

3 cloves garlic, crushed

3 fresh small red thai (serrano) chillies, sliced thinly

4 spring onions (100g), sliced thinly

2 tablespoons fish sauce

¼ cup (65g) grated palm sugar

1 cup firmly packed fresh coriander (cilantro) leaves

1 Place beef, in packaging, in a large saucepan, cover with cold water; bring to the boil, uncovered. Reduce heat; simmer, covered, for 1½ hours. Remove from pan, discard packaging; drain beef on a rack over a tray for 15 minutes.

2 Meanwhile, place noodles in a large heatproof bowl; cover with boiling water, separate with a fork. Drain.

3 Trim excess fat from beef; using two forks, shred beef finely. Heat oil in a wok; stir-fry beef, in batches, until browned all over and crisp. Drain on absorbent paper.

4 Stir-fry garlic, chilli and onion in same wok until onion softens. Add sauce and sugar; stir-fry until sugar dissolves. Return beef to wok with noodles; stir-fry gently until heated through. Remove from heat; toss coriander leaves through stir-fry. Season to taste.

nutritional count per serving
29.3g total fat
8.4g saturated fat
3198kJ (764 cal)
70.9g carbohydrate
53.3g protein
2.5g fibre

serving suggestion
Serve with steamed asian greens.

tip Corned silverside is best cooked in the cryovac packaging it is sold in; but, if you prefer, you can discard the packaging and simmer the meat submerged in water flavoured with some garlic and chillies, a few kaffir lime leaves and a stick of lemon grass. Allow the meat to cool slightly in the cooking liquid, then drain and, using two forks shred it roughly while still warm.

not suitable to freeze

HARIRA

prep + cook time 1 hour 40 minutes serves 4

½ cup (100g) french-style green lentils

500g (1 pound) diced lamb, cut into 1cm (½-inch) pieces

1 medium brown onion (150g), chopped finely

2 cloves garlic, crushed

½ teaspoon ground cinnamon

½ teaspoon ground ginger

½ teaspoon hot paprika

1 teaspoon ground turmeric

pinch saffron threads

1.5 litres (6 cups) water

400g (12½ ounces) canned chickpeas (garbanzo beans),
  drained, rinsed

½ cup (100g) white long-grain rice

3 small roma (egg) tomatoes (180g), chopped finely

¼ cup finely chopped fresh flat-leaf parsley

1 Cook lentils, lamb, onion, garlic and spices in a large flameproof baking dish, stirring, until lamb is browned. Add the water; bring to the boil. Reduce heat; simmer, covered, for 1 hour.

2 Add chickpeas, rice and tomato to dish; simmer, uncovered, for 20 minutes or until rice is just tender. Stir in parsley. Season to taste.

nutritional count per serving
13.1g total fat
5.3g saturated fat
1919kJ (459 cal)
41.4g carbohydrate
39.1g protein
8.3g fibre

serving suggestion
Serve with flat bread, preferably a Moroccan flat bread called khaubz.

note French-style green lentils are related to the famous French lentils du puy; these green-blue, tiny lentils have a nutty, earthy flavour and a hardy nature that allows them to be rapidly cooked without disintegrating. They are also known as australian, bondi or matilda lentils.

not suitable to freeze

PORK WITH STICKY ASIAN GLAZE

prep + cook time 2 hours 45 minutes **serves** 6

1 tablespoon vegetable oil

1.5kg (3-pound) piece pork neck

5 shallots (125g), sliced finely

2cm (¾-inch) piece fresh ginger (10g), sliced finely

5 cloves garlic, sliced finely

½ cup (125ml) dark soy sauce

½ cup (100g) crushed yellow rock sugar

2 whole star anise

2 cups (500ml) chicken stock

2 cups (500ml) water

8 dried whole shiitake mushrooms

½ cup (100g) canned bamboo shoots, drained, rinsed

1kg (2 pounds) fresh thick rice noodles

500g (1 pound) gai lan, chopped coarsely

3 green onions (scallions), sliced thinly

1   Heat oil in a large saucepan over a medium heat; cook pork until browned all over. Add shallots, ginger and garlic to pan; cook for 1 minute.

2   Add sauce, sugar, star anise, stock and the water; bring to the boil. Reduce heat; simmer, covered, for 1½ hours, turning pork occasionally.

3   Meanwhile, soak mushrooms in warm water for 20 minutes. Remove stems, cut in half. Add mushrooms and bamboo shoots to pan; simmer gently, uncovered, for further 30 minutes, turning pork occasionally.

4   Remove pork from pan; cover to keep warm. Strain cooking liquid into a large jug; reserve 2½ cups (625ml). Reserve mushroom mixture.

5   Bring reserved cooking liquid to the boil in a medium saucepan; boil, uncovered, for 10 minutes or until reduced by half.

6   Meanwhile, place noodles in a heatproof bowl; cover with boiling water. Stand until tender; drain.

7   Boil, steam or microwave gai lan until just tender. Slice pork thickly.

8   Place noodles on serving plates; top with gai lan, pork and reserved mushroom mixture. Drizzle with sauce, top with green onion.

nutritional count per serving
24.3g total fat
7.3g saturated fat
2884kJ (690 cal)
55.4g carbohydrate
60.1g protein
3g fibre

note Yellow rock sugar is available from Asian supermarkets. It's mainly used in braises and sauces as it gives them a lustre and glaze.

to freeze Pour stock into freezer-proof containers, leaving a 2.5cm (1 inch) space to allow for expansion. Seal, label and freeze for up to 3 months. Thaw overnight in the fridge. Reheat in a saucepan or microwave on medium power (50%) until heated through.

MAPLE SYRUP GLAZED LAMB SHANKS

prep + cook time 2 hours 15 minutes **serves** 4

⅓ cup (80ml) pure maple syrup

1 cup (250ml) chicken stock

1 tablespoon dijon mustard

1½ cups (375ml) orange juice

8 french-trimmed lamb shanks (1.6kg)

ROAST POTATOES

3 medium potatoes (600g), halved

2 tablespoons olive oil

1 Combine syrup, stock, mustard and juice in a large deep flameproof baking dish, add lamb; toss lamb to coat in syrup mixture. Bring to the boil, then cover tightly. Reduce heat; cook lamb, turning every 20 minutes, for 2 hours or until lamb is tender. Season to taste.

2 Meanwhile, make roast potatoes.

3 Serve lamb shanks with potatoes.

ROAST POTATOES Preheat oven to 220°C/425°F. Oil an oven tray. Boil, steam or microwave potatoes for 5 minutes; drain. Pat dry with absorbent paper; cool for 10 minutes. Gently rake the rounded sides of potatoes with the tines of a fork; place potato, in a single layer, cut-side down, on oven tray. Brush with oil; roast, uncovered, for 50 minutes or until browned lightly and crisp. Season to taste.

nutritional count per serving
29.1g total fat
10.3g saturated fat
2632kJ (629 cal)
42.2g carbohydrate
48.5g protein
2.4g fibre

serving suggestion
Serve with wilted baby spinach leaves.

tip Don't be tempted to use 'maple-flavoured' syrup, it is very different from pure maple syrup, which is far superior and well worth the extra cost.

to freeze Complete the recipe to the end of step 1. Pack into freezer-proof containers, leaving a 2.5cm (1 inch) space to allow for expansion. Seal, label and freeze for up to 3 months. Thaw overnight in the fridge. Reheat in a saucepan or microwave on medium power (50%) until heated through.

OREGANO LAMB STEW WITH GNOCCHI

prep + cook time 2 hours 45 minutes **serves** 6

2 tablespoons olive oil

1kg (2 pounds) boneless lamb shoulder,
  chopped coarsely

2 medium brown onions (300g), sliced thickly

2 cloves garlic, sliced thinly

2 teaspoons dried oregano

½ teaspoon ground cinnamon

400g (12½ ounces) canned diced tomatoes

3 cups (750ml) beef stock

1 tablespoon tomato paste

2 teaspoons caster (superfine) sugar

500g (1 pound) potato gnocchi

½ cup (40g) finely grated parmesan cheese

1 cup loosely packed fresh oregano leaves

1 Heat oil in a large saucepan; cook lamb, in batches, until browned. Remove from pan.

2 Meanwhile, cook onion in pan, stirring, until softened, add garlic to pan with dried oregano and cinnamon. Cook, stirring, until fragrant.

3 Return lamb to pan with tomatoes, stock, paste and sugar; bring to the boil. Reduce heat; simmer, covered, for 2 hours, stirring occasionally.

4 Uncover; bring to the boil. Boil, uncovered, for 10 minutes. Stir in gnocchi; cook, uncovered, for 5 minutes or until gnocchi is tender and sauce is thickened. Season to taste.

5 Serve stew topped with cheese and fresh oregano.

nutritional count per serving
19g total fat
7.2g saturated fat
1998kJ (478 cal)
31.8g carbohydrate
42.4g protein
3.9g fibre

serving suggestion
Serve with a green salad.

notes We used 'fresh' pre-made potato gnocchi available from the refrigerated section of most supermarkets. Oregano is a herb with a woody stalk and tiny, dark-green leaves. It has a pungent, peppery flavour that is delicious in stews, casseroles and roasts.

to freeze Complete the recipe to the end of step 3. Pack into freezer-proof containers, leaving a 2.5cm (1 inch) space to allow for expansion. Seal, label and freeze for up to 3 months. Thaw overnight in the fridge. Reheat in a large saucepan, then continue from step 4.

PASTA, BACON AND VEGETABLE SOUP

prep + cook time 1 hour 30 minutes **serves** 6

2 tablespoons olive oil

1 small brown onion (80g), chopped finely

6 rindless bacon slices (390g), chopped coarsely

2.5 litres (10 cups) water

1kg (2 pounds) bacon bones

2 tablespoons tomato paste

3 medium potatoes (600g), quartered

300g (9½ ounces) pumpkin, chopped coarsely

200g (6½ ounces) cauliflower, chopped coarsely

2½ cups (200g) finely shredded cabbage

1 medium carrot (120g), chopped coarsely

1 cup (110g) frozen beans

1 large zucchini (150g), chopped coarsely

¾ cup (95g) small pasta shells

1 Heat oil in a large saucepan; cook onion and bacon slices, stirring, until onion softens.

2 Add the water, bacon bones, paste, potato, pumpkin and cauliflower; bring to the boil. Reduce heat; simmer, covered, for 50 minutes.

3 Remove and discard bacon bones. Using potato masher, roughly crush vegetables.

4 Add cabbage, carrot, beans, zucchini and pasta; simmer, uncovered, for 10 minutes or until pasta is cooked. Season to taste.

nutritional count per serving
18.5g total fat
5.3g saturated fat
1760kJ (421 cal)
32.6g carbohydrate
27.5g protein
6.8g fibre

serving suggestion
Serve with toasted sour dough bread.

not suitable to freeze

IRISH LAMB AND BARLEY STEW

prep + cook time 2 hours 5 minutes **serves** 6

2 tablespoons olive oil

1kg (2 pounds) diced lamb shoulder

1 large brown onion (200g), chopped coarsely

2 medium carrots (240g), chopped coarsely

2 sticks celery (300g), trimmed, chopped coarsely

2 cloves garlic, crushed

1 litre (4 cups) chicken stock

2 cups (500ml) water

1 cup (200g) pearl barley

4 sprigs fresh thyme

3 medium potatoes (600g), chopped coarsely

2 cups (160g) finely shredded cabbage

⅓ cup finely chopped fresh flat-leaf parsley

1 Heat half the oil in a large saucepan; cook lamb, in batches, until browned. Remove from pan.

2 Heat remaining oil in same pan; cook onion, carrot, celery and garlic, stirring, until vegetables soften. Return lamb to pan with stock, the water, barley and thyme; bring to the boil. Reduce heat; simmer, covered, for 1 hour, skimming fat from surface occasionally.

3 Add potato; simmer, uncovered, for 20 minutes or until potato is tender. Add cabbage; simmer, uncovered, until cabbage is just tender. Discard thyme. Season to taste.

4 Serve stew sprinkled with parsley.

nutritional count per serving
22.6g total fat
8.2g saturated fat
2224kJ (532 cal)
37.4g carbohydrate
40.4g protein
8.6g fibre

serving suggestion
Serve with warmed irish soda bread.

to freeze Complete the recipe to the end of step 2. Pack into freezer-proof containers, leaving a 2.5cm (1 inch) space to allow for expansion. Seal, label and freeze for up to 3 months. Thaw overnight in the fridge. Reheat in a large saucepan, then continue from step 3.

rabbit stew

RABBIT STEW

prep + cook time 2 hours 5 minutes **serves** 4

2 tablespoons oil

1kg (2 pounds) rabbit pieces

3 medium brown onions (450g), sliced thickly

4 cloves garlic, crushed

1 cup (250ml) water

1 litre (4 cups) chicken stock

410g (13 ounces) canned diced tomatoes

5 medium potatoes (1kg), chopped coarsely

2 medium carrots (240g), sliced thickly

1 tablespoon balsamic vinegar

3 bay leaves

1 teaspoon dried chilli flakes

⅓ cup coarsely chopped fresh mint

1 cup (120g) frozen peas

1 Heat half the oil in a large saucepan; cook rabbit, in batches, until browned. Remove from pan.

2 Heat remaining oil in same pan; cook onion and garlic, stirring, until onion softens.

3 Add the water, stock, tomatoes, potato, carrot, vinegar, bay leaves, chilli and mint to pan. Return rabbit to pan; bring to the boil. Reduce heat; simmer, uncovered, for 1¼ hours. Add peas; simmer, uncovered, for 5 minutes. Season to taste.

nutritional count per serving   **not suitable to freeze**
19.4g total fat
5.1g saturated fat
2750kJ (658 cal)
44.4g carbohydrate
70.7g protein
10.6g fibre

PORK NECK, ORANGE AND WHITE BEAN STEW

prep + cook time 1 hour 40 minutes **serves** 4

1 tablespoon olive oil

800g (1½ pounds) pork neck, cut into 3cm (1¼-inch) pieces

1 large celeriac (celery root) (750g), trimmed, peeled, chopped coarsely

3 medium carrots (360g), chopped coarsely

3 cloves garlic, peeled

1 cup (250ml) dry white wine

1 cup (250ml) chicken stock

3 x 5cm (2-inch) strips orange rind

½ cup (125ml) orange juice

400g (12½ ounces) canned cannellini beans, drained, rinsed

1 Heat oil in a large flameproof baking dish; cook pork, in batches, until browned. Remove from pan.

2 Add vegetables, garlic, wine, stock, rind and juice to dish; bring to the boil. Return pork to dish, reduce heat; simmer, covered, for 40 minutes.

3 Add beans to dish; simmer, uncovered, for 20 minutes or until pork is tender. Season to taste.

(photograph page 92)

nutritional count per serving   **not suitable to freeze**
21.4g total fat
6.2g saturated fat
2215kJ (530 cal)
18.1g carbohydrate
50g protein
12.7g fibre

pork neck, orange and white bean stew (recipe page 91)

PORK BELLY AND CHORIZO STEW

prep + cook time 1 hour 35 minutes **serves** 4

2 chorizo sausages (340g), sliced thinly

600g (1¼-pound) piece pork belly, rind removed, cut into 3cm (1¼-inch) pieces

1 large brown onion (200g), sliced thinly

2 cloves garlic, crushed

1 teaspoon sweet smoked paprika

1 large red capsicum (bell pepper) (350g), chopped coarsely

800g (1½ pounds) canned chopped tomatoes

½ cup (125ml) dry red wine

½ cup (125ml) water

400g (12½ ounces) canned white beans, drained, rinsed

½ cup finely chopped fresh flat-leaf parsley

1   Cook chorizo and pork, stirring, in batches, in large flameproof baking dish until browned. Remove from dish. Add onion and garlic to dish; cook, stirring, until onion softens.

2   Return meats to dish with paprika, capsicum, tomatoes, wine and the water; bring to the boil. Reduce heat; simmer, covered, for 40 minutes.

3   Add beans; simmer, uncovered, for 20 minutes or until pork is tender and sauce thickens slightly. Season to taste. Serve sprinkled with parsley.

(photograph page 93)

nutritional count per serving   **not suitable to freeze**
55g total fat
19.1g saturated fat
3331kJ (797 cal)
26.7g carbohydrate
47g protein
7.9g fibre

CHICKEN AND ARTICHOKE POT ROAST

prep + cook time 2 hours **serves** 4

1.2kg (2½-pound) whole chicken

2 tablespoons olive oil

8 brown baby onions (320g), halved

600g (1¼ pounds) baby new potatoes, halved

6 cloves garlic

8 sprigs fresh thyme

1 cup (250ml) dry white wine

8 drained marinated artichoke hearts (100g), halved

1 cup (250ml) chicken stock

1   Rinse chicken under cold water; pat dry inside and out with absorbent paper. Tuck wing tips under chicken; tie legs together with kitchen string.

2   Heat oil in a large saucepan; cook onion, potato, unpeeled garlic and thyme, stirring occasionally, until browned. Remove from pan.

3   Cook chicken in same pan until browned all over. Add wine; boil, uncovered, for 1 minute.

4   Return vegetables to pan with artichokes and stock; bring to the boil. Reduce heat; simmer, covered, for 1½ hours or until chicken is cooked. Season to taste.

nutritional count per serving   **not suitable to freeze**
33.9g total fat
9g saturated fat
2516kJ (602 cal)
25.5g carbohydrate
36.2g protein
5.5g fibre

SHREDDED SPANISH BEEF

prep + cook time 3 hours **serves** 6

5 cloves garlic, quartered

1 large carrot (180g), chopped coarsely

1 stick celery (150g), trimmed, chopped coarsely

1.5kg (3 pounds) beef skirt steak

6 black peppercorns

2 teaspoons dried oregano

2 litres (8 cups) water

2 tablespoons olive oil

2 rindless bacon slices (130g), chopped finely

3 cloves garlic, extra, crushed

1 small brown onion (80g), chopped finely

½ small green capsicum (bell pepper) (75g),
  chopped finely

1 tablespoon tomato paste

2 tablespoons red wine vinegar

1 medium red capsicum (bell pepper) (200g),
  sliced thickly

1 medium green capsicum (bell pepper) (200g),
  sliced thickly

2 medium brown onions (300g), sliced thickly

400g (12½ ounces) canned whole tomatoes

1 teaspoon ground cumin

1 cup (150g) pimiento-stuffed green olives, halved

¼ cup (60ml) lemon juice

1   Place quartered garlic, carrot, celery, beef, peppercorns, half the oregano, and the water in a large deep saucepan; bring to the boil. Reduce heat; simmer, uncovered, 2 hours or until beef is tender.

2   Meanwhile, heat half the oil in a small frying pan; cook bacon, crushed garlic, finely chopped onion and finely chopped capsicum, stirring, until onion softens. Stir in paste and vinegar; cook until vinegar evaporates. Cool 10 minutes; blend or process until smooth.

3   Remove beef from braising liquid. Strain liquid over large bowl; discard solids. Using two forks, shred beef coarsely.

4   Heat remaining oil in same cleaned pan; cook capsicum mixture with thickly sliced capsicums and thickly sliced onion, stirring, until vegetables soften. Return beef and braising liquid to pan with undrained tomatoes, cumin and remaining oregano; bring to the boil. Reduce heat; simmer, uncovered, 20 minutes. Remove from heat; stir in olives and juice. Season to taste.

nutritional count per serving   **not suitable to freeze**

17.5g total fat

4.7g saturated fat

1969kJ (471 cal)

11 carbohydrate

64 protein

6.2g fibre

CHICKEN WITH FENNEL AND ORANGE

prep + cook time 1 hour 20 minutes **serves** 4

1 tablespoon olive oil

20g (¾ ounce) butter

12 chicken drumsticks (1.8kg)

4 baby fennel bulbs (520g), trimmed, quartered

1 medium brown onion (150g), chopped finely

2 cloves garlic, crushed

1 tablespoon finely grated orange rind

1 cup (250ml) orange juice

1 cup (250ml) dry white wine

2 cups (500ml) chicken stock

6 sprigs fresh thyme

1 medium kumara (orange sweet potato) (400g), chopped coarsely

1 Heat oil and butter in a large deep saucepan; cook chicken, in batches, until well browned. Remove from pan. Discard all but 1 tablespoon of the pan juices. Reheat juices in same pan; cook fennel, in batches, until browned and caramelised. Remove from pan.

2 Cook onion and garlic in same pan, stirring, until onion softens. Return chicken and fennel to pan with rind, juice, wine, stock and thyme; bring to the boil. Reduce heat; simmer, covered, for 30 minutes or until chicken is cooked.

3 Add kumara; simmer, uncovered, for 20 minutes or until kumara is tender. Discard thyme before serving. Season to taste.

nutritional count per serving
40.9g total fat
13.1g saturated fat
3031kJ (725 cal)
22.8g carbohydrate
55g protein
4.6g fibre

serving suggestion
Serve with fettuccine, tagliatelle or any of your favourite pasta.

not suitable to freeze

CHICKEN AND ASPARAGUS PILAF

prep + cook time 1 hour 20 minutes **serves** 4

40g (1½ ounces) butter

400g (12½ ounces) chicken breast fillets,
chopped coarsely

1 medium red onion (170g), chopped finely

3 cloves garlic, crushed

200g (6½ ounces) swiss brown mushrooms,
chopped coarsely

1½ cups (300g) basmati rice

¾ cup (180ml) dry white wine

1½ cups (375ml) chicken stock

2 teaspoons finely grated lemon rind

1 tablespoon lemon juice

2¼ cups (560ml) water

170g (5½ ounces) asparagus, trimmed,
chopped coarsely

100g (3 ounces) green beans, trimmed,
chopped coarsely

1 tablespoon fresh thyme leaves

2 tablespoons roasted pine nuts

1 Heat half the butter in a large saucepan; cook chicken, in batches, until cooked through.

2 Heat remaining butter in same pan; cook onion and garlic, stirring, until onion softens. Add mushrooms; cook, stirring, until just tender.

3 Add rice to pan; cook, stirring, for 1 minute. Add wine; cook, stirring, until liquid is absorbed.

4 Add stock, rind, juice and 2 cups of the water to pan; bring to the boil. Reduce heat; simmer, uncovered, stirring occasionally, for 20 minutes or until liquid is absorbed and rice is just tender.

5 Stir chicken, asparagus, beans, thyme and remaining water into pilaf; cook, covered, over low heat, for 5 minutes or until vegetables are tender and chicken is hot. Season to taste. Serve pilaf topped with nuts.

nutritional count per serving
16.6g total fat
6.6g saturated fat
2433kJ (582 cal)
64.3g carbohydrate
33.5g protein
4.3g fibre

tip Swiss brown mushrooms, also known as roman or cremini, are light-to-dark-brown in colour with a full bodied flavour. Store on a tray in a single layer, covered with dampened absorbent paper, in a spot where cool air can circulate freely around them.

not suitable to freeze

CREAM OF CHICKEN SOUP WITH PARMESAN CHEESE CROÛTONS

prep + cook time 3 hours **serves** 4

1.8kg (3½-pound) whole chicken

1 medium brown onion (150g), chopped coarsely

1 medium carrot (120g), chopped coarsely

1 stalk celery (150g), trimmed, chopped coarsely

2 litres (8 cups) water

1 litre (4 cups) chicken stock

40g (1½ ounces) butter

⅓ cup (50g) plain (all-purpose) flour

2 tablespoons lemon juice

½ cup (125ml) pouring cream

¼ cup finely chopped fresh flat-leaf parsley

PARMESAN CHEESE CROÛTONS

1 small french bread stick (150g), cut into
  2cm (¾-inch) slices

½ cup (40g) coarsely grated parmesan cheese

1   Place chicken, onion, carrot and celery in a large saucepan with the water and stock; bring to the boil. Reduce heat; simmer, covered, 1½ hours. Remove chicken; simmer broth, covered, 30 minutes.

2   Strain broth through muslin-lined sieve or colander into a large heatproof bowl; discard solids.

3   Melt butter in a large saucepan, add flour; cook, stirring, until mixture bubbles and thickens. Gradually stir in broth and juice; bring to the boil. Reduce heat; simmer, uncovered, 25 minutes or until thickened slightly. Remove from heat.

4   Remove and discard skin and bones from chicken; shred meat coarsely. Add chicken and cream to soup; stir over heat, without boiling, until soup is heated through.

5   Meanwhile, make parmesan cheese croûtons.

6   Serve bowls of soup topped with parsley; accompany with parmesan cheese croûtons.

PARMESAN CHEESE CROÛTONS Preheat grill (broiler). Toast bread on one side then turn and sprinkle with cheese; grill until cheese browns lightly.

nutritional count per serving
63.8g total fat
28.4g saturated fat
3984kJ (952 cal)
35.9g carbohydrate
57.9g protein
3.8g fibre

to freeze Complete the recipe to the end of step 4. Pack into freezer-proof containers, leaving a 2.5cm (1 inch) space to allow for expansion. Seal, label and freeze for up to 3 months. Thaw overnight in the fridge. Reheat in a saucepan or microwave on medium power (50%) until heated through.

BEEF AND VEGETABLE SOUP

prep + cook time 2 hours 25 minutes **serves** 4

2 tablespoons olive oil

1kg (2 pounds) gravy beef, trimmed,
  cut into 2cm (¾-inch) pieces

12 shallots (300g), halved

2 cloves garlic, crushed

2 small parsnips (240g), chopped coarsely

2 small turnips (300g), chopped coarsely

2 medium swedes (450g), chopped coarsely

300g (9½ ounces) pumpkin, chopped coarsely

1 cup (250ml) dry white wine

3 cups (750ml) beef stock

3 cups (750ml) water

1 tablespoon tomato paste

4 sprigs fresh thyme

⅓ cup (40g) crushed egg pasta vermicelli

1   Heat half the oil in a large saucepan; cook beef, in batches, until browned. Remove from pan.

2   Heat remaining oil in same pan; cook shallots and garlic, stirring, until onion softens.

3   Add vegetables, wine, stock, the water, paste and thyme; bring to the boil. Reduce heat; simmer, covered, for 1½ hours, stirring occasionally.

4   Add vermicelli; cook, uncovered, for 10 minutes or until just softened. Season to taste.

nutritional count per serving
21.4g total fat
6.5g saturated fat
2387kJ (571 cal)
22g carbohydrate
58.5g protein
7.6g fibre

tip Egg pasta vermicelli is sold in a packet as nests; you will need one nest for this recipe.

not suitable to freeze

HARISSA AND MINT VEGETABLE STEW

prep + cook time 1 hour 30 minutes **serves** 4

40g (1½ ounces) butter

10 shallots (250g), halved

6 cloves garlic, crushed

2 tablespoons plain (all-purpose) flour

2 cups (500ml) vegetable stock

2 cups (500ml) water

1kg (2 pounds) baby new potatoes, halved

410g (13 ounces) canned crushed tomatoes

2 tablespoons harissa paste

1 cinnamon stick

½ cup firmly packed fresh mint leaves

500g (1 pound) yellow patty-pan squash, halved

115g (3½ ounces) baby corn

½ cup (60g) frozen peas

250g (8 ounces) cherry tomatoes, halved

1 Heat butter in a large saucepan; cook shallots and garlic, stirring, until shallots soften. Add flour; cook, stirring, for 1 minute.

2 Add stock, the water, potatoes, canned tomatoes, harissa, cinnamon and about two-thirds of the mint leaves to pan; bring to the boil. Reduce heat; simmer, uncovered, for 30 minutes.

3 Add squash to pan; simmer, uncovered, for 20 minutes. Add corn, peas and cherry tomatoes; simmer, uncovered, for 10 minutes. Season to taste. Serve stew sprinkled with remaining mint.

nutritional count per serving   **not suitable to freeze**
10.3g total fat
5.7g saturated fat
1705kJ (408 cal)
55.7g carbohydrate
15.7g protein
14.3g fibre

ORANGE POACHED PEARS

prep + cook time 1 hour 20 minutes **serves** 6

6 medium pears (1.4kg)

2 cups (500ml) water

2 cups (500ml) dry red wine

2 tablespoons orange-flavoured liqueur

¾ cup (165g) caster (superfine) sugar

1 teaspoon vanilla bean paste

4 x 5cm (2-inch) strips orange rind

⅓ cup (80ml) orange juice

1   Peel pears, leaving stems intact.

2   Place remaining ingredients in a large saucepan; stir over heat, without boiling, until sugar dissolves. Add pears; bring to the boil. Reduce heat; simmer, covered, for 1 hour or until pears are tender. Transfer pears to serving bowls.

3   Bring syrup in pan to the boil. Boil, uncovered, for 10 minutes or until syrup thickens slightly.

4   Serve pears drizzled with warm syrup.

nutritional count per serving
0.2g total fat
0g saturated fat
1317kJ (315 cal)
57.1g carbohydrate
0.8g protein
3.5g fibre

tip Vanilla bean paste is made from vanilla beans and contains real seeds. It is highly concentrated and 1 teaspoon replaces a whole vanilla bean without mess or fuss, as you neither have to split or scrape the pod. It can also be used instead of vanilla extract. It is found in most supermarkets in the baking section.

not suitable to freeze

DATE AND APRICOT CREAMY RICE

prep + cook time 1 hour 10 minutes **serves** 6

1 litre (4 cups) milk

⅔ cup (150g) caster (superfine) sugar

1 cinnamon stick

2 teaspoons finely grated lemon rind

½ cup (100g) uncooked arborio rice

½ cup (75g) coarsely chopped dried apricots

½ cup (115g) coarsely chopped fresh dates

¼ cup (35g) coarsely chopped roasted
  unsalted pistachios

1 Bring milk, sugar, cinnamon and rind to the boil in a medium saucepan. Gradually stir rice into boiling milk mixture. Reduce heat; simmer, covered, stirring occasionally, for 1 hour or until rice is tender and liquid is almost absorbed.

2 Discard cinnamon stick; stir in apricots and dates. Serve rice, sprinkled with nuts.

nutritional count per serving   **not suitable to freeze**
9.6g total fat
4.6g saturated fat
1480kJ (354 cal)
56.5g carbohydrate
8.6g protein
2.4g fibre

FOR THE OVEN

The best thing about slow cooking is that you can use the cheaper cuts of meat that are normally tough and chewy; slow cooking tenderises the meat creating a delicious meal. Slow-cooked recipes are ideal for weeknight family meals especially as the weather grows cooler.

LAMB SHANKS IN FIVE SPICE, TAMARIND AND GINGER

prep + cook time 2 hours 30 minutes **serves** 4

2 teaspoons five-spice powder

1 teaspoon dried chilli flakes

1 cinnamon stick

2 whole star anise

¼ cup (60ml) soy sauce

½ cup (125ml) chinese cooking wine (shao hsing)

2 tablespoons tamarind concentrate

2 tablespoons light brown sugar

8cm (3¼-inch) piece fresh ginger (40g), grated

2 cloves garlic, chopped coarsely

1¼ cups (310ml) water

8 french-trimmed lamb shanks (1.6kg)

500g (1 pound) choy sum, cut into 10cm (4-inch) lengths

150g (4½ ounces) sugar snap peas, trimmed

1   Preheat oven to 180°C/350°F.

2   Dry-fry five-spice, chilli, cinnamon and star anise in a small frying pan, stirring, until fragrant. Combine spices with soy, wine, tamarind, sugar, ginger, garlic and the water in medium jug.

3   Place shanks, in a single layer, in a large shallow baking dish; drizzle with spice mixture. Roast, uncovered, turning shanks occasionally, for 2 hours or until meat is almost falling off the shanks. Remove shanks from dish; cover to keep warm. Skim away excess fat; strain sauce into a small saucepan.

4   Meanwhile, boil, steam or microwave choy sum and peas, separately, until tender; drain.

5   Divide vegetables among serving plates; serve with shanks, drizzled with reheated sauce.

nutritional count per serving
20g total fat
9g saturated fat
1885kJ (451 cal)
12.5g carbohydrate
48.3g protein
3.1g fibre

note Small, fresh and plump sugar snap peas are eaten whole, pod and all, similarly to snow peas. They are just as good tossed raw in a salad as they are boiled, steamed or microwaved.

not suitable to freeze

BEEF STEW WITH PARSLEY DUMPLINGS

prep + cook time 3 hours **serves** 4

1kg (2 pounds) beef chuck steak,
  cut into 5cm (2-inch) pieces
2 tablespoons plain (all-purpose) flour
2 tablespoons olive oil
20g (¾ ounce) butter
2 medium brown onions (300g), chopped coarsely
2 cloves garlic, crushed
2 medium carrots (240g), chopped coarsely
1 cup (250ml) dry red wine
2 tablespoons tomato paste
2 cups (500ml) beef stock
4 sprigs fresh thyme

PARSLEY DUMPLINGS

1 cup (150g) self-raising flour
50g (1½ ounces) butter
1 egg, beaten lightly
¼ cup (20g) coarsely grated parmesan cheese
¼ cup finely chopped fresh flat-leaf parsley
⅓ cup (50g) drained sun-dried tomatoes, chopped finely
¼ cup (60ml) milk, approximately

1 Preheat oven to 180°C/350°F.
2 Coat beef in flour; shake off excess. Heat oil in a large flameproof baking dish on the stove top; cook beef, in batches, until browned all over. Remove from dish.
3 Melt butter in same heated dish; cook onion, garlic and carrot, stirring, until vegetables soften. Add wine; cook, stirring, until liquid reduces to ¼ cup. Return beef to dish with paste, stock and thyme; bring to the boil. Season to taste. Roast, covered, for 1¾ hours.
4 Meanwhile, make parsley dumpling mixture.
5 Remove dish from oven; drop level tablespoons of the dumpling mixture, about 2cm (¾ inch) apart, on top of stew. Return to oven, cook, uncovered, for 20 minutes or until dumplings are browned lightly and cooked through.

PARSLEY DUMPLINGS Place flour in a medium bowl; rub in butter. Stir in egg, cheese, parsley, tomato and enough milk to make a soft, sticky dough.

nutritional count per serving
39.7g total fat
17.4g saturated fat
3457kJ (827 cal)
43g carbohydrate
63.9g protein
6.7g fibre

serving suggestion
Serve with a mixed leaf salad dressed with vinaigrette.

to freeze Complete the recipe to the end of step 3. Pack into freezer-proof containers, leaving a 2.5cm (1 inch) space to allow for expansion. Seal, label and freeze for up to 3 months. Thaw overnight in the fridge. Reheat in a saucepan or microwave on medium power (50%) until heated through.

LAMB CASSEROLE WITH HERB DUMPLINGS

prep + cook time 2 hours 45 minutes **serves** 6

1kg (2-pound) boneless lamb shoulder

1 tablespoon olive oil

1 medium leek (350g), sliced

1 medium carrot (120g), sliced thickly

2 sticks celery (300g), trimmed, chopped coarsely

40g (1½-ounce) packet french onion soup mix

2 cups (500ml) salt-reduced chicken stock

½ cup (125ml) water

20g (¾ ounce) butter

HERB DUMPLINGS

1 cup (150g) self-raising flour

40g (1½ ounces) cold butter, chopped finely

1 egg, beaten lightly

2 tablespoons finely chopped fresh flat-leaf parsley

2 tablespoons finely chopped fresh chives

⅓ cup (80ml) milk

1   Preheat oven to 160°C/325°F.

2   Trim excess fat from lamb. Cut lamb into 4cm (1½-inch) pieces.

3   Heat half the oil in a small flameproof baking dish; cook lamb, in batches, until browned.

4   Return lamb to dish with leek, carrot and celery; stirring until combined. Stir in the soup mix, stock and the water. Roast, covered, for 1¾ hours.

5   Meanwhile, make herb dumpling mixture.

6   Remove the dish from the oven. Stir the lamb mixture well. Season to taste. Drop rounded dessertspoons of the dumpling mixture on top of the lamb mixture about 2cm (¾ inch) apart.

7   Melt the butter in a small saucepan on the stove over low heat. Brush the tops of the dumplings with butter. Roast, uncovered, for 20 minutes or until the dumplings are browned and cooked through.

HERB DUMPLINGS Place flour in a medium bowl; rub in butter. Stir in egg, herbs and milk to make a soft, sticky dough.

nutritional count per serving
22.9g total fat
11.2g saturated fat
1960kJ (469 cal)
24.2g carbohydrate
39.9g protein
3.6g fibre

serving suggestion
Serve with steamed green beans or broccoli.

tip You can buy chopped lamb for stewing from the butcher or supermarket to save time.

to freeze Complete the recipe to end of step 4. Pack into freezer-proof containers, leaving a 2.5cm (1 inch) space to allow for expansion. Seal, label and freeze for up to 3 months. Thaw overnight in the fridge. Reheat in a saucepan or microwave on medium power (50%) until heated through.

SLOW-ROASTED BEEF AND GARLIC WITH MUSTARD CREAM

prep + cook time 4 hours 50 minutes (+ standing) **serves** 6

18 brown baby onions (720g)

2.5kg (5-pound) piece beef bolar blade or chuck

2 tablespoons olive oil

½ cup (125ml) red wine

2 sprigs fresh thyme

2 bulbs garlic, tops removed

1 cup (250ml) beef stock

MUSTARD CREAM

½ cup (120g) sour cream

2 tablespoons wholegrain mustard

1 Preheat oven to 120°C/250°F.

2 Place onions in a heatproof bowl; cover with boiling water and stand for 5 minutes. Drain, peel away the skins.

3 Brush beef all over with oil; cook in heated large flameproof baking dish until browned all over. Add wine, simmer, uncovered, until reduced by half. Remove dish from heat; sprinkle beef with thyme. Season to taste.

4 Add garlic, peeled onions and stock to dish, cover tightly; roast for 2½ hours. Uncover; baste meat with pan juices. Roast, uncovered, for further 2 hours. Cover; stand for 30 minutes before slicing.

5 Meanwhile, make mustard cream.

6 Serve beef with onions, garlic, strained pan juices and mustard cream.

MUSTARD CREAM Combine ingredients in a small bowl.

nutritional count per serving
33.5g total fat
14.1g saturated fat
2876kJ (688 cal)
4.5g carbohydrate
87.1g protein
3.1g fibre

serving suggestion
Serve with steamed green beans.

not suitable to freeze

LEBANESE LAMB AND POTATO BAKE

prep + cook time 1 hour 15 minutes **serves** 6

500g (1 pound) potatoes, sliced thinly

1 teaspoon ground coriander

2 tablespoons olive oil

1 small brown onion (80g), chopped finely

2 cloves garlic, crushed

800g (1½ pounds) minced (ground) lamb

½ teaspoon ground cinnamon

½ teaspoon ground allspice

½ cup (50g) packaged breadcrumbs

1 egg, beaten lightly

½ cup (140g) onion marmalade

2 tablespoons raisins

2 tablespoons roasted pine nuts

1 Preheat oven to 200°C/400°F. Oil a small baking dish; line the base and sides with baking paper.

2 Combine potato, coriander and half the oil in dish; season. Roast, uncovered, for 30 minutes.

3 Meanwhile, combine onion, garlic, lamb, cinnamon, allspice, breadcrumbs and egg in a medium bowl; season.

4 Spread lamb mixture over potato; drizzle with remaining oil. Roast, uncovered, for 20 minutes or until cooked through.

5 Spread onion marmalade over lamb; sprinkle with raisins and nuts.

nutritional count per serving
21.7g total fat
6g saturated fat
1736kJ (415 cal)
21.5g carbohydrate
32.3g protein
2.5g fibre

serving suggestion
Serve with a tomato, mint and red onion salad, and accompany with hummus, baba ghanoush or yoghurt.

note Onion marmalade, also called caramelised onion relish or onion jam, is available, in jars, from large supermarkets and delicatessens.

not suitable to freeze

family beef casserole

FAMILY BEEF CASSEROLE

prep + cook time 2 hours 30 minutes **serves** 6

2 tablespoons vegetable oil

2kg (4 pounds) beef chuck steak,
  chopped coarsely

2 medium brown onions (300g), sliced thinly

2 medium carrots (240g), sliced thickly

3 cloves garlic, crushed

¼ cup finely chopped fresh flat-leaf parsley

¼ cup (70g) tomato paste

2 teaspoons dijon mustard

1 cup (250ml) dry red wine

½ cup (125ml) beef stock

1 Preheat oven to 150°C/300°F.

2 Heat oil in a 2.5 litre (10-cup) flameproof baking
   dish; cook beef, in batches, until browned.
   Remove from dish.

3 Cook onion, carrot and garlic in same dish,
   stirring over heat, until onion is soft.

4 Return beef to dish; stir in parsley, paste, mustard,
   wine and stock. Season to taste. Roast, covered,
   for 1¾ hours or until beef is tender.

nutritional count per serving
21.4g total fat
7.1g saturated fat
2203kJ (527 cal)
6.1g carbohydrate
69.2g protein
2.6g fibre

serving suggestion
Serve with creamy mash.

tip Ask the butcher to cut
the meat for you, this saves
you some time.

to freeze Pack into freezer-
proof containers, leaving
a 2.5cm (1 inch) space to
allow for expansion. Seal,
label and freeze for up to
3 months. Thaw overnight
in the fridge. Reheat in a
saucepan or microwave on
medium power (50%) until
heated through.

ITALIAN VEAL CASSEROLE

prep + cook time 2 hours 30 minutes **serves** 4

1 tablespoon olive oil

4 thick pieces veal osso buco (1.2kg)

¾ cup (90g) pitted green olives, chopped coarsely

1 medium lemon (140g), quartered

2 cups (520g) bottled tomato pasta sauce

2 cups (500ml) water

4 drained anchovy fillets, chopped coarsley

½ cup (120g) firm ricotta cheese

½ cup (40g) finely grated parmesan cheese

½ cup coarsely chopped fresh flat-leaf parsley

1 Preheat oven to 160°C/325°F.

2 Heat oil in a large flameproof baking dish;
   cook veal until browned.

3 Add olives, lemon, sauce, and the water to dish;
   season. Roast, covered, for 2 hours.

4 Increase oven to 200°C/400°F.

5 Stir anchovy into veal mixture; top with ricotta,
   sprinkle with parmesan. Roast, uncovered,
   for 15 minutes or until cheese is browned.
   Serve sprinkled with parsley.

(photograph page 126)

nutritional count per serving
16.5g total fat
5.9g saturated fat
1788kJ (427 cal)
15.7g carbohydrate
52g protein
3.5g fibre

tips Place a piece of baking
paper, cut to fit inside the
dish, onto the surface of the
food before it goes into the
oven. This will stop the food
from browning too much.
Cover the dish itself with
a lid or foil.

Use a casserole dish big
enough to fit one layer of
the tightly-packed osso
buco, as they will shrink
during cooking. Buy pieces
of uniform thickness and
size and stand them up in
the dish to ensure that each
person receives a portion of
the rich bone marrow that
is found in the veal shin.

not suitable to freeze

italian veal casserole (recipe page 125)

braised lamb shanks with tzatziki and tomato salad (recipe pages 128 & 129)

BRAISED LAMB SHANKS WITH TZATZIKI AND TOMATO SALAD

prep + cook time 3 hours 30 minutes **serves** 6

⅓ cup (80ml) light olive oil

6 french-trimmed lamb shanks (1.2kg)

1 large brown onion (200g), chopped finely

1 large carrot (180g), chopped coarsely

1 stick celery (150g), trimmed, chopped finely

4 cloves garlic, chopped finely

2 cups (500ml) chicken stock

1 cup (250ml) dry white wine

2 tablespoons tomato paste

½ cup (100g) pearl barley

½ cup (100g) dried brown lentils

400g (12½ ounces) canned chickpeas
   (garbanzo beans), drained, rinsed

4 sprigs fresh thyme

1 cup (250ml) water

4 medium roma (egg) tomatoes (300g),
   chopped coarsely

1 tablespoon lemon juice

2 tablespoons extra virgin olive oil

⅓ cup finely chopped fresh flat-leaf parsley

TZATZIKI

1 lebanese cucumber (130g), peeled, seeded,
   grated finely

1 cup (280g) yoghurt

1 tablespoon lemon juice

2 cloves garlic, crushed

2 tablespoons finely chopped fresh mint

1 Preheat oven to 120°C/250°F.

2 Heat light olive oil in a 6-litre (24-cup) flameproof baking dish; cook lamb, in batches, until browned all over. Remove from dish.

3 Add onion, carrot and celery to same dish; cook, covered, over low heat, stirring occasionally, until soft. Add garlic, stock, wine, paste, barley, lentils, chickpeas and thyme; bring to the boil. Return lamb to dish, cover; cook, in oven, for 2 hours. Stir in the water; roast, covered, for 1 hour or until lamb is almost falling off the bone. Season to taste.

4 Meanwhile, combine tomato, juice, extra virgin olive oil and half the parsley in a small bowl; season to taste.

5 Make tzatziki.

6 Serve lamb topped with tomato salad and tzatziki; sprinkle with remaining parsley.

TZATZIKI Squeeze excess liquid from cucumber; combine cucumber with remaining ingredients in a small bowl. Season to taste.

(photograph page 127)

nutritional count per serving
31.9g total fat
8.5g saturated fat
2506kJ (599 cal)
31.3g carbohydrate
35.6g protein
9.6g fibre

serving suggestion
Serve with warmed or grilled pitta bread.

tip Remove lamb from the bone; add a little more stock to the mixture and serve as a thick soup.

to freeze Complete recipe to the end of step 3. Pack into freezer-proof containers, leaving a 2.5cm (1 inch) space to allow for expansion. Seal, label and freeze for up to 3 months. Thaw overnight in the fridge. Reheat in a saucepan or microwave on medium power (50%) until heated through.

LAMB RENDANG

prep + cook time 3 hours 45 minutes **serves** 4

2 teaspoons coriander seeds

¼ teaspoon ground turmeric

2 large brown onions (400g), chopped coarsely

4 cloves garlic, quartered

2 x 10cm (4-inch) sticks fresh lemon grass (40g), chopped coarsely

2cm (¾-inch) piece fresh galangal (10g), sliced thinly

4 fresh small red thai (serrano) chillies, chopped coarsely

2 fresh long red chillies, chopped coarsely

2 tablespoons coarsely chopped coriander (cilantro) root and stem mixture

2 tablespoons peanut oil

1.5kg (3-pound) butterflied leg of lamb

1⅔ cups (410ml) coconut milk

1 Dry-fry spices in a small frying pan, stirring, for 1 minute or until fragrant. Blend or process spices with onion, garlic, lemon grass, galangal, chillies and coriander root and stem mixture until mixture forms a paste.

2 Preheat oven to 150°C/300°F.

3 Heat half the oil in a large flameproof baking dish; cook lamb, turning occasionally, until browned all over. Remove from dish.

4 Heat remaining oil in same dish; cook paste, stirring, until fragrant. Add coconut milk; bring to the boil.

5 Return lamb to dish; roast, uncovered, turning occasionally, for 3 hours or until liquid has evaporated. Cover lamb; stand for 10 minutes before serving. Serve sprinkled with fresh coriander leaves, if you like.

nutritional count per serving
50.2g total fat
28.8g saturated fat
3490kJ (835 cal)
8.1g carbohydrate
86.5g protein
3.7g fibre

serving suggestion
Serve with steamed rice.

note We've given a spin to a classic rendang, the Malaysian meat curry that is also eaten throughout Indonesia and Singapore. Traditionally slowly cooked until the coconut milk sauce thickens and is quite dry, the succulent meat becomes so tender it virtually falls apart.

not suitable to freeze

VEAL SHANKS WITH HONEY AND LEMON

prep + cook time 4 hours 15 minutes **serves** 4

30g (1 ounce) butter, softened

4 french-trimmed veal shanks (2kg)

1 medium lemon (140g), quartered

⅓ cup (115g) honey

4 cloves garlic, crushed

⅓ cup (80ml) dry white wine

⅓ cup (80ml) veal or beef stock

1 Preheat oven to 160°C/325°F.

2 Grease four 30cm x 40cm (12-inch x 16-inch) pieces of baking paper with butter; place one shank on each piece of paper. Top each shank with a lemon quarter, 1 tablespoon of the honey and 1 garlic clove; season. Stand shanks upright, enclose with paper; tie loosely with kitchen string. Carefully pour combined wine and stock into packages; tighten string to secure firmly.

3 Stand packages in a small deep casserole dish, so they fit snugly. Cover; roast for 4 hours.

4 Serve shanks in their packages, to be opened at the table.

nutritional count per serving
11.3g total fat
4.1g saturated fat
1562kJ (467 cal)
24.9g carbohydrate
61.7g protein
1.4g fibre

serving suggestion
Serve with cheesy mash
(see page 174) and steamed
green vegetables.

not suitable to freeze

SLOW-COOKED LAMB SHANK AND BEAN RAGU

prep + cook time 3 hours (+ standing) **serves** 4

½ cup (100g) dried haricot beans

½ cup (100g) dried borlotti beans

8 french-trimmed lamb shanks (1.6kg)

2 tablespoons plain (all-purpose) flour

1 tablespoon olive oil

1 large brown onion (200g), chopped coarsely

1 medium carrot (120g), chopped coarsely

1 stick celery (150g), trimmed, chopped coarsely

1 fresh long red chilli, chopped finely

¼ cup (60ml) balsamic vinegar

425g (13½ ounces) canned crushed tomatoes

8 drained anchovies in oil

½ cup (125ml) dry white wine

1 cup (250ml) water

⅓ cup coarsely chopped fresh flat-leaf parsley

1 Place beans in a large bowl, cover with water; stand overnight. Rinse under cold water; drain. Place beans in a medium saucepan, cover with boiling water; bring to the boil. Reduce heat; simmer, uncovered, about 15 minutes or until beans are just tender. Drain.

2 Preheat oven to 180°C/350°F.

3 Toss lamb in flour; shake away excess. Heat oil in a large flameproof baking dish; cook lamb, in batches, until browned. Remove from dish.

4 Cook onion, carrot, celery and chilli in same dish, stirring, for 5 minutes or until onion softens. Return lamb to dish with beans, vinegar, tomatoes, anchovies, wine and the water; bring to the boil. Roast, covered, for 1 hour, stirring occasionally. Uncover; roast, for 1 hour or until meat is almost falling off the bone. Just before serving, stir parsley through ragu. Season to taste.

nutritional count per serving
18.1g total fat
6.5g saturated fat
2077kJ (497 cal)
24g carbohydrate
54.9g protein
5.2g fibre

note Haricot and borlotti beans are just two members of the legume family. From the humble baked bean to the chickpea, legumes contain healthy components linked with protection against diseases such as cancer, diabetes and heart problems. They are high in soluble fibre and low in fat.

not suitable to freeze

SPANISH CHICKEN CASSEROLE

prep + cook time 1 hour 35 minutes **serves** 4

1 tablespoon olive oil

4 chicken drumsticks (600g)

4 chicken thigh cutlets (800g)

1 large brown onion (200g), chopped finely

4 medium potatoes (800g), quartered

½ cup (80g) roasted pine nuts

½ cup (80g) roasted blanched almonds

3 cups (750ml) chicken stock

1 cup (250ml) dry white wine

⅓ cup (80ml) lemon juice

4 cloves garlic, crushed

2 tablespoons fresh thyme leaves

½ cup coarsely chopped fresh flat-leaf parsley

500g (1 pound) baby green beans, trimmed

1   Preheat oven to 180°C/350°F.

2   Heat oil in a large flameproof baking dish; cook chicken, in batches, over heat until browned. Remove from dish.

3   Cook onion in same dish, stirring over heat, until soft. Return chicken to dish with potato, nuts, stock, wine, juice, garlic, thyme and half the parsley; bring to the boil. Cover; bake, for 1 hour or until chicken is cooked through.

4   Meanwhile, boil, steam or microwave beans until tender; drain.

5   Serve chicken topped with remaining parsley; accompany with beans.

nutritional count per serving
61.4g total fat
12.4g saturated fat
4050kJ (969 cal)
35g carbohydrate
57g protein
10.4g fibre

serving suggestion
Serve with a green salad.

tip Carlingford, desiree, kestrel or mondial potatoes are good varieties to use in this dish.

not suitable to freeze

ASIAN BROTH WITH CRISP PORK BELLY

prep + cook time 2 hours 20 minutes (+ standing & refrigeration) **serves** 4

½ cup (100g) dried soy beans

1kg (2 pounds) boned pork belly, rind-on

1½ teaspoons cooking salt (kosher salt)

1 teaspoon five-spice powder

2 cups (500ml) water

1 litre (4 cups) chicken stock

1 fresh small red thai (serrano) chilli, chopped finely

2 whole star anise

5cm (2-inch) piece fresh ginger (25g), slivered

⅓ cup (80ml) hoisin sauce

500g (1 pound) choy sum, sliced thinly

3 green onions (scallions), sliced thinly

1 Place beans in small bowl, cover with cold water; stand overnight.

2 Place pork on a board, rind-side up; using a sharp knife, score pork by making shallow cuts diagonally in both directions at 1cm (½-inch) intervals. Rub combined salt and half the five-spice into cuts; slice pork into 10 pieces. Place pork, rind-side up, on tray, cover loosely; refrigerate overnight.

3 Preheat oven to 240°C/475°F.

4 Rinse beans under cold water; drain. Place beans in a medium saucepan of boiling water; bring to the boil. Reduce heat; simmer, uncovered, until tender. Drain.

5 Meanwhile, place pork on a wire rack in a shallow baking dish; roast, uncovered, for 30 minutes. Reduce oven to 160°C/325°F; roast, uncovered, for 45 minutes or until crackling is browned and crisp. Cut pork pieces in half.

6 Place beans in large saucepan with the water, stock, chilli, star anise, ginger, sauce and remaining five-spice; bring to the boil. Reduce heat; simmer, covered, for 30 minutes. Stir in choy sum and onion.

7 Serve bowls of soup topped with pork.

nutritional count per serving
59.6g total fat
20.2g saturated fat
3687kJ (882 cal)
12.4g carbohydrate
72.2g protein
6.2g fibre

tip Since the beans are soaked overnight, the pork also benefits from being prepared the day before and refrigerated overnight. This helps the rind dry out, which ensures a crisp crackling at the end of cooking.

not suitable to freeze

APPLES, PORK AND PRUNES

prep + cook time 1 hour 55 minutes **serves** 4

2 tablespoons vegetable oil

2 small leeks (400g), sliced thinly

800g (1½ pounds) diced pork

½ cup (75g) plain (all-purpose) flour

1 litre (4 cups) chicken stock

½ cup (100g) white long-grain rice

4 medium apples (600g), sliced thickly

1 cup (170g) pitted prunes

2 tablespoons coarsely chopped fresh sage

1 Preheat oven to160°C/325°F.

2 Heat half the oil in a 2.5-litre (10-cup) flameproof baking dish; cook leek, stirring, until soft. Remove from dish.

3 Toss pork in flour; shake away excess flour.

4 Heat remaining oil in same dish; cook pork, stirring, until browned. Add leek and stock; roast, covered, for 45 minutes.

5 Remove dish from oven; skim off any fat. Stir in rice, apple, prunes and half the sage; roast, covered, for 20 minutes or until pork is tender. Serve topped with remaining sage.

nutritional count per serving
27.1g total fat
7.1g saturated fat
3022kJ (723 cal)
63.9g carbohydrate
51.4g protein
8.3g fibre

tip You can use apples such as granny smith, golden delicious, sundowner, fuji or jonagolds in this recipe.

not suitable to freeze

RED BEAN, PORK AND RICE

prep + cook time 3 hours 30 minutes **serves** 4

1kg (2-pound) piece boneless pork belly

2 teaspoons caster (superfine) sugar

4cm (1½-inch) piece fresh ginger (20g), grated

2 cloves garlic, crushed

2 green onions (scallion), chopped coarsely

¼ cup (60ml) chinese cooking wine (shao hsing)

2 tablespoons sweetened red bean paste

2 tablespoons light soy sauce

1 whole star anise

½ teaspoon ground cardamom

2½ cups (625ml) water

1 cup (200g) white long-grain rice

1½ cups (375ml) water, extra

4 frozen chinese steamed rice buns

1 green onion (scallion), sliced thinly, extra

1 Preheat oven to 150°C/300°F.

2 Remove rind from pork, trim excess fat; chop pork coarsely. Heat a large flameproof dish; cook pork, in batches, until browned. Remove from dish.

3 Discard all but about 2 tablespoons of fat from dish. Add sugar to dish; cook, stirring, over low heat, until browned. Return pork to dish with ginger, garlic, chopped onion, wine, paste, sauce, star anise, cardamom and the water. Cover dish; roast, for 3 hours.

4 Meanwhile, rinse rice in a sieve under cold water until water runs clear; drain well. Remove dish from oven; stir in rice and the extra water. Roast, covered, for 18 minutes or until rice is tender. Season to taste.

5 Meanwhile, steam or microwave buns according to directions on packet.

6 Serve pork and rice with buns and sliced onion.

nutritional count per serving
66.2g total fat
23.9g saturated fat
4834kJ (1155 cal)
74.6g carbohydrate
60.9g protein
4.3g fibre

tip Frozen steamed rice buns are available in the freezer section of Asian supermarkets and most large supermarkets.

not suitable to freeze

PROSCIUTTO-WRAPPED PORK AND VEAL MEATLOAF

prep + cook time 1 hour 20 minutes **serves** 4

4 slices white bread (180g)

½ cup (125ml) milk

300g (9½ ounces) minced (ground) pork

450g (14½ ounces) minced (ground) veal

1 small leek (200g), chopped finely

2 cloves garlic, crushed

2 teaspoons fresh thyme leaves

½ cup finely chopped fresh flat-leaf parsley

½ cup (40g) finely grated parmesan cheese

2 eggs

8 slices prosciutto (120g)

1 tablespoon dijon mustard

1   Preheat oven to 200°C/400°F.

2   Remove crusts from bread; tear bread into pieces, place in a large bowl. Pour milk over bread; stand for 2 minutes.

3   Add pork and veal to bowl with leek, garlic, herbs, cheese and eggs; mix well. Roughly shape mixture into a mound.

4   Lay 6 slices of prosciutto on a board, overlapping slightly; brush with mustard. Place mince mound onto prosciutto slices; using wet hands, pat mixture into a loaf shape. Lay remaining 2 slices of prosciutto lengthways on top of meatloaf. Wrap bottom prosciutto slices around sides of meatloaf to meet slices on top. Turn meatloaf over carefully; place on a wire rack in a large shallow baking dish.

5   Cook meatloaf, uncovered, for 1 hour or until juices run clear. Cover meatloaf; stand for 10 minutes before serving.

nutritional count per serving
23.4g total fat
9.6g saturated fat
2266kJ (542 cal)
23.4g carbohydrate
58g protein
2.9g fibre

serving suggestion
Serve with any of the mashes on pages 174 & 175.

not suitable to freeze

CLASSIC ROAST CHICKEN

prep + cook time 2 hours (+ cooling) **serves** 4

40g (1½ ounces) butter
2 rindless bacon slices (130g), chopped finely
1 small leek (200g), sliced thinly
2 sticks celery (300g), trimmed, chopped finely
2 cups (140g) stale breadcrumbs
1 egg, beaten lightly
1 tablespoon coarsely chopped fresh sage
1.8kg (3½-pound) whole chicken
2 tablespoons olive oil
6 medium potatoes (1.2kg), halved
2 tablespoons plain (all-purpose) flour
2 cups (500ml) chicken stock
1 cup (250ml) water

1   Melt butter in a medium frying pan; cook bacon, leek and celery until vegetables are tender. Cool. Combine bacon mixture, breadcrumbs, egg and sage in a medium bowl.
2   Preheat oven to 200°C/400°F.
3   Wash chicken under cold running water; pat dry inside and out with absorbent paper. Tuck wing tips under chicken. Trim skin around neck; secure to underside of chicken with toothpicks.

4   Fill chicken cavity with bacon mixture; tie legs together with string. Place chicken on an oiled wire rack in a large flameproof baking dish. Rub chicken all over with half the oil; roast, uncovered, for 1½ hours.
5   Meanwhile, boil, steam or microwave potato for 5 minutes; drain. Combine potatoes and remaining oil in a large shallow baking dish; roast alongside chicken for 1 hour, turning occasionally during roasting. Remove chicken from oven; cover to keep warm. Discard toothpicks.
6   Increase oven to 240°C/475°F; roast potatoes for a further 15 minutes or until browned and crisp.
7   Meanwhile, drain all but 2 tablespoons of the juices from chicken dish, add flour; cook, stirring over medium heat, until mixture thickens and bubbles. Gradually add combined stock and the water, stirring until gravy boils and thickens. Strain into a large jug.
8   Serve chicken and potatoes with gravy.

nutritional count per serving
50.2g total fat
16.8g saturated fat
4138kJ (989 cal)
61.5g carbohydrate
68.3g protein
8.2g fibre

serving suggestion
Serve with steamed broccoli, green beans and baby carrots.

tip Coliban, delaware and kestrel potatoes are ideal varieties for roasting.

not suitable to freeze

BAKED CHICKEN WITH RATATOUILLE

prep + cook time 1 hours 15 minutes **serves** 4

1 small brown onion (80g), chopped coarsely

1 medium red capsicum (bell pepper) (200g), chopped coarsely

1 small eggplant (300g), chopped coarsely

2 medium zucchini (240g), chopped coarsley

250g (8 ounces) cherry tomatoes

4 cloves garlic, peeled

¼ cup fresh oregano sprigs

1 tablespoon red wine vinegar

1 teaspoon caster (superfine) sugar

¼ cup (60ml) olive oil

4 x 200g (6½-ounce) chicken breast fillets

240g (7½ ounces) semi-soft goat's cheese, sliced thickly

½ cup loosely packed fresh small basil leaves

1 Preheat oven to 220°C/425°F.

2 Combine onion, capsicum, eggplant, zucchini, tomatoes, garlic, oregano, vinegar, sugar and 2 tablespoons of the oil in a large baking dish. Cover dish with foil; bake for 45 minutes.

3 Uncover dish; top vegetable mixture with chicken and cheese, season. Drizzle with remaining oil. Bake, uncovered, for 15 minutes or until chicken is cooked.

4 Serve chicken topped with basil leaves.

nutritional count per serving
27g total fat
9.2g saturated fat
2140kJ (512 cal)
9.1g carbohydrate
55.6g protein
5.3g fibre

serving suggestion
Serve with soft polenta (see page 313).

tip Ratatouille is a classic French dish, popular for its hearty flavour and attractive, rustic presentation. It is the perfect accompaniment not only for chicken but also for meat and fish.

not suitable to freeze

CLAY POT CHICKEN

prep + cook time 1 hour 10 minutes (+ refrigeration) **serves** 4

800g (1½ pounds) chicken thigh fillets, halved

4 cloves garlic, crushed

1 tablespoon fish sauce

1 tablespoon soy sauce

1 tablespoon hoisin sauce

2 tablespoons lime juice

10cm (4-inch) stick fresh lemon grass (20g),
  chopped finely

1 large brown onion (200g), quartered

1 fresh long red chilli, sliced thinly

½ cup (125ml) chicken stock

100g (3 ounces) fresh shiitake mushrooms, halved

4 green onions (scallions), cut into 4cm (1½-inch) pieces

½ small cabbage (600g), cut into 6cm (2½-inch) squares

1 Combine chicken, garlic, sauces, juice and lemon grass in a large bowl. Cover; refrigerate for 3 hours or overnight.

2 Preheat oven to 180°C/350°F.

3 Place chicken mixture in a clay pot or a 2.5-litre (10-cup) ovenproof dish with brown onion, chilli and stock; mix gently to combine. Bake, covered, for 45 minutes.

4 Add mushrooms, green onion and cabbage; bake, covered, stirring occasionally, for 15 minutes or until chicken is cooked through.

nutritional count per serving
9.2g total fat
2.5g saturated fat
1296kJ (310 cal)
9.4g carbohydrate
46.6g protein
8.2g fibre

serving suggestion
Serve with steamed rice.

note Clay pots are typically soaked in water for 15 to 30 minutes before cooking. The food is then placed in the pot and baked. As the pot warms it produces steam, allowing the food to lose less moisture creating a tender, flavoursome meal.

not suitable to freeze

CHICKEN POT ROAST WITH MUSTARD CREAM SAUCE

prep + cook time 2 hours 15 minutes **serves** 4

1.6kg (3¼-pounds) whole chicken

1 tablespoon olive oil

12 shallots (300g), halved

20 baby carrots (400g), trimmed

3 small parsnips (360g), chopped coarsely

1 cup (250ml) dry white wine

2 cups (500ml) chicken stock

2 dried bay leaves

200g (6½ ounces) swiss brown mushrooms

2 tablespoons pouring cream

2 tablespoons wholegrain mustard

1 Preheat oven to 200°C/400°F.

2 Wash chicken under cold water; pat dry inside and out with absorbent paper.

3 Heat oil in a large flameproof baking dish; cook chicken until browned all over. Remove chicken.

4 Cook shallot, carrot and parsnip in same dish, stirring, for 5 minutes or until vegetables are browned lightly.

5 Return chicken to dish with wine, stock and bay leaves; bring to the boil. Roast, covered, for 30 minutes. Uncover; roast, for 30 minutes or until chicken is cooked through. Add mushrooms; roast, uncovered, for 10 minutes or until mushrooms are tender.

6 Remove chicken and vegetables from dish; cover to keep warm. Add cream and mustard to dish; bring to the boil. Boil, uncovered, for 5 minutes or until sauce thickens slightly, stirring occasionally.

7 Serve chicken, cut into pieces, with vegetables and mustard cream sauce.

nutritional count per serving
42.2g total fat
13.8g saturated fat
2859kJ (684 cal)
16.9g carbohydrate
46.7g protein
6.6g fibre

tip Swiss brown mushrooms, also known as roman or cremini, are light-to-dark brown in colour with a full bodied flavour. Store on a tray in a single layer, covered with damp, absorbent paper and keep where cool air can circulate around them.

not suitable to freeze

BAKED PRAWN, ASPARAGUS AND BROAD BEAN RISOTTO

prep + cook time 1 hour 15 minutes **serves** 4

1 tablespoon olive oil

1 large brown onion (200g), chopped finely

2 cloves garlic, crushed

2 cups (400g) arborio rice

½ cup (125ml) dry white wine

1 litre (4 cups) chicken stock

1½ cups (375ml) water

1 tablespoon finely grated lemon rind

⅓ cup (80ml) lemon juice

1kg (2 pounds) uncooked medium king prawns (shrimp)

170g (5½ ounces) asparagus, trimmed,
  cut into 3cm (1¼-inch) lengths

1 cup (150g) shelled, peeled fresh broad (fava) beans

⅓ cup coarsely chopped fresh mint

1 Preheat oven to 180°C/350°F.

2 Heat oil in a shallow large flameproof baking dish; cook onion and garlic, stirring, until onion softens. Add rice; stir to coat in onion mixture. Add wine; bring to the boil. Boil, uncovered, stirring, until liquid is absorbed. Stir in stock, the water, rind and juice; bring to the boil. Cover tightly, transfer to oven; cook for 25 minutes, stirring halfway through cooking time.

3 Meanwhile, shell and devein prawns, leaving tails intact.

4 Uncover risotto, return to oven; cook for 15 minutes. Stir in prawns, asparagus and broad beans, return to oven; cook, uncovered, for 10 minutes or until prawns change colour and rice is tender.

5 Serve bowls of risotto topped with mint.

nutritional count per serving
7.2g total fat
1.4g saturated fat
2512kJ (601 cal)
85.9g carbohydrate
39.5g protein
4.9g fibre

tip You will need about 500g (1 pound) fresh broad beans in the pod to get the required amount of shelled beans.

not suitable to freeze

TUNA POTATO BAKE

prep + cook time 1 hours 45 minutes **serves** 6

1.2kg (2½ pounds) potatoes, sliced thinly

425g (13½ ounces) canned tuna in springwater,
 drained, flaked

1 small brown onion (80g), sliced thinly

1 cup loosely packed fresh flat-leaf parsley leaves

2 cups (200g) coarsely grated havarti cheese

1 cup (250ml) pouring cream

2 cloves garlic, crushed

2 teaspoons finely grated lemon rind

1 Preheat oven to 200°C/400°F. Grease a shallow 2-litre (8-cup) ovenproof dish.

2 Layer about one-third of the potato in dish; top with half the tuna, half the onion and half the parsley. Sprinkle with ½ cup of the cheese. Repeat layering, finishing with potato; press down firmly. Cover dish with foil; bake for 1 hour.

3 Combine cream, garlic and the rind in a small bowl; season to taste. Pour cream mixture over potato. Sprinkle with remaining cheese.

4 Bake, uncovered, for 30 minutes or until potato is tender and top is browned.

nutritional count per serving
32.3g total fat
20.5g saturated fat
2119kJ (506 cal)
23.2g carbohydrate
29.1g protein
3.4g fibre

serving suggestion
Serve with a green salad.

tip Havarti cheese is a soft, mild, cow's-milk cheese from Denmark; it is a good melting cheese, but you could use mozzarella or a colby cheddar instead. Pale yellow in colour, it has small irregular holes throughout. When young, havarti has a mild, yet tangy, taste. As the cheese ages, its flavour intensifies and sharpens.

not suitable to freeze

POTATO AND OLIVE-FILLED BANANA CHILLIES

prep + cook time 2 hours serves 4

40g (1½ ounces) butter

2 tablespoons olive oil

3 cloves garlic, crushed

2 teaspoons ground cumin

2 teaspoons dried oregano

600g (1¼ pounds) potatoes, cut into 1cm (½-inch) pieces

3 large tomatoes (660g), cut into 1cm (½-inch) pieces

1 cup (120g) pitted green olives, chopped coarsely

2 cups (240g) coarsely grated cheddar cheese

8 red or yellow banana chillies (1.3kg)

TOMATO SAUCE

1 tablespoon olive oil

1 medium red onion (170g), chopped coarsely

1 clove garlic, crushed

1 tablespoon ground cumin

2 teaspoons dried oregano

800g (1½ pounds) canned diced tomatoes

½ cup (125ml) water

1 Preheat oven to 180°C/350°F.

2 Heat butter and oil in a large frying pan; cook garlic, cumin, oregano and potato, stirring occasionally, for 10 minutes or until potato is browned. Add tomato and olives; cook, stirring, for 10 minutes or until liquid has evaporated. Transfer to a large bowl; stir in cheese.

3 Meanwhile, using a sharp knife, make a small horizontal cut in each chilli 1cm (½ inch) below the stem, then make lengthways slit in chilli, starting from the horizontal cut and ending 1cm (½ inch) from tip, taking care not to cut all the way through; discard membrane and seeds. Carefully divide filling among chillies, securing each with a toothpick.

4 Make tomato sauce.

5 Pour tomato sauce into a small ovenproof dish; place chillies on sauce. Cover; bake for 40 minutes or until chillies are tender.

TOMATO SAUCE Heat oil in a large saucepan; cook onion, garlic, cumin and oregano, stirring, until onion softens. Add tomatoes and the water; bring to the boil. Reduce heat; simmer, uncovered, for 10 minutes.

nutritional count per serving
43.8g total fat
20.3g saturated fat
2725kJ (652 cal)
39.9g carbohydrate
24.4g protein
11.2g fibre

serving suggestion
Serve with a green salad.

note Banana chillies are sweet in flavour when ripe, a lighter flavour than capsicum (bell pepper), with very little heat.

not suitable to freeze

VEGETABLE PITHIVIERS WITH TOMATO SAUCE

prep + cook time 3 hours serves 4

10 large roma (egg) tomatoes (900g), quartered
2 teaspoons light brown sugar
⅓ cup (80ml) olive oil
2 tablespoons red wine vinegar
2 large red capsicums (bell peppers) (700g), halved
30g (1 ounce) butter
2 large green zucchini (300g), sliced thinly
7 flat mushrooms (560g), sliced thinly
1 clove garlic, crushed
1 tablespoon port
5 sheets puff pastry
1 egg yolk
1 tablespoon milk
50g (1½ ounces) baby spinach leaves

1   Preheat oven to 180°C/350°F. Oil oven trays.

2   Combine tomato, sugar, half the oil and half the vinegar in a large bowl. Place tomato pieces, skin-side down, on an oven tray; roast for 1 hour 40 minutes. Remove from oven; return to same bowl; crush with potato masher. Cover to keep warm; reserve tomato sauce.

3   Place capsicum pieces skin-side up, on an oven tray. Roast in oven for 40 minutes or until softened. Place capsicum in a plastic bag; close tightly. Cool. Discard skin, membrane and seeds; slice thinly.

4   Meanwhile, melt butter in a large frying pan; cook zucchini, stirring, for 5 minutes or until softened. Place zucchini in a small bowl; cover to keep warm. Cook mushrooms and garlic in same pan, stirring, for 5 minutes or until mushrooms soften. Add port; cook, stirring, until liquid evaporates.

5   Cut 4 pastry sheets into 16cm (6½-inch) squares; cut remaining sheet into quarters. Place one of the small squares on an oven tray; centre 9cm (3¾-inch) cutter on pastry. Layer one-quarter of the mushroom mixture, one-quarter of the zucchini and one-quarter of the capsicum on pastry; remove cutter. Brush border with a little combined egg yolk and milk; top with one of the large squares, press edges together to seal.

6   Using a sharp knife, cut around pithiviers, leaving a 5mm (¼-inch) border; mark pastry with a swirl design from centre to side, without cutting through. Brush with egg mixture. Repeat with remaining pastry, vegetables and egg mixture. Bake for 25 minutes.

7   Combine spinach, remaining oil and remaining vinegar in small bowl.

8   Serve pithivier with tomato sauce and salad.

nutritional count per serving   **not suitable to freeze**
74.3g total fat
10.5g saturated fat
4824kJ (1154 cal)
90.9g carbohydrate
23.5g protein
12.3g fibre

ROASTED ROOT VEGETABLE RATATOUILLE

prep + cook time 2 hours 10 minutes **serves** 6

800g (1½ pounds) celeriac (celery root), trimmed, chopped coarsely

2 large carrots (360g), chopped coarsely

2 medium parsnips (500g), chopped coarsely

2 medium kumara (800g), chopped coarsely

⅓ cup (80ml) olive oil

1 large brown onion (200g), chopped finely

3 cloves garlic, crushed

¼ cup loosely packed fresh oregano leaves

1 tablespoon tomato paste

850g (1¾ pounds) canned crushed tomatoes

½ cup (125ml) dry red wine

1 cup (250ml) water

½ cup (40g) coarsely grated parmesan cheese

2½ cups (250g) coarsely grated mozzarella cheese

1 cup (70g) fresh breadcrumbs

2 teaspoons finely grated lemon rind

½ cup coarsely chopped fresh flat-leaf parsley

2 tablespoons coarsely chopped fresh oregano

1 Preheat oven to 220°C/425°F.

2 Combine celeriac, carrot, parsnip, kumara and half the oil in a large deep baking dish. Roast, uncovered, for 50 minutes or until vegetables are tender and browned lightly, stirring halfway through cooking.

3 Meanwhile, heat remaining oil in a large saucepan; cook onion, garlic and oregano leaves, stirring, until onion softens. Add paste; cook, stirring, for 1 minute. Add tomatoes, wine and the water; bring to the boil. Boil, uncovered, for 10 minutes, stirring occasionally.

4 Add tomato mixture to roasted vegetables; toss gently to combine. Top with combined cheeses, breadcrumbs, rind, parsley and chopped oregano. Bake, uncovered, for 20 minutes or until top browns lightly.

nutritional count per serving
24.7g total fat
9.1g saturated fat
2090kJ (500 cal)
43.9g carbohydrate
22.1g protein
12.7g fibre

serving suggestion
Serve with a green salad.

not suitable to freeze

BEEF AND SHIITAKE MUSHROOM PIE

prep + cook time 2 hours 45 minutes **serves** 4

30g (1 ounce) butter

900g (1¾ pounds) beef brisket, chopped coarsely

¼ cup (35g) plain (all-purpose) flour

¼ cup (60ml) light soy sauce

½ cup (125ml) mirin

½ cup (125ml) sake

1 cup (250ml) water

100g (3 ounces) oyster mushrooms, chopped coarsely

100g (3 ounces) fresh shiitake mushrooms,
  chopped coarsely

1 sheet puff pastry

1 egg, beaten lightly

½ teaspoon black sesame seeds

½ teaspoon white sesame seeds

1 Preheat oven to 160°C/325°F.

2 Melt butter, on stove top, in shallow 22cm (9-inch) flameproof dish; cook beef, in batches, stirring, until browned. Return beef to dish; sprinkle with flour, stir to combine. Gradually stir in sauce, mirin, sake and the water until smooth. Roast, covered, for 2 hours or until beef is tender. Season to taste.

3 Increase oven to 180°C/350°F.

4 Stir mushrooms into dish; season. Cover dish with pastry; brush with egg and sprinkle with seeds.

5 Bake pie for 15 minutes or until pastry is browned.

nutritional count per serving
47.5g total fat
18.7g saturated fat
3641kJ (871 cal)
23.8g carbohydrate
72.5g protein
2.7g fibre

tip You can use any of your favourite mushrooms for this recipe.

not suitable to freeze

BAKED PASSIONFRUIT TART

prep + cook time 1 hour 30 minutes (+ refrigeration & cooling) **serves** 8

1½ cups (225g) plain (all-purpose) flour

⅓ cup (55g) icing (confectioners') sugar

150g (4½ ounces) cold unsalted butter, chopped

2 egg yolks

PASSIONFRUIT FILLING

7 egg yolks

1 cup (220g) caster (superfine) sugar

1 teaspoon finely grated lemon rind

⅓ cup (80ml) passionfruit pulp

1 cup (250ml) thickened (heavy) cream

1 Process flour, sugar and butter until crumbly. Add egg yolks, process until ingredients just come together. Knead dough on a floured surface until smooth. Enclose in plastic wrap; refrigerate 30 minutes.

2 Roll pastry between sheets of baking paper until large enough to line a 24cm (9½-inch) round loose-based tart tin. Ease pastry into base and side of tin; trim edge. Cover; refrigerate 1 hour.

3 Preheat oven to 200°C/400°F.

4 Line pastry with baking paper, fill with dried beans or rice. Place tin on an oven tray; bake 10 minutes. Remove paper and beans; bake further 10 minutes or until pastry is lightly browned. Cool.

5 Reduce oven to 150°C/300°F.

6 Meanwhile, make passionfruit filling; pour into pastry case.

7 Bake tart for 1 hour or until just set; cool. Serve at room temperature, dusted with a little sifted icing sugar, if you like.

PASSIONFRUIT FILLING Combine ingredients in a medium bowl.

nutritional count per serving
33g total fat
19.6g saturated fat
2282kJ (546 cal)
56.3g carbohydrate
7.1g protein
2.5g fibre

serving suggestion
Serve with thick (double) cream or vanilla ice-cream.

tip You will need about 4 passionfruit for this recipe.

not suitable to freeze

LOW-FAT LEMON AND BLACKBERRY CHEESECAKE

prep +cooking time 1 hour 20 minutes (+ refrigeration) **serves** 12

200g (6½ ounces) low-fat cottage cheese

250g (8 ounces) light spreadable cream cheese

2 teaspoons finely grated lemon rind

¾ cup (165g) caster (superfine) sugar

2 eggs

⅓ cup (55g) semolina

¼ cup (35g) self-raising flour

¼ cup (60ml) buttermilk

200g (6½ ounces) fresh or frozen blackberries

1 Preheat oven to 160ºC/325ºF. Grease a 20cm (8-inch) round springform tin; line the base with baking paper. Place tin on an oven tray.

2 Beat cheeses, rind and sugar in a medium bowl with an electric mixer until smooth. Beat in eggs, one at a time. Stir in semolina and sifted flour, then buttermilk. Pour mixture into tin; top with blackberries.

3 Bake cheesecake for 1 hour. Cool cheesecake in oven with door ajar.

4 Refrigerate cheesecake 3 hours or overnight.

5 Serve dusted with sifted icing (confectioners') sugar, if you like.

nutritional count per serving
7.6g total fat
4.5g saturated fat
752kJ (180 cal)
21.3g carbohydrate
6.6g protein
1.3g fibre

tip This cheesecake is best made a day before serving.

not suitable to freeze

ACCOMPANIMENTS
potatoes & mashes

ROAST POTATOES

prep + cook time 1 hour 15 minutes **serves** 4

Preheat oven to 220°C/425°F. Oil an oven tray. Cut 6 medium potatoes in half horizontally. Boil, steam or microwave potatoes for 5 minutes; drain. Pat dry; cool for 10 minutes. Gently rake rounded sides with the tines of fork; place, in a single layer, cut-side down, on oven tray. Brush with 2 tablespoons light olive oil; season. Roast for 50 minutes or until potatoes are browned and crisp.

nutritional count per serving 9.4g total fat (1.3g saturated fat); 1246kJ (298 cal); 42.6g carbohydrate; 7.8g protein; 5.2g fibre

HASSELBACK POTATOES

prep + cook time 1 hour 15 minutes **serves** 4

Preheat oven to 180°C/350°F. Cut 6 medium potatoes in half horizontally; slice thinly, without cutting all the way through. Brush 40g (1½ ounces) melted butter combined with 2 tablespoons olive oil over potatoes; place in a baking dish. Roast for 45 minutes, brushing with butter mixture. Roast for a further 15 minutes, without brushing, or until potatoes are tender. Sprinkle potatoes with ¼ cup stale breadcrumbs combined with ½ cup finely grated cheddar cheese. Roast a further 10 minutes or until browned lightly.

nutritional count per serving 22.9g total fat (10g saturated fat); 1756kJ (420 cal); 40.2g carbohydrate; 11.3g protein; 4.7g fibre

POTATO CRUSH

prep + cook time 20 minutes **serves** 4

Boil, steam or microwave 1kg (2 pounds) baby new potatoes until tender; drain. Mash about half the potatoes with ½ cup sour cream and 40g (1½ ounces) softened butter in a large bowl until smooth. Using the back of a fork or a potato masher, gently crush remaining potatoes until skins burst and flesh is just flattened; fold into mash mixture. Season to taste. Sprinkle with 2 tablespoons coarsely chopped fresh flat-leaf parsley.

nutritional count per serving 20.4g total fat (13.2g saturated fat); 1480kJ (354 cal); 33.7g carbohydrate; 6.8g protein; 5g fibre

POTATOES ANNA

prep + cook time 1 hour 15 minutes **serves** 6

Preheat oven to 240°C/475°F. Oil a shallow 2-litre (8-cup) 26cm (10½-inch) round baking dish. Slice 1.2kg (2½ pounds) potatoes into 2mm (⅛-inch) slices; pat dry. Melt 100g (3 ounces) butter. Place a single layer of potato, slightly overlapping, into dish; brush with a little of the butter. Layer with remaining potato and butter. Cover with foil; bake for 20 minutes. Discard foil; press down on potato with a metal spatula. Reduce oven to 220°C/425°F; bake for 30 minutes or until top is crisp and browned lightly.

nutritional count per serving 13.9g total fat (9g saturated fat); 1066kJ (255 cal); 26.3g carbohydrate; 4.9g protein; 3.2g fibre

CHEESY MASH

prep + cook time 30 minutes **serves** 4

Coarsely chop 1kg (2 pounds) potatoes; boil, steam or microwave until tender, drain. Mash potato with 1 cup finely grated parmesan cheese, ⅔ cup finely grated mozzarella cheese, 1 cup mascarpone cheese and ½ cup hot milk in large bowl. Season to taste.

nutritional count per serving 48.1g total fat (31.3g saturated fat); 2763kJ (661 cal); 35.4g carbohydrate; 20.7g protein; 4g fibre

KUMARA MASH

prep + cook time 30 minutes **serves** 4

Coarsely chop 500g (1 pound) kumara (orange sweet potato) and 500g (1 pound) potatoes; boil, steam or microwave, together, until tender; drain. Mash in a large bowl; stir in ¼ cup hot chicken stock and 40g (1½ ounces) melted butter. Season to taste.

nutritional count per serving 8.5g total fat (5.4g saturated fat); 1024kJ (245 cal); 34.2g carbohydrate; 5.6g protein; 4.3g fibre

PEA MASH

prep + cook time 30 minutes **serves** 4

Coarsely chop 1kg (2 pounds) potatoes; boil, steam or microwave potato and 1½ cups frozen peas, separately, until tender; drain. Mash potato in a large bowl; stir in ¾ cup hot milk and 50g (1½ ounces) softened butter. Using a fork, mash peas in a small bowl; stir into potato mixture. Season to taste.

nutritional count per serving 12.6g total fat (8g saturated fat); 1392kJ (333 cal); 39.8g carbohydrate; 11.1g protein; 7.5g fibre

CAPSICUM MASH

prep + cook time 30 minutes **serves** 4

Quarter 2 red capsicums (bell peppers); discard seeds and membranes. Roast under a hot grill (broiler), skin-side up, until skin blisters and blackens. Cover capsicum with plastic for 5 minutes, then peel away skin; chop capsicum coarsely. Blend capsicum until smooth. Meanwhile, boil, steam or microwave 1kg (2 pounds) coarsely chopped potato until tender; drain. Mash potato in a large bowl; stir in ½ cup hot pouring cream and 20g (¾ ounce) softened butter. Add capsicum to mash; stir until combined. Season to taste.

nutritional count per serving 18g total fat (11.6g saturated fat); 1446kJ (346 cal); 36.2g carbohydrate; 7.7g protein; 4.7g fibre

FREEZER FRIENDLY

FOR THE SLOW COOKER

Slow cookers are perfect for creating large quantities of delicious food that you can freeze and enjoy later. Casseroles and curries in particular benefit from slow cooking, freezing and then slow reheating. Try one today instead of opting for take-away.

MEXICAN PULL-APART PORK

prep + cook time 8 hours 30 minutes **serves** 6

2 medium red capsicums (bell peppers) (400g),
  sliced thinly
2 medium brown onions (300g), sliced thinly
375g (12 ounces) bottled chunky mild tomato salsa
1 cup (280g) barbecue sauce
4 cloves garlic, crushed
3 teaspoons ground cumin
2 teaspoons cayenne pepper
1 teaspoon dried oregano
1kg (2-pound) boneless pork shoulder
12 large flour tortillas
1 cup (240g) sour cream
1 cup coarsely chopped fresh coriander (cilantro)

1 Combine capsicum, onion, salsa, sauce, garlic, spices and oregano in a 4.5-litre (18-cup) slow cooker; add pork, turn to coat in mixture. Cook, covered, on low, for 8 hours.

2 Carefully remove pork from cooker; shred meat using two forks. Return pork to cooker; stir gently. Season to taste.

3 Divide pork between tortillas. Serve topped with sour cream and coriander, and accompany with lime wedges, if you like.

nutritional count per serving
26.3g total fat
13.2g saturated fat
2842kJ (680 cal)
66.5g carbohydrate
42.5g protein
5.4g fibre

tip You can quickly peel the capsicum with a vegetable peeler if you don't like the skin peeling off when it's cooked.

to freeze Complete the recipe to the end of step 2. Pack into freezer-proof containers, leaving a 2.5cm (1 inch) space to allow for expansion. Seal, label and freeze for up to 3 months. Thaw overnight in the fridge. Reheat in a saucepan or microwave on medium power (50%) until heated through.

MEATBALLS WITH TOMATO SAUCE

prep + cook time 6 hours 45 minutes **serves** 6

2 slices white bread (90g), crusts removed

½ cup (125ml) milk

1kg (2 pounds) minced (ground) beef

1 large brown onion (200g), chopped finely

1 medium carrot (120g), grated finely

3 cloves garlic, crushed

1 egg

2 tablespoons tomato paste

½ teaspoon dried oregano leaves

2 tablespoons finely chopped fresh basil

1 tablespoon olive oil

1 medium brown onion (150g), chopped finely, extra

2 cloves garlic, crushed, extra

400g (12½ ounces) canned diced tomatoes

400g (12½ ounces) canned cherry tomatoes

2 tablespoons tomato paste, extra

1 cup (250ml) beef stock

¼ cup loosely packed fresh basil leaves

1 Combine bread and milk in a large bowl; stand 10 minutes. Add beef, onion, carrot, garlic, egg, paste, oregano and chopped basil; season, mix well. Shape level tablespoons of mixture into balls. Transfer to a 4.5-litre (18-cup) slow cooker.

2 Heat oil in a large frying pan; cook extra onion and garlic, stirring, until onion softens. Stir in tomatoes, extra paste and stock; transfer to cooker. Cook, covered, on low, for 6 hours. Season to taste.

3 Serve meatballs sprinkled with basil leaves.

nutritional count per serving
18.1g total fat
7.5g saturated fat
1689kJ (404 cal)
18.4g carbohydrate
39.7g protein
4.4g fibre

serving suggestion
Serve with spaghetti, sprinkled with grated parmesan cheese.

to freeze Complete the recipe to the end of step 2. Pack into freezer-proof containers, leaving a 2.5cm (1 inch) space to allow for expansion. Seal, label and freeze for up to 3 months. Thaw overnight in the fridge. Reheat in a saucepan or microwave on medium power (50%) until heated through.

VEAL AND ROSEMARY CASSEROLE

prep + cook time 8 hours 35 minutes **serves** 6

1.2kg (2½ pounds) boned veal shoulder,
  chopped coarsely
¼ cup (35g) plain (all-purpose) flour
1 tablespoon olive oil
1 medium brown onion (150g), chopped coarsely
2 cloves garlic, crushed
½ cup (125ml) dry red wine
2 medium carrots (240g), chopped coarsely
2 sticks celery (300g), trimmed, chopped coarsely
2 medium parsnips (500g), chopped coarsely
2½ cups (625ml) beef stock
3 sprigs fresh rosemary

1 Toss veal in flour to coat, shake off excess. Heat half the oil in a large frying pan; cook veal, in batches, until browned. Transfer to a 4.5-litre (18-cup) slow cooker.

2 Heat remaining oil in same pan; cook onion and garlic, stirring, until onion softens. Add wine; bring to the boil. Boil, uncovered, until liquid reduces by half.

3 Stir onion mixture into cooker with carrot, celery, parsnip, stock and rosemary. Cook, covered, on low, for 8 hours. Season to taste.

nutritional count per serving
8.6g total fat
2g saturated fat
1513kJ (362 cal)
15.6g carbohydrate
49.5g protein
4.2g fibre

serving suggestion
Serve with soft polenta (see page 313).

tip The butcher might have some good stewing veal available – it's fine to use in this recipe.

to freeze Pack into freezer-proof containers, leaving a 2.5cm (1 inch) space to allow for expansion. Seal, label and freeze for up to 3 months. Thaw overnight in the fridge. Reheat in a saucepan or microwave on medium power (50%) until heated through.

CHORIZO, CHILLI AND BEAN STEW

prep + cook time 3 hours 20 minutes **serves** 6

1 tablespoon olive oil

1 large red onion (300g), chopped coarsely

3 chorizo sausages (510g), chopped coarsely

4 cloves garlic, crushed

1 teaspoon dried chilli flakes

1 medium red capsicum (bell pepper) (200g), chopped coarsely

150g (4½ ounces) baby green beans, halved

800g (1½ pounds) canned cannellini beans, drained, rinsed

800g (1½ pounds) canned diced tomatoes

⅓ cup (80ml) chicken stock

2 dried bay leaves

⅓ cup coarsely chopped fresh flat-leaf parsley

1 Heat oil in a large frying pan; cook onion and chorizo, stirring, until browned lightly. Add garlic and chilli flakes; cook, stirring, until fragrant.

2 Combine capsicum, both beans, tomatoes, stock, bay leaves and chorizo mixture in a 4.5-litre (18-cup) slow cooker. Cook, covered, on low, for 3 hours.

3 Discard bay leaves. Season to taste; sprinkle with parsley.

nutritional count per serving
28.7g total fat
9.6g saturated fat
1689kJ (404 cal)
13.1g carbohydrate
21.3g protein
5.8g fibre

serving suggestion
Serve with a green salad and some crusty bread.

to freeze Complete the recipe to the end of step 2. Pack into freezer-proof containers, leaving a 2.5cm (1 inch) space to allow for expansion. Seal, label and freeze for up to 3 months. Thaw overnight in the fridge. Reheat in a saucepan or microwave on medium power (50%) until heated through.

OXTAIL STEW WITH RED WINE AND PORT

prep + cook time 9 hours 15 minutes **serves** 8

2kg (4 pounds) oxtails, cut into 5cm (2-inch) pieces

2 tablespoons plain (all-purpose) flour

2 tablespoons vegetable oil

12 brown baby onions (480g)

2 medium carrots (240g), chopped coarsely

1 stick celery (150g), trimmed, sliced thickly

8 cloves garlic, peeled

1½ cups (375ml) dry red wine

2 cups (500ml) port

2 cups (500ml) beef stock

4 sprigs fresh thyme

1 dried bay leaf

1 Trim excess fat from oxtail; toss oxtail in flour to coat, shake off excess. Heat half the oil in a large frying pan; cook oxtail, in batches, until browned. Transfer to a 4.5-litre (18-cup) slow cooker.

2 Meanwhile, peel onions, leaving root ends intact.

3 Heat remaining oil in same pan; cook onions, carrot, celery and garlic, stirring, for 5 minutes or until vegetables are browned lightly. Transfer to cooker. Add wine and port to pan; bring to the boil. Boil, uncovered, until reduced to 1 cup. Transfer to cooker with stock, thyme and bay leaf. Cook, covered, on low, for 8 hours.

4 Discard thyme and bay leaf. Remove oxtail; cover to keep warm. Cook sauce, uncovered, on high, for 30 minutes or until thickened. Skim fat from surface. Season to taste. Return oxtail to sauce to heat through.

nutritional count per serving
48.4g total fat
17.4g saturated fat
2959kJ (708 cal)
14.5g carbohydrate
30.9g protein
2g fibre

serving suggestion
Serve with potato or kumara mash (see page 174).

notes Oxtails are often sold frozen or may need to be ordered from the butcher. Beef brisket, beef cheeks and chuck steak are also suitable to use in this recipe. The stew is best made a day ahead and refrigerated to set the fat, which can then be removed from the surface of the stew.
Baby onions are also known as pickling onions.

to freeze Pack oxtail into freezer-proof containers; pour sauce over, leaving a 2.5cm (1 inch) space to allow for expansion. Seal, label and freeze for up to 3 months. Thaw overnight in the fridge. Reheat in a saucepan or microwave on medium power (50%) until heated through.

ITALIAN-STYLE CHILLI BEEF

prep + cook time 6 hours 45 minutes **serves** 6

1 tablespoon olive oil

750g (1½ pounds) lean minced (ground) beef

1 large brown onion (200g), chopped finely

3 cloves garlic, crushed

1 teaspoon dried chilli flakes

½ cup (125ml) dry red wine

½ cup (125ml) beef stock

2 medium red capsicums (bell peppers) (400g), chopped finely

500g (1 pound) bottled tomato pasta sauce

2 small zucchini (240g), chopped finely

400g (12½ ounces) canned cannellini beans, drained, rinsed

½ cup firmly packed fresh small basil leaves

1 Heat oil in a large frying pan; cook beef and onion, stirring, until beef is browned. Add garlic and chilli; cook, stirring, until fragrant. Add wine; bring to the boil. Boil, uncovered, about 1 minute or until liquid is almost evaporated. Transfer beef mixture to a 4.5-litre (18-cup) slow cooker.

2 Stir in stock, capsicum and passata. Cook, covered, on low, for 5 hours.

3 Stir in zucchini and beans. Cook, covered, on low, for 1 hour.

4 Shred half the basil. Just before serving, stir in shredded basil; season to taste. Serve sprinkled with remaining basil.

nutritional count per serving
14.2g total fat
5.2g saturated fat
1329kJ (318 cal)
12.5g carbohydrate
29.7g protein
4.9g fibre

serving suggestion
Serve with soft polenta or crusty bread.

tip Tomato passata is simply sieved tomato puree and is available in supermarkets. If you can't find it, you can also use canned tomato puree instead.

to freeze Complete the recipe to the end of step 3. Pack into freezer-proof containers, leaving a 2.5cm (1 inch) space to allow for expansion. Seal, label and freeze for up to 3 months. Thaw overnight in the fridge. Reheat in a saucepan or microwave on medium power (50%) until heated through.

LAMB SHANK, FENNEL AND VEGETABLE SOUP

prep + cook time 10 hours 30 minutes **serves** 6

1 tablespoon olive oil

4 french-trimmed lamb shanks (800g)

1 medium brown onion (150g), chopped coarsely

2 baby fennel bulbs (260g), sliced thinly

2 medium carrots (240g), chopped coarsely

4 cloves garlic, crushed

2 fresh small red thai (serrano) chillies, chopped finely

2 teaspoons ground cumin

2 teaspoons ground coriander

1 teaspoon ground cinnamon

1 teaspoon caraway seeds

pinch saffron threads

1.5 litres (6 cups) water

2 cups (500ml) beef stock

400g (12½ ounces) canned diced tomatoes

400g (12½ ounces) canned chickpeas (garbanzo beans), drained, rinsed

¾ cup (90g) frozen baby peas

1 cup loosely packed fresh coriander (cilantro) leaves

1 Heat half the oil in a large frying pan; cook lamb, until browned all over, then place in a 4.5-litre (18-cup) slow cooker.

2 Heat remaining oil in same pan; cook onion, fennel, carrot, garlic and chilli, stirring, until onion softens. Add spices; cook, stirring, until fragrant. Place vegetable mixture into cooker. Stir in the water, stock, tomatoes and chickpeas. Cook, covered, on low, for 10 hours.

3 Remove lamb from cooker. When cool enough to handle, remove meat from bones, shred meat; discard bones. Stir meat, peas and coriander leaves into cooker. Season to taste.

nutritional count per serving
11.4g total fat
3.7g saturated fat
1098kJ (262 cal)
15.2g carbohydrate
21.5g protein
6.9g fibre

serving suggestion
Serve with Greek-style yoghurt, lemon wedges and crusty bread.

to freeze Complete the recipe to end of step 2. Pack into freezer-proof containers, leaving a 2.5cm (1 inch) space to allow for expansion. Seal, label and freeze for up to 3 months. Thaw overnight in the fridge. Reheat in a saucepan or microwave on medium power (50%) until heated through.

BALTIC LAMB AND RICE MEATBALLS

prep + cook time 4 hours 30 minutes (+ refrigeration) **serves** 6

750g (1½ pounds) minced (ground) lamb

¾ cup (150g) uncooked jasmine rice

1 cup (70g) stale breadcrumbs

1 egg

2 tablespoons finely chopped fresh coriander (cilantro)

½ cup (150g) balti curry paste

2½ cups (625ml) water

400g (12½ ounces) canned diced tomatoes

2 medium brown onions (300g), chopped finely

650g (1¼ pounds) baby eggplant, halved lengthways, chopped coarsely

½ cup loosely packed fresh coriander (cilantro) leaves, extra

1 Combine lamb, rice, breadcrumbs, egg and coriander in a large bowl, season; roll level tablespoons of mixture into balls. Place on a tray, cover; refrigerate 20 minutes.

2 Combine paste and the water in a large jug; pour into a 4.5-litre (18-cup) slow cooker. Stir in tomatoes and onion; add meatballs and eggplant. Cook, covered, on high, for 4 hours. Season to taste.

3 Serve sprinkled with extra coriander leaves.

nutritional count per serving
19g total fat
5.4g saturated fat
1969kJ (471 cal)
37.5g carbohydrate
33.7g protein
7.3g fibre

tip Make sure the meatballs are completely submerged in the liquid during cooking.

to freeze Complete recipe to end of step 2. Pack into freezer-proof containers, leaving a 2.5cm (1 inch) space to allow for expansion. Seal, label and freeze for up to 3 months. Thaw overnight in the fridge. Reheat in a saucepan or microwave on medium power (50%) until heated through.

LAMB KORMA

prep + cook time 6 hours 30 minutes **serves** 6

1.5kg (3 pounds) boned lamb shoulder,
  chopped coarsely

2 medium brown onions (300g), sliced thinly

5cm (2-inch) piece fresh ginger (25g), grated

3 cloves garlic, crushed

⅔ cup (200g) korma paste

3 medium tomatoes (450g), chopped coarsely

½ cup (125ml) chicken stock

300ml (½ pint) pouring cream

1 cinnamon stick

2 teaspoons poppy seeds

½ cup loosely packed fresh coriander (cilantro) leaves

1 fresh long red chilli, sliced thinly

⅓ cup (25g) roasted flaked almonds

1   Combine lamb, onion, ginger, garlic, paste,
    tomatoes, stock, cream, cinnamon and seeds
    in a 4.5-litre (18-cup) slow cooker. Cook, covered,
    on low, for 6 hours. Season to taste.

2   Discard cinnamon stick. Serve korma sprinkled
    with coriander, chilli and nuts.

nutritional count per serving
49.4g total fat
22.4g saturated fat
2977kJ (719 cal)
9.3g carbohydrate
55.7g protein
6.2g fibre

serving suggestion
Serve with steamed basmati
rice, grilled naan bread
and yoghurt.

to freeze Complete the
recipe to the end of step 1.
Pack into freezer-proof
containers, leaving a 2.5cm
(1 inch) space to allow for
expansion. Seal, label and
freeze for up to 3 months.
Thaw overnight in the fridge.
Reheat in a saucepan or
microwave on medium power
(50%) until heated through.

CUBAN BLACK BEAN SOUP

prep + cook time 8 hours 55 minutes (+ standing) **serves** 6

1½ cups (300g) dried black turtle beans

1 ham hock (1kg)

2 tablespoons olive oil

1 large brown onion (200g), chopped finely

1 medium red capsicum (bell pepper) (200g), chopped finely

3 garlic cloves, crushed

3 teaspoons ground cumin

1 teaspoon dried chilli flakes

400g (12½ ounces) canned crushed tomatoes

2 litres (8 cups) water

3 teaspoons dried oregano leaves

1 teaspoon ground black pepper

2 tablespoons lime juice

1 large tomato (220g), chopped finely

¼ cup coarsely chopped fresh coriander (cilantro)

1 Place beans in a medium bowl, cover with cold water; stand overnight.

2 Drain and rinse beans, place in a medium saucepan, cover with cold water; bring to the boil. Boil, uncovered, 15 minutes; drain.

3 Meanwhile, preheat oven to 220°C/425°F.

4 Roast ham on oven tray for 30 minutes.

5 Heat oil in a large frying pan; cook onion, capsicum and garlic, stirring, until onion is soft. Add cumin and chilli; cook, stirring, until fragrant.

6 Combine beans, ham, onion mixture, tomatoes, the water, oregano and pepper in a 4.5-litre (18-cup) slow cooker. Cook, covered, on low, for 8 hours.

7 Remove ham from cooker. When cool enough to handle, remove meat from bone; shred coarsely. Discard skin, fat and bone. Cool soup 10 minutes, then blend or process 2 cups soup mixture until smooth. Return meat to cooker with pureed soup, stir in juice and tomato; sprinkle with coriander. Season to taste.

nutritional count per serving
18.1g total fat
2.9g saturated fat
1350kJ (323 cal)
9.6g carbohydrate
24.7g protein
12.4g fibre

note Black beans, also known as black turtle beans, have long been a staple food in Latin America and South America. They are commonly used in soups and stews, and are an extremely good source of antioxidants. They have a meaty, dense texture and a flavour similar to mushrooms.

to freeze Complete the recipe to the end of step 6. Pack into freezer-proof containers, leaving a 2.5cm (1 inch) space to allow for expansion. Seal, label and freeze for up to 3 months. Thaw overnight in the fridge. Reheat in a saucepan or microwave on medium power (50%) until heated through.

ITALIAN PORK AND CAPSICUM RAGU

prep + cook time 8 hours 30 minutes **serves** 8

2 tablespoons olive oil

1.6kg (3¼-pound) rindless boneless pork belly, chopped coarsely

4 Italian-style thin pork sausages (310g)

3 medium red capsicums (bell peppers) (600g), sliced thickly

2 medium brown onions (300g), sliced thinly

1.2kg (2½ pounds) canned white beans, drained, rinsed

6 cloves garlic, crushed

400g (12½ ounces) canned diced tomatoes

1¼ cups (310ml) salt-reduced chicken stock

1 tablespoon tomato paste

1 teaspoon dried oregano

½ teaspoon chilli flakes

¼ cup loosely packed fresh oregano leaves

1 Heat oil in a large frying pan; cook pork, in batches, until browned. Transfer to a 4.5-litre (18-cup) slow cooker.

2 Cook sausages in same pan until browned; transfer to cooker with capsicum, onion, beans, garlic, tomatoes, stock, paste, dried oregano and chilli. Cook, covered, on low, for 8 hours.

3 Skim fat from surface. Remove sausages from cooker; chop coarsely, return to cooker. Season to taste; serve sprinkled with fresh oregano.

nutritional count per serving
24.8g total fat
8g saturated fat
2006kJ (480 cal)
10.9g carbohydrate
51.6g protein
5g fibre

serving suggestion
Serve with pasta or soft polenta (see page 313).

tip You can quickly peel the capsicum with a vegetable peeler if you don't like the skin peeling off when it's cooked.

to freeze Complete the recipe to the end of step 2. Pack into freezer-proof containers, leaving a 2.5cm (1 inch) space to allow for expansion. Seal, label and freeze for up to 3 months. Thaw overnight in the fridge. Reheat in a saucepan or microwave on medium power (50%) until heated through.

cauliflower soup

CAULIFLOWER SOUP

prep + cook time 7 hours 30 minutes **serves** 8

40g (1½ ounces) butter

2 large brown onions (400g), chopped coarsely

3 cloves garlic, crushed

1 litre (4 cups) vegetable stock

1.2kg (2½ pounds) cauliflower, cut into florets

2 medium potatoes (400g), chopped coarsely

2 cups (500ml) water

300ml (½ pint) pouring cream

2 tablespoons finely chopped fresh
  flat-leaf parsley

1 Heat butter in large frying pan; cook onion, stirring, until softened. Add garlic; cook, stirring, until fragrant. Add stock; bring to the boil.

2 Transfer onion mixture to 4.5-litre (18-cup) slow cooker with cauliflower, potato and the water. Cook, covered, on low, for 6½ hours.

3 Blend or process soup, in batches, until smooth. Return to cooker; stir in cream. Cook, covered, on high, about 30 minutes or until soup is hot. Season to taste. Serve sprinkled with parsley.

nutritional count per serving
17.3g total fat
10.9g saturated fat
1021kJ (244 cal)
114.9g carbohydrate
6g protein
4.1g fibre

tip You will need about 2 small cauliflowers for this recipe.

to freeze Pack into freezer-proof containers, leaving a 2.5cm (1 inch) space to allow for expansion. Seal, label and freeze for up to 3 months. Thaw overnight in the fridge. Reheat in a saucepan or microwave on medium power (50%) until heated through.

CHICKEN TIKKA MASALA

prep + cook time 4 hours 15 minutes **serves** 6

1kg (2 pounds) skinless chicken thigh cutlets

800g (1½ pounds) canned diced tomatoes

2 large brown onions (400g), sliced thinly

⅔ cup (200g) tikka masala paste

¼ cup (60ml) pouring cream

1 cup loosely packed fresh coriander
  (cilantro) leaves

1 Combine chicken, tomatoes, onion and paste in a 4.5-litre (18-cup) slow cooker; cook, covered, on high, for 4 hours. Season to taste.

2 Serve drizzled with cream, topped with coriander.

(photograph page 204)

nutritional count per serving
22.3g total fat
5.9g saturated fat
1467kJ (351 cal)
10.8g carbohydrate
24.2g protein
6g fibre

serving suggestion
Serve with steamed rice, naan bread and raita.

to freeze Complete the recipe to the end of step 1. Pack into freezer-proof containers, leaving a 2.5cm (1 inch) space to allow for expansion. Seal, label and freeze for up to 3 months. Thaw overnight in the fridge. Reheat in a saucepan or microwave on medium power (50%) until heated through.

chicken tikka masala (recipe page 203)

petit sale aux lentilles
(salted pork with lentils)
(recipe page 206)

PETIT SALE AUX LENTILLES

(SALTED PORK WITH LENTILS)

prep + cook time 4 hours 30 minutes **serves** 8

1 tablespoon olive oil

2 large brown onions (400g), chopped finely

4 toulouse sausages (400g)

1.75 litres (7 cups) water

3 cups (600g) french-style green lentils

1.5kg (3-pounds) ham hock

5 cloves garlic, crushed

3 dried bay leaves

1 Heat oil in large frying pan; cook onion, stirring, until softened. Transfer to a 4.5-litre (18-cup) slow cooker.

2 Cook sausages in same pan until browned; transfer to cooker with remaining ingredients. Cook, covered, on high, for 4 hours. Season to taste.

(photograph page 205)

nutritional count per serving
17.3g total fat
5.8g saturated fat
2082kJ (498 cal)
32.3g carbohydrate
49.5g protein
11.7g fibre

tips Taste before adding any salt as the ham and sausages are quite salty. Toulouse is a small French sausage made of coarsely diced pork and flavoured with wine, garlic and various seasonings. It is available from speciality butchers. You can also use thick pork sausages.

to freeze Shred meat from the ham bones and return to the lentil mixture. Pack into freezer-proof containers, leaving a 2.5cm (1 inch) space to allow for expansion. Seal, label and freeze for up to 3 months. Thaw overnight in the fridge. Reheat in a saucepan or microwave on medium power (50%) until heated through.

CHANA MASALA

prep + cook time 3 hours **serves** 6

2 large brown onions (400g), chopped coarsely

8 cloves garlic, quartered

6cm (2½-inch) piece fresh ginger (60g), grated

2 tablespoons tomato paste

125g (4 ounces) ghee

2 teaspoons ground coriander

2 teaspoons garam masala

1 teaspoon ground turmeric

½ teaspoon ground chilli

800g (1½ pounds) canned chickpeas (garbanzo beans), drained, rinsed

1½ cups (375ml) water

½ cup loosely packed fresh coriander (cilantro) leaves

1 Blend or process onion, garlic, ginger and paste until smooth.

2 Heat ghee in large saucepan; cook onion mixture, stirring, 5 minutes. Add spices; cook, stirring, 2 minutes. Transfer to 4.5-litre (18-cup) slow cooker with chickpeas and the water. Cook, covered, on high, 2½ hours. Season to taste.

3 Serve sprinkled with coriander.

nutritional count per serving
22.1g total fat
13.4g saturated fat
1283kJ (307 cal)
17.9g carbohydrate
7.2g protein
6.3g fibre

serving suggestion
Serve with steamed rice, yoghurt and naan (flat) bread.

note Chana masala is a spicy vegetarian chickpea curry, with a slightly sour taste.

to freeze Complete the recipe to the end of step 2. Pack into freezer-proof containers, leaving a 2.5cm (1 inch) space to allow for expansion. Seal, label and freeze for up to 3 months. Thaw overnight in the fridge. Reheat in a saucepan or microwave on medium power (50%) until heated through.

chana masala

ANDALUSIAN PORK

prep + cook time 8 hours 30 minutes (+ refrigeration) **serves** 8

1.5kg (3 pounds) pork neck, chopped coarsely

1 tablespoon ground cumin

2 teaspoons sweet smoked paprika

2 teaspoons cayenne pepper

5 cloves garlic, crushed

2 tablespoons lemon juice

3 dried bay leaves

⅓ cup (80ml) olive oil

2 chorizo sausages (340g), sliced thinly

2 large brown onions (400g), sliced thinly

2 medium red capsicums (bell peppers) (400g),
  sliced thickly

1 cup (250ml) salt-reduced chicken stock

⅓ cup (80ml) sherry vinegar

⅓ cup coarsely chopped fresh flat-leaf parsley

1 Combine pork with spices, garlic, juice, bay leaves and half the oil in a large bowl; turn to coat. Cover; refrigerate overnight.

2 Heat a large frying pan; cook chorizo until browned. Transfer to a 4.5-litre (18-cup) slow cooker; discard pan drippings.

3 Heat remaining oil in same pan; cook pork, in batches, until browned all over. Transfer to cooker; stir in onion, capsicum, stock and vinegar. Cook, covered, on slow, for 8 hours. Skim fat from surface. Season to taste. Sprinkle with parsley.

nutritional count per serving
28.1g total fat
8.2g saturated fat
1990kJ (476 cal)
6.7g carbohydrate
48.3g protein
1.7g fibre

serving suggestion
Serve with a spinach and pine nut pilaf.

tip You can quickly peel the capsicum with a vegetable peeler if you don't like the skin peeling off when it's cooked.

to freeze Pack into freezer-proof containers, leaving a 2.5cm (1 inch) space to allow for expansion. Seal, label and freeze for up to 3 months. Thaw overnight in the fridge. Reheat in a saucepan or microwave on medium power (50%) until heated through.

MULLIGATAWNY SOUP WITH CHICKEN

prep + cook time 6 hours 30 minutes **serves** 8

1 tablespoon vegetable oil

800g (1½ pounds) chicken thigh fillets, chopped coarsely

20g (¾ ounce) ghee

1 large brown onion (200g), chopped coarsely

2 sticks celery (300g), trimmed, chopped coarsely

2 medium carrots (240g), chopped coarsely

3 cloves garlic, chopped finely

¼ cup (75g) madras curry paste

2 medium potatoes (400g), chopped coarsely

1 medium kumara (orange sweet potato) (400g), chopped coarsely

½ cup (100g) dried red lentils, rinsed

1.5 litres (6 cups) salt-reduced chicken stock

2 cups (500ml) coconut milk

¼ cup coarsely chopped fresh coriander (cilantro)

1 Heat oil in a large frying pan; cook chicken, in batches, until browned. Transfer to a 4.5-litre (18-cup) slow cooker.

2 Heat ghee in same pan; cook onion, celery and carrot, stirring, until onion softens. Add garlic and curry paste; cook, stirring, until fragrant. Transfer to cooker with potato, kumara, lentils, stock and coconut milk. Cook, covered, on low, for 6 hours.

3 Serve topped with coriander; season to taste.

nutritional count per serving
28.5g total fat
16g saturated fat
1981kJ (474 cal)
24.7g carbohydrate
27.9g protein
6.8g fibre

serving suggestion
Serve with yoghurt, lemon wedges and roti bread.

tip Mulligatawny is a chicken soup flavoured with Indian spices; it is a product of the British Raj in India. Mulligatawny means 'pepper water', which the Indians used to drink as a digestive. Beef or lamb could be used in this recipe, instead of the chicken.

to freeze Complete the recipe to the end of step 2. Pack into freezer-proof containers, leaving a 2.5cm (1 inch) space to allow for expansion. Seal, label and freeze for up to 3 months. Thaw overnight in the fridge. Reheat in a saucepan or microwave on medium power (50%) until heated through.

SWEET AND SOUR CHICKEN

prep + cook time 4 hours 30 minutes **serves** 4

1 tablespoon vegetable oil

4 chicken lovely legs (520g)

4 skinless chicken thigh cutlets (800g)

2 medium red onions (340g), cut into wedges

½ cup (125ml) japanese soy sauce

½ cup (130g) bottled tomato pasta sauce

⅓ cup (80ml) pineapple juice

2 tablespoons light brown sugar

2 tablespoons white vinegar

1 fresh long red chilli, chopped finely

2 cloves garlic, crushed

1 large red capsicum (bell pepper) (350g),
   chopped coarsely

1 large green capsicum (bell pepper) (350g),
   chopped coarsely

225g (7 ounces) canned pineapple pieces in juice

2 tablespoons cornflour (cornstarch)

2 tablespoons water

2 green onions (scallions), shredded finely

1 Heat oil in large frying pan; cook chicken, in batches, until browned. Transfer to a 4.5-litre (18-cup) slow cooker. Add red onion, sauces, juice, sugar, vinegar, chilli, garlic, capsicum and undrained pineapple. Cook, covered, on low, for 4 hours.

2 Blend cornflour with the water in a small bowl until smooth. Add cornflour mixture to cooker. Cook, uncovered, on high, for 5 minutes or until thickened. Season to taste.

3 Serve sprinkled with shredded green onion.

nutritional count per serving
16.1g total fat
4.6g saturated fat
1986kJ (475 cal)
31.7g carbohydrate
47.8g protein
4.7g fibre

tip Lovely legs are trimmed, skinless chicken drumsticks, available from supermarkets. Use whatever cuts of chicken you like – choose cuts on the bone for a moist result.

to freeze Complete the recipe to the end of step 2. Pack into freezer-proof containers, leaving a 2.5cm (1 inch) space to allow for expansion. Seal, label and freeze for up to 3 months. Thaw overnight in the fridge. Reheat in a saucepan or microwave on medium power (50%) until heated through.

*Soups can be an elegant first course to a
formal dinner but during the week, they're perfect
stand-alone meals in their own right, served
simply with a crusty bread roll. And it takes no extra
effort to double the quantities in each recipe to make
a larger pot, ensuring you end up with leftovers
for a take-to-work lunch or for dinner another
night and of course, they're perfect
to freeze for much later.*

OKRA CURRY

prep + cook time 3 hours serves 4

¼ cup (60ml) peanut oil

2 large brown onions (400g), sliced thinly

2 fresh long green chillies, quartered lengthways

4cm (1½-inch) piece fresh ginger (20g), grated

5 cloves garlic, crushed

2 teaspoons ground coriander

1 teaspoon garam masala

½ teaspoon ground turmeric

½ teaspoon chilli powder

2 medium tomatoes (300g), chopped coarsely

1kg (2 pounds) okra, trimmed

2½ cups (625ml) coconut milk

1   Heat oil in a large saucepan; cook onion, stirring, until soft and browned lightly. Add chilli, ginger and garlic; cook, stirring, until fragrant. Stir in spices; cook, stirring, 1 minute. Add tomato; cook, stirring, for 2 minutes.

2   Transfer tomato mixture to a 4.5-litre (18-cup) slow cooker with okra and coconut milk; season. Cook, covered, on high, for 2½ hours.

nutritional count per serving
46.8g total fat
30.9g saturated fat
2395kJ (573 cal)
17.4g carbohydrate
14g protein
16.9g fibre

serving suggestion
Serve with steamed rice and lime wedges.

tips This recipe serves 4 as a vegetarian main meal with rice, but you can also serve it as part of an Indian banquet to serve 8.
Okra, also known as lady fingers, is a green, ridged, oblong pod with a furry skin. While native to Africa, this vegetable is used in Indian, Middle-Eastern and southern US cooking. It often serves as a thickener in stews.

to freeze Pack into freezer-proof containers, leaving a 2.5cm (1 inch) space to allow for expansion. Seal, label and freeze for up to 3 months. Thaw overnight in the fridge. Reheat in a saucepan or microwave on medium power (50%) until heated through.

SPINACH AND RICOTTA LASAGNE

prep + cook time 4 hours 30 minutes **serves** 6

500g (1 pound) frozen spinach, thawed

3 cups (720g) ricotta cheese

2 eggs

1 cup (80g) finely grated parmesan cheese

cooking-oil spray

750g (1½ pounds) bottled tomato pasta sauce

⅓ cup (90g) basil pesto

6 dried instant lasagne sheets

1 cup (100g) coarsely grated mozzarella cheese

1 Squeeze excess moisture from spinach; place spinach in a large bowl. Add ricotta, eggs and half the parmesan; season, mix well.

2 Spray the bowl of a 4.5-litre (18-cup) slow cooker lightly with cooking oil. Combine sauce and pesto in a medium bowl, season; spread ½ cup of the sauce mixture over base of cooker.

3 Place 2 lasagne sheets in cooker, breaking to fit. Spread one-third of the spinach mixture over pasta; top with one-third of the sauce, then 2 more lasagne sheets. Repeat layering, finishing with sauce. Sprinkle with mozzarella and remaining parmesan. Cook, covered, on low, for 4 hours or until pasta is tender.

nutritional count per serving
31.9g total fat
15.8g saturated fat
2211kJ (529 cal)
25.1g carbohydrate
32.7g protein
8.3g fibre

serving suggestion
Serve with a rocket salad and some thick crusty bread.

to freeze Pack into freezer-proof containers, leaving a 2.5cm (1 inch) space to allow for expansion. Seal, label and freeze for up to 3 months. Thaw overnight in the fridge. Reheat in a microwave on medium power (50%) until heated through.

CHILLI BEANS WITH TOMATO SAUCE

prep + cook time 8 hours 30 minutes **serves** 6

1 tablespoon olive oil

6 rindless bacon slices (390g), chopped finely

1 stick celery (150g), trimmed, chopped finely

1 small brown onion (80g), chopped finely

1 small carrot (70g), chopped finely

1 fresh long red chilli, chopped finely

¼ cup (70g) tomato paste

3 cups (700g) bottled tomato pasta sauce

¾ cup (180ml) chicken stock

2 teaspoons caster (superfine) sugar

800g (1½ pounds) canned cannellini beans,
   drained, rinsed

¼ cup coarsely chopped fresh flat-leaf parsley

1 Heat oil in a medium frying pan; cook bacon, celery, onion, carrot and chilli, stirring, until onion softens. Add paste; cook, stirring, 1 minute. Transfer mixture to a 4.5-litre (18-cup) slow cooker. Stir in sauce, stock, sugar and beans. Cook, covered, on low, for 8 hours.

2 Stir in parsley; season to taste.

nutritional count per serving
12.9g total fat
3.9g saturated fat
1112kJ (266 cal)
17.8g carbohydrate
17.3g protein
5.2g fibre

serving suggestion
Serve with toasted sourdough or cornbread.

tips While we've used cannellini beans here, you can use any canned white beans you like, such as great northern, navy or haricot. Use a plain (unflavoured) tomato-based sauce suitable for serving over pasta. These sauces can be bought in cans and jars and are often labelled "sugo" or "passata".

to freeze Complete the recipe to the end of step 1. Pack into freezer-proof containers, leaving a 2.5cm (1 inch) space to allow for expansion. Seal, label and freeze for up to 3 months. Thaw overnight in the fridge. Reheat in a saucepan or microwave on medium power (50%) until heated through.

SMOKY CHICKPEA AND TOMATO SOUP

prep + cook time 8 hours 30 minutes **serves** 6

1.5kg (3 pounds) tomatoes, quartered

1 large brown onion (200g), chopped coarsely

3 cloves garlic, chopped coarsely

1 stick celery (150g), trimmed, sliced thickly

1.2kg (2½ pounds) canned chickpeas (garbanzo beans), drained, rinsed

1¾ cups (430ml) chicken stock

2 teaspoons smoked paprika

1 tablespoon caster (superfine) sugar

⅓ cup (80g) sour cream

1 Place tomato, onion, garlic, celery, chickpeas, stock, paprika and sugar in a 4.5-litre (18-cup) slow cooker. Cook, covered, on low, for 8 hours.

2 Using a slotted spoon, transfer 2 cups of chickpeas to a medium bowl; reserve. Stand remaining soup 10 minutes, then process soup until smooth. Stir in reserved chickpeas. Season to taste.

3 Serve soup topped with sour cream.

nutritional count per serving
10.1g total fat
4g saturated fat
1418kJ (339 cal)
39.3g carbohydrate
16.6g protein
14.2g fibre

serving suggestion
Serve with char-grilled slices of bread.

tips Choose the ripest tomatoes you can get. If you hate tomato skins, you can either peel the tomatoes before adding to the cooker or strain the pureed soup before adding the reserved chickpeas.

to freeze Complete the recipe to the end of step 2. Pack into freezer-proof containers, leaving a 2.5cm (1 inch) space to allow for expansion. Seal, label and freeze for up to 3 months. Thaw overnight in the fridge. Reheat in a saucepan or microwave on medium power (50%) until heated through.

STICKY DATE AND FIG PUDDING

prep + cook time 5 hours 30 minutes serves 12

2 cups (300g) finely chopped seeded dried dates

½ cup (100g) finely chopped dried figs

1 cup (250ml) water

1 cup (220g) firmly packed light brown sugar

90g (3 ounces) butter, chopped coarsely

1 teaspoon bicarbonate of soda (baking soda)

2 eggs, beaten lightly

¾ cup (110g) plain (all-purpose) flour

¾ cup (110g) self-raising flour

BUTTERSCOTCH SAUCE

¾ cup (165g) firmly packed light brown sugar

1 cup (250ml) pouring cream

125g (4 ounces) unsalted butter, chopped coarsely

1   Combine fruit, the water, sugar and butter in a medium saucepan; stir over heat until butter melts and sugar dissolves. Bring to the boil. Reduce heat; simmer, uncovered, for 5 minutes. Transfer mixture to a large heatproof bowl, stir in soda; cool 10 minutes.

2   Stir eggs and sifted dry ingredients into the fruit mixture.

3   Grease a 2-litre (8-cup) pudding steamer; spoon mixture into steamer. Top with pleated baking paper and foil; secure with kitchen string or lid.

4   Place steamer in a 4.5-litre (18-cup) slow cooker; pour enough boiling water into cooker to come halfway up the side of the steamer. Cook, covered, on high, for 5 hours, replenishing with boiling water as necessary to maintain level.

5   Remove pudding from cooker. Stand for 10 minutes before turning onto plate.

6   Meanwhile, make butterscotch sauce.

7   Serve pudding with butterscotch sauce.

BUTTERSCOTCH SAUCE Stir ingredients in a medium saucepan over heat, without boiling, until sugar dissolves; bring to the boil. Reduce heat; simmer, uncovered, 2 minutes.

nutritional count per serving
24.9g total fat
15.9g saturated fat
2174kJ (520 cal)
70.6g carbohydrate
4.4g protein
4.3g fibre

serving suggestion
Serve with a dollop of thick (double) cream.

tips The pleated paper and foil simply allow space for the pudding mixture to rise. Butterscotch will keep in a jar in the fridge for about 2 weeks.

to freeze Wrap pudding in two layers of plastic wrap. Seal, label and freeze for up to 2 months. Thaw overnight at room temperature. Reheat in a microwave on medium power (50%) until heated through.

MANDARIN AND ALMOND PUDDING

prep + cook time 5 hours 30 minutes **serves** 8

4 small mandarins (mandarin oranges) (400g)

4 eggs

⅔ cup (150g) caster (superfine) sugar

1⅓ cups (160g) ground almonds

⅔ cup (100g) self-raising flour

1 Place washed unpeeled mandarins in a 4.5-litre (18-cup) slow cooker; cover with hot water. Cook, covered, on high, for 2 hours.

2 Trim the ends from mandarins; discard. Halve mandarins; discard seeds. Process mandarins, including rind, until mixture is pulpy.

3 Grease a 2-litre (8-cup) pudding steamer.

4 Beat eggs and sugar in a small bowl with an electric mixer until thick and creamy. Fold in ground almonds, sifted flour and mandarin pulp. Spoon mixture into steamer. Top with pleated baking paper and foil; secure with kitchen string or a lid.

5 Place pudding in cooker with enough boiling water to come halfway up the side of the steamer. Cook, covered, on high, for 3 hours, replenishing with boiling water as necessary to maintain level. Stand pudding for 5 minutes before turning onto a plate.

nutritional count per serving
13.9g total fat
1.6g saturated fat
1246kJ (298 cal)
32.5g carbohydrate
9g protein
3.2g fibre

serving suggestion
Serve with cream, custard or vanilla ice-cream.

tips The pleated paper and foil simply allow space for the pudding mixture to rise. Although this pudding has only a few ingredients, it is a labour of love to create. The result is well worth the effort, but keep in mind the time you will need to make it.

to freeze Wrap pudding in two layers of plastic wrap. Seal, label and freeze for up to 2 months. Thaw overnight at room temperature. Reheat in a microwave on medium power (50%) until heated through.

FOR
THE STOVE

Enjoy the luxury of a no-cook meal throughout
the week when you freeze one of these recipes.
Combine these with one of the fresh and
delicious recipe accompaniments on offer for
a delicious and nutritious meal.

BRAISED BEEF BRISKET

prep + cook time 2 hours 30 minutes serves 4

1kg (2 pounds) beef brisket, trimmed

2 tablespoons vegetable oil

1 small brown onion (80g), sliced thinly

2 cloves garlic, crushed

2cm (¾-inch) piece fresh ginger (10g), grated

2 tablespoons fish sauce

1 tablespoon dark soy sauce

1 tablespoon light brown sugar

1 teaspoon five-spice powder

2 x 10cm (4-inch) sticks fresh lemon grass (40g),
  halved crossways

2 cups (500ml) water

150g (4½ ounces) snake beans, chopped coarsely

¾ cup (105g) crushed peanuts

⅓ cup loosely packed fresh vietnamese mint leaves

1 Cut beef into 3cm (1¼-inch) pieces. Heat half the oil in a large saucepan; cook beef, in batches, until browned. Remove from pan.

2 Heat remaining oil in same pan; cook onion, garlic and ginger until onion softens.

3 Return beef to pan with sauces, sugar, five-spice, lemon grass and the water; bring to the boil. Reduce heat; simmer, covered, about 1¼ hours or until beef is tender. Discard lemon grass. Add beans and ½ cup of the nuts; simmer, uncovered, for 15 minutes. Season to taste.

4 Serve beef, sprinkled with remaining nuts and mint leaves.

nutritional count per serving
35.6g total fat
8.3g saturated fat
2458kJ (588 cal)
8.3g carbohydrate
56.8g protein
4.2g fibre

to freeze Complete the recipe to the end of step 3. Pack into freezer-proof containers, leaving a 2.5cm (1 inch) space to allow for expansion. Seal, label and freeze for up to 3 months. Thaw overnight in the fridge. Reheat in a saucepan or microwave on medium power (50%) until heated through.

BEEF AND BARLEY SOUP

prep + cook time 2 hours 15 minutes **serves** 6

1 tablespoon olive oil

500g (1 pound) gravy beef, trimmed,
  cut into 2.5cm (1-inch) pieces

2 cloves garlic, crushed

2 medium brown onions (300g), chopped finely

¾ cup (150g) pearl barley

3 cups (750ml) beef stock

1.5 litres (6 cups) water

1 bay leaf

1 sprig fresh thyme

1 sprig fresh rosemary

2 medium potatoes (400g)

2 medium carrots (240g)

2 medium zucchini (240g)

2 medium yellow patty-pan squash (60g)

100g (3 ounces) swiss brown mushrooms,
  chopped coarsely

½ cup finely chopped fresh flat-leaf parsley

1 Heat half the oil in a large saucepan; cook beef, in batches, until browned.

2 Heat remaining oil in a same pan; cook garlic and onion, stirring, until onion softens. Return beef to pan with barley, stock, the water, bay leaf, thyme and rosemary; bring to the boil. Reduce heat; simmer, covered, for 1 hour or until beef and barley are tender, skimming fat occasionally.

3 Meanwhile, chop potatoes, carrots and zucchini into 1cm (½-inch) pieces. Add potato, carrot, zucchini, squash and mushrooms to soup; simmer, covered, for 25 minutes or until vegetables are softened. Remove and discard bay leaf, thyme and rosemary. Season to taste.

4 Serve bowls of soup sprinkled with parsley.

nutritional count per serving
8.8g total fat
2.6g saturated fat
1350kJ (323 cal)
30g carbohydrate
26.9g protein
7.8g fibre

to freeze Complete the recipe to the end of step 2. Cool to room temperature. Spoon into freezer-proof containers, leaving a 2.5cm (1 inch) space to allow for expansion. Seal, label and freeze for up to 3 months. Thaw overnight in the fridge. Reheat in a saucepan or microwave on medium power (50%) until heated through.

POTATO AND LEEK SOUP

prep + cook time 1 hour 20 minutes (+ cooling) **serves** 4

2 medium potatoes (400g), chopped coarsely

2 medium carrots (240g), chopped coarsely

1 large brown onion (200g), chopped coarsely

1 medium tomato (150g), chopped coarsely

1 stick celery (150g), trimmed, chopped coarsely

1.5 litres (6 cups) water

1 tablespoon olive oil

50g (1½ ounces) butter

4 medium potatoes (800g), chopped coarsely, extra

1 large leek (500g), sliced thickly

300ml (½ pint) pouring cream

2 tablespoons finely chopped fresh chives

1 tablespoon finely chopped fresh basil

1 tablespoon finely chopped fresh dill

1 Place potato, carrot, onion, tomato, celery and the water in a large saucepan; bring to the boil. Reduce heat; simmer, uncovered, for 25 minutes. Strain broth through a muslin-lined sieve or colander into a large heatproof bowl; discard solids.

2 Heat oil and butter in same cleaned pan; cook extra potato and leek, covered, for 20 minutes, stirring occasionally. Add broth; bring to the boil. Reduce heat; simmer, covered, for 15 minutes. Cool 15 minutes.

3 Blend or process soup, in batches, until smooth.

4 Return soup to same cleaned pan, add cream; stir over medium heat until hot.

5 Serve soup sprinkled with combined herbs and, if you like, topped with croûtons.

nutritional count per serving
46.9g total fat
28.1g saturated fat
2812kJ (665 cal)
46.3g carbohydrate
11g protein
9.8g fibre

to freeze Complete the recipe to the end of step 3. Pour into freezer-proof containers, leaving a 2.5cm (1 inch) space to allow for expansion. Seal, label and freeze for up to 3 months. Thaw overnight in the fridge. Reheat in a saucepan or microwave on medium power (50%) until heated through.

BRAISED OXTAIL IN PEANUT SAUCE

prep + cook time 3 hours 50 minutes **serves** 4

2 oxtails (2kg), cut into 5cm (2-inch) pieces

2 tablespoons plain (all-purpose) flour

2 tablespoons vegetable oil

1 large brown onion (200g), chopped coarsely

6 cloves garlic, crushed

1 tablespoon ground coriander

1 tablespoon ground cumin

2 whole star anise

2 fresh long red chillies, halved lengthways

1 litre (4 cups) beef stock

1 litre (4 cups) water

⅔ cup (150g) red curry paste

⅔ cup (90g) roasted unsalted peanuts, chopped coarsely

300g (9½ ounces) green beans, trimmed, chopped coarsely

2 green onions (scallions), sliced thinly

1 Coat oxtail in flour; shake off excess. Heat half the oil in a large flameproof baking dish; cook oxtail, in batches, until browned.

2 Heat remaining oil in same dish; cook onion and garlic, stirring, until onion softens. Add spices and chilli; cook, stirring, until fragrant. Return oxtail to dish with stock and the water; simmer, covered, for 2 hours.

3 Strain beef over a large bowl; reserve braising liquid and oxtail, discard solids. Skim fat from braising liquid.

4 Cook paste in same cleaned dish, stirring, until fragrant. Add 1 litre of the reserved braising liquid; bring to the boil. Add oxtail; simmer, uncovered, for 45 minutes or until oxtail is tender.

5 Add nuts and beans to dish; cook, uncovered, for 5 minutes or until beans are tender.

6 Serve curry topped with green onion.

nutritional count per serving
111.7g total fat
36.8g saturated fat
5626kJ (1346 cal)
15.6g carbohydrate
70g protein
6.7 g fibre

serving suggestion
Serve with steamed rice.

to freeze Pack into freezer-proof containers, leaving a 2.5cm (1 inch) space to allow for expansion. Seal, label and freeze for up to 3 months. Thaw overnight in the fridge. Reheat in a large saucepan or microwave on medium power (50%) until heated through.

MEXICAN BEANS WITH SAUSAGES

prep +cooking time 2 hours 35 minutes (+ standing) **serves** 4

1 cup (200g) dried kidney beans

800g (1½ pounds) beef sausages, chopped coarsely

1 tablespoon olive oil

1 large white onion (200g), chopped coarsely

3 cloves garlic, crushed

1 large red capsicum (bell pepper) (350g), chopped coarsely

½ teaspoon ground cumin

2 teaspoons sweet smoked paprika

1 teaspoon dried chilli flakes

800g (1½ pounds) canned crushed tomatoes

2 tablespoons coarsely chopped fresh oregano

1 Soak beans in a medium bowl of cold water overnight; drain. Rinse under cold water; drain.

2 Place beans in a medium saucepan of boiling water; return to the boil. Reduce heat; simmer, uncovered, for 30 minutes or until beans are almost tender. Drain.

3 Cook sausages, in batches, in a large deep saucepan until browned; drain on absorbent paper.

4 Heat oil in same pan; cook onion, garlic and capsicum, stirring, until onion softens. Add cumin, paprika and chilli; cook, stirring, for 2 minutes or until fragrant. Add beans and tomatoes; bring to the boil. Reduce heat; simmer, covered, for 1 hour or until beans are tender.

5 Return sausages to pan; simmer, covered, for 10 minutes or until sausages are cooked through. Remove from heat; stir in oregano.

nutritional count per serving
56.9g total fat
25.2g saturated fat
3323kJ (795 cal)
33.5g carbohydrate
38.1g protein
20.2g fibre

serving suggestion
Serve with tortillas.

to freeze Complete the recipe to the end of step 4. Pack into freezer-proof containers, leaving a 2.5cm (1 inch) space to allow for expansion. Seal, label and freeze for up to 3 months. Thaw overnight in the fridge. Reheat in a saucepan or microwave on medium power (50%) until heated through.

CHILLI BEEF WITH CORNBREAD DUMPLINGS

prep + cook time 1 hour 15 minutes **serves** 4

1 tablespoon olive oil

1 medium brown onion (150g), chopped coarsley

800g (1½ pounds) minced (ground) beef

3 cloves garlic, crushed

2 teaspoons ground cumin

2 teaspoons smoked paprika

½ teaspoon cayenne pepper

400g (12½ ounces) canned kidney beans, drained, rinsed

800g (1½ pounds) canned diced tomatoes

1 cup (250ml) beef stock

1 cup (250ml) water

1 tablespoon light brown sugar

CORNBREAD DUMPLINGS

1⅓ cups (200g) self-raising flour

⅓ cup (55g) polenta

¼ cup (30g) coarsely grated cheddar cheese

¼ cup (60g) creamed corn

1 egg, beaten lightly

½ cup (125ml) milk

1   Heat oil in a large saucepan; cook onion, beef, garlic and spices, stirring, until beef is browned.

2   Add beans and tomatoes to pan with stock, the water and sugar; bring to the boil. Reduce heat; simmer, uncovered, for 30 minutes, stirring occasionally. Season to taste.

3   Meanwhile, make cornbread dumplings.

4   Roll level tablespoons of the dumpling mixture into balls and place on top of chilli. Cook, covered, for 15 minutes or until dumplings are cooked.

CORNBREAD DUMPLINGS Combine sifted flour, polenta and cheese in a medium bowl; stir in corn, egg and milk.

nutritional count per serving
26.6g total fat
11.2g saturated fat
3047kJ (729 cal)
70.8g carbohydrate
58.2g protein
10.5g fibre

tips Use wet hands when rolling the dumplings to stop them sticking. Use a wide saucepan so you have more surface area for the dumplings to cook.

to freeze Complete the recipe to the end of step 2. Pack into freezer-proof containers, leaving a 2.5cm (1 inch) space to allow for expansion. Seal, label and freeze for up to 3 months. Thaw overnight in the fridge. Reheat in a large saucepan, then continue from step 3.

SLOW-COOKED LAMB AND WHITE BEAN SOUP

prep + cook time 3 hours 55 minutes (+ standing) **serves** 4

1 cup (200g) dried white beans

2 medium red capsicums (bell peppers) (400g)

1 tablespoon olive oil

1.5kg (3 pounds) french-trimmed lamb shanks

1 large brown onion (200g), chopped coarsely

2 cloves garlic, quartered

2 medium carrots (240g), chopped coarsely

2 sticks celery (300g), trimmed, chopped coarsely

2 tablespoons tomato paste

1 cup (250ml) dry red wine

3 litres (12 cups) water

90g (3 ounces) baby spinach leaves

1 Place beans in a medium bowl, cover with water, stand overnight; drain. Rinse under cold water; drain.

2 Quarter capsicums; discard seeds and membranes. Roast under grill (broiler) or in a very hot oven, skin-side up, until skin blisters and blackens. Cover capsicum pieces with plastic or paper for 5 minutes; peel away skin, dice capsicum finely.

3 Heat oil in a large saucepan; cook lamb, in batches, until browned all over. Cook onion and garlic in same pan, stirring, until onion softens. Add carrot and celery; cook, stirring, for 2 minutes. Add paste and wine; bring to the boil. Reduce heat; simmer, uncovered, for 5 minutes.

4 Return lamb to pan with the water; bring to the boil. Reduce heat; simmer, uncovered, for 2 hours, skimming fat from surface occasionally.

5 Meanwhile, place beans in a medium saucepan of boiling water; return to the boil. Reduce heat; simmer, uncovered, for 30 minutes or until beans are almost tender. Drain.

6 Remove lamb from pan. Strain broth through muslin-lined sieve or colander into a large heatproof bowl; discard solids. When lamb is cool enough to handle, remove meat from shanks; shred coarsely. Discard bones.

7 Return broth to same cleaned pan with capsicum, beans and lamb; bring to the boil. Reduce heat; simmer, uncovered, 5 minutes. Remove from heat.

8 Add spinach, stir until wilted.

nutritional count per serving
1.8g total fat
0.7g saturated fat
171kJ (41 cal)
1.4g carbohydrate
3.8g protein
0.7g fibre

to freeze Complete the recipe to the end of step 7. Pack into freezer-proof containers, leaving a 2.5cm (1 inch) space to allow for expansion. Seal, label and freeze for up to 3 months. Thaw overnight in the fridge. Reheat in a large saucepan, then continue from step 8.

SOUTH AFRICAN BEAN CURRY

prep + cook time 1 hour 20 minutes (+ standing) **serves** 4

1 cup (200g) dried red kidney beans

2 tablespoons vegetable oil

½ teaspoon brown mustard seeds

½ teaspoon cumin seeds

15 fresh curry leaves

¼ teaspoon turmeric

1 teaspoon ground coriander

1 teaspoon ground cumin

2 fresh long green chillies, seeded, chopped finely

3 cloves garlic, chopped finely

1cm (½-inch) piece fresh ginger (5g), grated

2 teaspoons sugar

1½ teaspoons salt

4 medium tomatoes (600g), chopped finely

1 cup (250ml) vegetable stock

1 cup (150g) frozen broad (fava) beans, thawed, peeled

1 Cover kidney beans with cold water in a medium bowl; stand overnight.

2 Drain beans, rinse under cold water. Place beans in a medium saucepan of water; bring to the boil, drain. Add fresh water to the pan; bring to the boil. Reduce heat; simmer, partially covered, for 1 hour or until beans are tender. Drain.

3 Meanwhile, heat oil in a medium saucepan over medium-high heat; cook seeds, curry leaves, spices, chilli, garlic and ginger, stirring, for 1 minute or until seeds begin to pop. Stir in sugar, salt, tomato and stock; bring to the boil. Reduce heat; simmer, uncovered, for 5 minutes.

4 Add kidney beans and broad beans; simmer, partially covered, for 5 minutes or until beans are heated through and tender. Season to taste.

nutritional count per serving
20.5g total fat
2.7g saturated fat
1412kJ (337 cal)
14.4g carbohydrate
19.8g protein
14.9g fibre

serving suggestion
Serve topped with yoghurt and fresh mint leaves.

to freeze Pack into freezer-proof containers, leaving a 2.5cm (1 inch) space to allow for expansion. Seal, label and freeze for up to 3 months. Thaw overnight in the fridge. Reheat in a saucepan or microwave on medium power (50%) until heated through.

*All the recipes in this chapter are suitable to freeze,
either as the complete dish or part-way through —
just reheat and stir in the final fresh ingredients.
Label and store in individual containers for handy dinners
for one or in larger containers for the family.
Thaw overnight in the fridge and reheat in a saucepan
over medium heat, or in the microwave oven on
medium power, until warmed through.*

LAMB CHOPS WITH BARLEY, MINT AND CUMIN

prep + cook time 2 hour 15 minutes **serves** 4

1 tablespoon olive oil

8 lamb forequarter chops (1.5kg)

20g (¾ ounce) butter

1 large brown onion (200g), chopped coarsely

2 cloves garlic, chopped finely

1 tablespoon ground cumin

2 large red capsicums (bell peppers) (700g), chopped coarsely

1 cup (200g) pearl barley

2 teaspoons finely grated orange rind

1 cup (250ml) orange juice

1 litre (4 cups) chicken stock

2 cups (500ml) water

¼ cup firmly packed fresh mint leaves

1 Heat oil in a large deep saucepan; cook lamb, in batches, until browned all over.

2 Heat butter in same pan; cook onion and garlic, stirring, until onion softens. Add cumin and capsicum; cook, stirring, until fragrant.

3 Return lamb to pan with barley, rind, juice, stock and the water; bring to the boil. Reduce heat; simmer, covered, for 45 minutes. Uncover; simmer for 30 minutes or until lamb is tender.

4 Strain mixture over a large bowl; cover lamb mixture to keep warm. Return cooking liquid to pan; bring to the boil. Boil, uncovered, stirring occasionally, for 15 minutes or until sauce thickens slightly.

5 Divide lamb mixture among plates; top with sauce then with mint.

nutritional count per serving
28.5g total fat
12.2g saturated fat
3031kJ (725 cal)
45.7g carbohydrate
70.9g protein
8.9g fibre

to freeze Complete the recipe to the end of step 3. Pack into freezer-proof containers, leaving a 2.5cm (1 inch) space to allow for expansion. Seal, label and freeze for up to 3 months. Thaw overnight in the fridge. Reheat in a large saucepan, then continue from step 4.

LAMB AND OKRA IN RICH TOMATO SAUCE WITH GARLIC CONFIT

prep + cook time 2 hours 30 minutes **serves** 4

1 tablespoon olive oil

1kg (2-pounds) boned lamb shoulder, trimmed, chopped coarsely

2 medium brown onions (300g), chopped coarsely

7 medium tomatoes (1kg), chopped coarsely

1 litre (4 cups) water

200g (6½ ounces) okra

½ cup loosely packed fresh mint leaves

GARLIC CONFIT

1 teaspoon coriander seeds

½ teaspoon cardamom seeds

30g (1 ounce) butter

5 cloves garlic, sliced thinly

1 teaspoon dried chilli flakes

1 teaspoon salt

1   Heat oil in a large deep saucepan; cook lamb, in batches, until browned all over.

2   Cook onion in same pan, stirring, until soft. Add tomato and the water; bring to the boil. Return lamb to pan, reduce heat; simmer, uncovered, stirring occasionally, for 1¾ hours or until lamb is tender.

3   Add okra to lamb mixture; simmer, uncovered, for 15 minutes or until okra is tender.

4   Meanwhile, make garlic confit.

5   Serve with garlic confit and mint.

GARLIC CONFIT Crush seeds in a mortar and pestle. Melt butter in a small saucepan; cook seeds, garlic, chilli and salt over low heat, stirring, for 10 minutes or until garlic softens.

nutritional count per serving
33.5g total fat
15g saturated fat
2286kJ (547 cal)
8g carbohydrate
53.4g protein
6.4g fibre

serving suggestion
Serve with steamed rice.

to freeze Complete the recipe to the end of step 2. Cool to room temperature. Pack into freezer-proof containers, leaving a 2.5cm (1 inch) space to allow for expansion. Seal, label and freeze for up to 3 months. Thaw overnight in the fridge. Reheat in a large saucepan, then continue from step 3.

LAMB AND MACADAMIA CURRY

prep + cook time 2 hours 30 minutes **serves** 4

1 cup (140g) roasted unsalted macadamias

2 tablespoons vegetable oil

800g (1½ pounds) diced lamb shoulder

1 medium brown onion (150g), chopped coarsely

1 clove garlic, crushed

2 fresh small red thai (serrano) chillies, chopped finely

2cm (¾-inch) piece fresh ginger (10g), grated

1 teaspoon ground cumin

1 teaspoon ground turmeric

½ teaspoon ground cinnamon

½ teaspoon ground cardamom

½ teaspoon ground fennel

400g (12½ ounces) canned diced tomatoes

1⅔ cups (410ml) coconut milk

1 cup (250ml) beef stock

½ cup loosely packed fresh coriander (cilantro) leaves

1   Blend or process half the nuts until finely ground; coarsely chop remaining nuts.

2   Heat half the oil in a large saucepan; cook lamb, in batches, until browned.

3   Heat remaining oil in same pan; cook onion, garlic, chilli and ginger, stirring, until onion softens. Add spices; cook, stirring, until fragrant. Return lamb to pan with ground nuts, tomatoes, coconut milk and stock; bring to the boil. Reduce heat; simmer, covered, for 1¼ hours or until lamb is tender. Uncover; simmer for 15 minutes or until sauce thickens slightly. Season to taste.

4   Serve lamb topped with remaining nuts and coriander leaves.

nutritional count per serving
68.4g total fat
28.4g saturated
3561kJ (852 cal)
11.6g carbohydrate
47g protein
5.9g fibre

to freeze Complete the recipe to the end of step 3. Cool to room temperature. Pack into freezer-proof containers, leaving a 2.5cm (1 inch) space to allow for expansion. Seal, label and freeze for up to 3 months. Thaw overnight in the fridge. Reheat in a saucepan or microwave on medium power (50%) until heated through.

MINTED BROAD BEAN AND HAM SOUP

prep + cook time 2 hour 30 minutes **serves** 4

2 teaspoons olive oil

1 large brown onion (200g), chopped coarsely

2 sticks celery (300g), trimmed, chopped coarsely

1 medium carrot (120g), chopped coarsely

2 cloves garlic, crushed

1kg (2-pound) ham hock

2 litres (8 cups) water

3 cups (450g) frozen broad (fava) beans

1 tablespoon lemon juice

⅓ cup finely chopped fresh mint

1   Heat oil in a large saucepan; cook onion, celery, carrot and garlic, stirring, until vegetables soften. Add ham hock and the water; bring to the boil. Reduce heat; simmer, covered, for 1½ hours. Uncover; simmer for 30 minutes.

2   Meanwhile, place beans in a medium heatproof bowl, cover with boiling water; stand for 5 minutes, drain. Peel away grey skins.

3   Remove ham hock from soup; when cool enough to handle, remove meat from bone, shred coarsely. Discard skin and bone.

4   Add beans to soup; simmer, uncovered, for 5 minutes or until beans are tender. Cool soup for 10 minutes.

5   Using a hand-held blender, blend soup, in pan, until soup is almost smooth. Return ham meat to soup with juice; cook, stirring, until hot. Season to taste.

6   Serve soup topped with mint.

nutritional count per serving
7.4g total fat
2g saturated fat
890kJ (213 cal)
13.4g carbohydrate
17.7g protein
11.4g fibre

to freeze Complete the recipe to the end of step 5. Pack into freezer-proof containers, leaving a 2.5cm (1 inch) space to allow for expansion. Seal, label and freeze for up to 3 months. Thaw overnight in the fridge. Reheat in a saucepan or microwave on medium power (50%) until heated through.

PORK, MUSHROOM AND MARSALA STEW

prep + cook time 2 hours 15 minutes **serves** 4

1kg (2 pounds) boneless pork shoulder, chopped coarsely
¼ cup (35g) plain (all-purpose) flour
2 tablespoons olive oil
4 shallots (100g), sliced thinly
2 cloves garlic, sliced thinly
300g (9½ ounces) swiss brown mushrooms, halved
1 tablespoon coarsely chopped fresh rosemary
1 cup (250ml) marsala
1 cup (250ml) chicken stock
1 cup (250ml) water
1 tablespoon tomato paste
½ cup coarsely chopped fresh flat-leaf parsley

1 Coat pork in flour; shake off excess. Heat oil in a large saucepan or flameproof baking dish; cook pork, in batches, until browned.

2 Cook shallot, garlic, mushrooms and rosemary in same pan, stirring occasionally, until mushrooms are browned. Add marsala; cook, stirring, for 30 seconds.

3 Return pork to pan with stock, the water and paste; bring to the boil. Reduce heat; simmer, covered, for 1¾ hours, stirring occasionally, or until pork is tender. Season to taste.

4 Serve sprinkled with parsley.

nutritional count per serving
19.3g total fat
4.9g saturated fat
2299kJ (550 cal)
17g carbohydrate
58.4g protein
3.3g fibre

tips You can use another type of stewing cut of pork for this dish. You can use the more expensive pork neck too.
Marsala is an Italian fortified wine recognisable by its intense amber colour and complex aroma. It is used in Italian cooking, however, you can substitute madeira, port or dry sherry.

to freeze Complete the recipe to the end of step 3. Cool to room temperature. Pack into freezer-proof containers, leaving a 2.5cm (1 inch) space to allow for expansion. Seal, label and freeze for up to 3 months. Thaw overnight in the fridge. Reheat in a saucepan or microwave on medium power (50%) until heated through.

BOLLITO MISTO

prep + cook time 3 hours **serves** 4

2 tablespoons olive oil

4 thin italian pork sausages (320g)

500g (1 pound) beef chuck steak,
  cut into 2cm (¾-inch) pieces

500g (1 pound) chicken thigh fillets,
  cut into 2cm (¾-inch) pieces

1 medium brown onion (150g), chopped coarsely

1 clove garlic, crushed

2 cups (500ml) beef stock

1 cup (250ml) water

2 bay leaves

2 medium carrots (240g), chopped coarsely

2 medium potatoes (400g), chopped coarsely

¼ cup (50g) drained capers, rinsed, chopped coarsely

4 anchovy fillets, chopped finely

2 teaspoons finely grated lemon rind

1 tablespoon lemon juice

1 cup coarsely chopped fresh flat-leaf parsley

1 Heat half the oil in a large saucepan; cook sausages until browned. Remove from pan; chop coarsely.

2 Cook beef and chicken, in batches, in same pan, until browned. Remove from pan.

3 Heat remaining oil in same pan; cook onion and garlic, stirring, until onion softens. Return meats to pan with stock, the water and bay leaves; bring to the boil. Reduce heat; simmer, covered, for 1½ hours.

4 Add carrot and potato to pan; simmer, uncovered, for 30 minutes or until vegetables soften. Add capers, anchovy, rind and juice; cook, stirring, until hot. Remove from heat; stir in parsley.

nutritional count per serving
42.2g total fat
13.8g saturated fat
3035kJ (726 cal)
20.5g carbohydrate
64.1g protein
5.7g fibre

to freeze Complete the recipe to the end of step 3. Cool to room temperature. Pack into freezer-proof containers, leaving a 2.5cm (1 inch) space to allow for expansion. Seal, label and freeze for up to 3 months. Thaw overnight in the fridge. Reheat in a large saucepan, then continue from step 4.

PORK AND VEGETABLE VINDALOO

prep + cook time 1 hour 40 minutes serves 6

2 teaspoons cumin seeds

2 teaspoons garam masala

1 teaspoon ground cinnamon

2 cloves garlic, quartered

4 fresh small red thai (serrano) chillies, chopped coarsely

2.5cm (1-inch) piece fresh ginger (15g), sliced thinly

1 large brown onion (200g) chopped coarsely

2 tablespoons white vinegar

2 tablespoons vegetable oil

1kg (2 pounds) boneless pork shoulder,
  cut into 2.5cm (1-inch) pieces

2 cups (500ml) beef stock

2 medium potatoes (400g), cut into 2.5cm (1-inch) pieces

2 medium carrots (240g), cut into 2.5cm (1-inch) pieces

155g (5 ounces) green beans, trimmed,
  chopped coarsely

1 Dry-fry spices in small frying pan, stirring, until fragrant; cool.

2 Blend or process spices with garlic, chilli, ginger, onion and vinegar until mixture forms a smooth paste.

3 Heat half the oil in a large saucepan; cook pork, in batches, until browned. Remove from pan.

4 Heat remaining oil in same pan; cook paste, stirring, for 5 minutes. Return pork to pan with stock; bring to the boil. Reduce heat; simmer, covered, for 40 minutes.

5 Add potato, carrot and beans to pan; simmer, uncovered, for 20 minutes or until pork is tender and sauce thickens slightly.

nutritional count per serving
19.9g total fat
5.4g saturated fat
1664kJ (398 cal)
13.6g carbohydrate
39.3g protein
3.8g fibre

to freeze Complete the recipe to the end of step 4. Pack into freezer-proof containers, leaving a 2.5cm (1 inch) space to allow for expansion. Seal, label and freeze for up to 3 months. Thaw overnight in the fridge. Reheat in a large saucepan, then continue from step 5.

CHICKEN, CHORIZO AND OKRA GUMBO

prep + cook time 3 hours 15 minutes **serves** 8

1.5kg (3-pound) whole chicken

2 medium carrots (240g), chopped coarsely

2 sticks celery (300g), trimmed, chopped coarsely

1 medium brown onion (150g), chopped coarsely

12 black peppercorns

1 dried bay leaf

3 litres (12 cups) water

60g (2 ounces) butter

1 small brown onion (80g), chopped finely, extra

2 cloves garlic, crushed

1 medium red capsicum (bell pepper) (200g),
   chopped finely

2 teaspoons dried oregano

1 teaspoon sweet paprika

¼ teaspoon cayenne pepper

¼ teaspoon ground clove

¼ cup (35g) plain (all-purpose) flour

¼ cup (70g) tomato paste

400g (12½ ounces) canned crushed tomatoes

100g (3 ounces) fresh okra, halved diagonally

1 cup (200g) white medium-grain rice

1 chorizo sausage (170g), sliced thinly

1 Place chicken in a large saucepan with carrot, celery, onion, peppercorns, bay leaf and the water; bring to the boil. Reduce heat; simmer, covered, for 1½ hours.

2 Remove chicken from pan. Strain broth through muslin-lined sieve or colander into large heatproof bowl; discard solids. When chicken is cool enough to handle, remove and discard skin and bones; shred meat coarsely.

3 Melt butter in a large saucepan; cook extra onion and garlic, stirring, until onion softens. Add capsicum, oregano and spices; cook, stirring, until fragrant. Add flour and paste; cook, stirring, for 1 minute. Gradually stir in reserved broth and tomatoes; bring to the boil, stirring. Stir in okra and rice; simmer, uncovered, stirring occasionally, for 15 minutes or until rice is tender.

4 Heat a large oiled frying pan; cook sausage until browned, drain.

5 Add sausage and chicken to gumbo; stir over medium heat until hot. Season to taste.

nutritional count per serving
26.8g total fat
5.7g saturated fat
2011kJ (481 cal)
30.5g carbohydrate
27.8g protein
3.9g fibre

tips If you want to cook this gumbo a day ahead, the flavours will meld and deepen, making the soup even more delicious. Follow the recipe through to the end of step 2, then cool the stock, cover and refrigerate it overnight.

to freeze Complete the recipe to the end of step 2. Pack into freezer-proof containers, leaving a 2.5cm (1 inch) space to allow for expansion. Seal, label and freeze for up to 3 months. Thaw overnight in the fridge. Reheat in a large saucepan, then continue from step 2.

CREAMY CHICKEN AND VEGETABLE CASSEROLE

prep + cook time 1 hour 30 minutes **serves** 4

1kg (2 pounds) chicken thigh fillets,
  cut into 2cm (¾-inch) pieces

2 tablespoons plain (all-purpose) flour

2 tablespoons olive oil

1 large brown onion (200g), chopped coarsely

1 clove garlic, crushed

2 medium carrots (240g), chopped coarsely

2 medium potatoes (400g), chopped coarsely

2 sticks celery (300g), trimmed, chopped coarsely

1 cup (250ml) dry white wine

1½ cups (375ml) chicken stock

2 bay leaves

2 sprigs fresh thyme

200g (6½ ounces) green beans, trimmed,
  cut into 3cm (1¼-inch) pieces

2 large zucchini (300g), chopped coarsely

2 medium tomatoes (300g), chopped coarsely

300ml (½ pint) pouring cream

1 tablespoon wholegrain mustard

1 Coat chicken in flour; shake off excess. Heat half the oil in a large saucepan; cook chicken, in batches, until browned.

2 Heat remaining oil in same pan; cook onion, garlic, carrot, potato and celery, stirring, for 5 minutes or until vegetables are browned lightly. Add wine; bring to the boil. Boil, uncovered, until liquid reduces by half.

3 Return chicken to pan with stock, bay leaves and thyme; bring to the boil. Reduce heat; simmer, covered, for 30 minutes or until chicken is tender.

4 Add beans, zucchini, tomato, cream and mustard; simmer, uncovered, for 15 minutes or until vegetables are tender and sauce thickens slightly.

nutritional count per serving
60.8g total fat
28.4g saturated fat
3853kJ (921 cal)
28.7g carbohydrate
56.2g protein
8.5g fibre

serving suggestion
Serve with steamed white rice or small pasta shells.

to freeze Complete the recipe to the end of step 3. Pack into freezer-proof containers, leaving a 2.5cm (1 inch) space to allow for expansion. Seal, label and freeze for up to 3 months. Thaw overnight in the fridge. Reheat in a large saucepan, then continue from step 4.

SPICY CARIBBEAN-STYLE CHICKEN STEW

prep + cook time 2 hours **serves** 6

1kg (2 pounds) chicken thigh fillets,
  cut into 2cm (¾-inch) strips

2 teaspoons ground allspice

1 teaspoon ground cinnamon

pinch ground nutmeg

1 tablespoon finely chopped fresh thyme

¼ cup (60ml) olive oil

2 medium brown onions (300g), sliced thinly

2 cloves garlic, crushed

4cm (1½-inch) piece fresh ginger (20g), grated

1 teaspoon sambal oelek

5 medium tomatoes (650g), peeled, seeded,
  chopped finely

2 tablespoons light brown sugar

2 teaspoons finely grated orange rind

2 tablespoons soy sauce

1 medium kumara (orange sweet potato) (400g),
  chopped coarsely

2 fresh corn cobs (800g), trimmed, sliced thickly

125g (4 ounces) baby spinach leaves

1 Toss chicken in combined spices and thyme.

2 Heat half the oil in a large saucepan; cook chicken, in batches, stirring, until browned. Drain on absorbent paper.

3 Heat remaining oil in same pan; cook onion, garlic, ginger and sambal oelek, stirring, until onion is soft.

4 Add tomato, sugar, rind, sauce, kumara, corn and chicken; cook, covered, for 15 minutes or until chicken and vegetables are tender. Remove cover; simmer for 5 minutes.

5 Remove from heat. Stir in spinach until wilted.

nutritional count per serving
22.3g total fat
5g saturated fat
2015kJ (482 cal)
29.7g carbohydrate
37.5g protein
6.7g fibre

to freeze Complete the recipe to the end of step 4. Pack into freezer-proof containers, leaving a 2.5cm (1 inch) space to allow for expansion. Seal, label and freeze for up to 3 months. Thaw overnight in the fridge. Reheat in a large saucepan, then continue from step 5.

tomato-braised lamb shanks

TOMATO-BRAISED LAMB SHANKS

prep + cook time 2 hours 20 minutes serves 4

1 tablespoon olive oil

4 french-trimmed lamb shanks (1kg)

1 medium brown onion (150g), sliced thinly

2 medium carrots (240g), chopped finely

2 sticks celery (300g), trimmed, sliced thinly

2 cloves garlic, crushed

½ cup (125ml) dry red wine

1¾ cup (430ml) beef stock

4 medium tomatoes (600g), chopped coarsely

410g (13 ounces) canned crushed tomatoes

2 tablespoons tomato paste

4 sprigs fresh thyme

1 Heat oil in a large saucepan; cook lamb, in batches, until browned.

2 Cook onion, carrot, celery and garlic in same pan, stirring, until celery softens.

3 Return lamb to pan with wine, stock, fresh and canned tomatoes, paste and thyme; bring to the boil. Reduce heat; simmer, covered, for 1 hour, stirring occasionally. Uncover; simmer for 1 hour or until lamb is tender.

nutritional count per serving
7.7g total fat
1.9g saturated fat
1250kJ (299 cal)
13.2g carbohydrate
35.2g protein
6.8g fibre

to freeze Cool to room temperature. Pack into freezer-proof containers, leaving a 2.5cm (1 inch) space to allow for expansion. Seal, label and freeze for up to 3 months. Thaw overnight in the fridge. Reheat in a saucepan or microwave on medium power (50%) until heated through.

DHAL WITH EGG AND EGGPLANT

prep + cook time 1 hour 10 minutes serves 4

2 cups (400g) red lentils

2 teaspoons vegetable oil

1 medium brown onion (150g), chopped finely

1 clove garlic, crushed

2 teaspoons ground cumin

½ teaspoon cumin seeds

1 tablespoon tomato paste

2 cups (500ml) vegetable stock

1 litre (4 cups) water

1 large tomato (250g), chopped coarsely

3 baby eggplants (180g), chopped coarsely

4 hard-boiled eggs

1 Rinse lentils in large colander under cold water until water runs clear.

2 Heat oil in a large heavy-based saucepan; cook onion, garlic, cumin, seeds and paste, stirring, for 5 minutes. Add lentils, stock and the water; bring to the boil. Reduce heat; simmer, uncovered, stirring occasionally, for 40 minutes or until mixture thickens slightly.

3 Add tomato and eggplant to pan; simmer, uncovered, stirring occasionally, for 20 minutes or until dhal is thickened and eggplant is tender.

4 Add whole eggs; stir gently until eggs are heated through.

(photograph page 270)

nutritional count per serving
10.9g total fat
2.6g saturated fat
1698kJ (406 cal)
44.6g carbohydrate
34.1g protein
16.7g fibre

to freeze Complete the recipe to the end of step 3. Pack into freezer-proof containers, leaving a 2.5cm (1 inch) space to allow for expansion. Seal, label and freeze for up to 3 months. Thaw overnight in the fridge. Reheat in a large saucepan, then continue from step 4.

dhal with egg and eggplant (recipe page 269)

dhansak with caramelised onion brown rice
(recipe pages 272 & 273)

DHANSAK WITH CARAMELISED ONION BROWN RICE

prep + cook time 3 hours (+ standing) **serves** 8

1 cup (200g) yellow split peas

½ cup (100g) dried chickpeas

½ cup (100g) red lentils

⅓ cup (80ml) vegetable oil

1kg (2 pounds) diced lamb

1 large eggplant (500g), chopped coarsely

800g (1½ pounds) pumpkin, chopped coarsely

5 medium tomatoes (750g), peeled, chopped coarsely

7 medium brown onions (1kg), sliced thinly

GARAM MASALA

1 tablespoon ground coriander

2 teaspoons ground cumin

2 teaspoons ground turmeric

½ teaspoon ground cinnamon

½ teaspoon ground cardamom

½ teaspoon black mustard seeds

¼ teaspoon ground clove

MASALA PASTE

6 dried small red chillies

6 long green chillies, seeded

4cm (1½-inch) piece fresh ginger (20g), chopped

6 cloves garlic, quartered

½ cup firmly packed fresh mint leaves

½ cup firmly packed fresh coriander (cilantro) leaves

¼ cup (60ml) hot water

CARAMELISED ONION BROWN RICE

2½ cups (500g) basmati rice

2 tablespoons vegetable oil

20g (¾ ounce) butter

4 medium brown onions (600g), sliced thinly

1.25 litres (5 cups) water

1   Place split peas and chickpeas in a large bowl, cover with water; stand overnight.

2   Drain split peas and chickpeas. Rinse under cold water; drain. Rinse lentils under cold water; drain. Add lentils, split peas and chickpeas in a large saucepan of boiling water; return to the boil. Reduce heat; simmer, uncovered, for 40 minutes or until chickpeas are tender.

3   Meanwhile, make garam masala and masala paste.

4   Heat half the oil in a large frying pan; cook lamb, in batches, until just browned. Reserve.

5   Drain pea mixture through a sieve over a large bowl. Return 1 litre of the cooking liquid to same pan, discard remainder. Reserve pea mixture in same bowl.

6   Place eggplant, pumpkin, tomato and a third of the sliced onion in pan with reserved cooking liquid, cover; bring to the boil. Reduce heat; simmer, covered, for 10 minutes, stirring occasionally. Drain vegetable mixture through a sieve over another large bowl; reserve 2 cups of the cooking liquid, discard remainder.

7   Combine half the split pea mixture and half the vegetable mixture in a large bowl; mash until smooth.

8   Heat same cleaned pan; dry-fry garam masala and masala paste, stirring, until fragrant. Add mashed, whole split pea and vegetable mixtures, lamb and reserved cooking liquid to pan; bring to the boil. Reduce heat; simmer, uncovered, for 45 minutes, stirring occasionally.

9   Meanwhile, make caramelised onion brown rice.

10 Heat remaining oil in a large frying pan; cook remaining sliced onion, stirring, for 15 minutes or until softened and caramelised lightly. Serve dhansak and rice, topped with caramelised onion.

GARAM MASALA Combine ingredients in a small bowl.

MASALA PASTE Blend or process ingredients until mixture forms a smooth paste.

CARAMELISED ONION BROWN RICE Wash rice in a strainer under cold water until water runs clear; drain. Heat oil and butter in a medium saucepan; cook onion, stirring, for 15 minutes or until softened and lightly caramelised. Carefully add the water to pan; bring to the boil. Stir in rice; return to the boil. Reduce heat; simmer rice, partially covered, for 10 minutes or until steam holes appear on the surface. Cover rice tightly, reduce heat to as low as possible; steam for 10 minutes (do not remove lid). Remove from heat; stand for 10 minutes without removing the lid. Fluff with a fork before serving.

(photograph page 271)

nutritional count per serving
33.7g total fat
9.2g saturated fat
3637kJ (869 cal)
87.4g carbohydrate
45.9g protein
17.2g fibre

to freeze Complete the recipe to the end of step 8. Pack into freezer-proof containers, leaving a 2.5cm (1 inch) space to allow for expansion. Seal, label and freeze for up to 3 months. Thaw overnight in the fridge. Reheat in a large saucepan, then continue from step 9.

LAMB STOBA

prep + cook time 1 hour 40 minutes **serves** 4

2 tablespoons vegetable oil

1kg (2-pound) lamb shoulder, trimmed,
 cut into 3cm (1¼-inch) pieces

2 medium brown onions (300g), sliced thinly

3cm (1¼-inch) piece fresh ginger (15g), sliced thinly

2 fresh long red chillies, sliced thinly

1 medium red capsicum (bell pepper) (200g),
 chopped coarsely

2 teaspoons ground cumin

2 teaspoons ground allspice

1 cinnamon stick

800g (1½ pounds) canned chopped tomatoes

2 teaspoons finely grated lime rind

2 tablespoons lime juice

¼ cup (55g) firmly packed light brown sugar

1 Heat half the oil in a large saucepan; cook lamb, in batches, until browned all over.

2 Heat remaining oil in same pan; cook onion, ginger, chilli, capsicum and spices, stirring, until onion softens.

3 Return lamb to pan with remaining ingredients; simmer, covered, for 1 hour or until lamb is tender.

nutritional count per serving
31.8g total fat
11.2g saturated fat
2567kJ (614 cal)
24.4g carbohydrate
55.8g protein
4.1g fibre

serving suggestion
Serve with steamed rice.

to freeze Pack into freezer-proof containers, leaving a 2.5cm (1 inch) space to allow for expansion. Seal, label and freeze for up to 3 months. Thaw overnight in the fridge. Reheat in a saucepan or microwave on medium power (50%) until heated through.

STEAMED GINGER PUDDING

prep + cook time 1 hour 15 minutes **serves** 6

60g (2 ounces) butter

¼ cup (90g) golden syrup

½ teaspoon bicarbonate of soda (baking soda)

1 cup (150g) self-raising flour

2 teaspoons ground ginger

½ cup (125ml) milk

1 egg

SYRUP

⅓ cup (115g) golden syrup

2 tablespoons water

30g (1 ounce) butter

1   Grease a 1.25-litre (5-cup) pudding steamer.

2   Stir butter and syrup in a small saucepan over low heat until smooth. Remove from heat, stir in soda; transfer mixture to a medium bowl. Stir in sifted dry ingredients then combined milk and egg, in two batches.

3   Spread mixture into steamer. Cover with pleated baking paper and foil; secure with the lid.

4   Place pudding steamer in a large saucepan with enough boiling water to come halfway up the side of the steamer; cover pan with a tight-fitting lid. Boil for 1 hour, replenishing water as necessary to maintain level. Stand pudding for 5 minutes before turning onto plate.

5   Meanwhile, make syrup.

6   Serve pudding topped with syrup.

SYRUP Stir ingredients in a small saucepan over heat until smooth; bring to the boil. Reduce heat; simmer, uncovered, for 2 minutes.

nutritional count per serving
14.4g total fat
9g saturated fat
1342kJ (321 cal)
44.3g carbohydrate
4.6g protein
1g fibre

serving suggestion
Serve with cream or ice-cream.

tip Cut leftover pudding into serving-size wedges. Wrap and freeze as per instructions opposite. Reheat as needed for a quick dessert.

to freeze Complete the recipe up to the end of step 4. Cool to room temperature. Wrap pudding in two layers of plastic wrap. Seal, label and freeze for up to 3 months. Thaw overnight in the fridge. Reheat in microwave on medium power (50%) until heated through.

FOR THE OVEN

Turn your slow-cooked recipes from weekend-only-cooking to everyday-weeknight-meals. Make sure to freeze the food in appropriate-sized freezer-friendly containers so they are easy to defrost for an on-the-go lunch or speedy dinner.

RAGU ALLA BOLOGNESE

prep + cook time 5 hours **serves** 4

250g (8 ounces) sliced hot pancetta,
chopped coarsely

20g (¾ ounce) butter

800g (1½ pounds) beef chuck steak,
chopped coarsely

¾ cup (180ml) dry red wine

1 small brown onion (80g), chopped finely

1 medium carrot (120g), chopped finely

1 stick celery (150g), trimmed, chopped finely

10g (½ ounce) dried porcini mushrooms

10 fresh sage leaves (10g)

⅓ cup (95g) tomato paste

3 cups (750ml) beef stock

⅓ cup (25g) finely grated parmesan cheese

2 teaspoons finely grated lemon rind

1 Preheat oven to 150°C/300°F.

2 Cook pancetta in a heated large flameproof dish,
stirring, until browned lightly.

3 Add butter and beef to dish; cook, stirring, until
beef is browned. Add wine; cook, uncovered,
for 5 minutes.

4 Add onion, carrot and celery with mushrooms
and sage; cook, stirring, for 5 minutes. Add paste;
cook, stirring, for 5 minutes. Add stock; roast,
covered, for 4 hours. Uncover dish; return to oven,
roast for 30 minutes.

5 Skim and discard excess fat from surface. Season
to taste. Using two forks, shred meat coarsely.

6 Serve bolognese topped with cheese and rind.

nutritional count per serving
24.3g total fat
11.2g saturated fat
2182kJ (522 cal)
7.4g carbohydrate
59.5g protein
2.9g fibre

serving suggestion
Serve with your favourite
pasta.

to freeze Complete the
recipe to the end of step 5.
Pack into freezer-proof
containers, leaving a 2.5cm
(1 inch) space to allow for
expansion. Seal, label and
freeze for up to 3 months.
Thaw overnight in the fridge.
Reheat in a saucepan or
microwave on medium power
(50%) until heated through.

CHICKEN WITH LEEK AND BACON

prep + cook time 1 hour 45 minutes **serves** 4

4 chicken thigh cutlets (800g), skin on

¼ cup (35g) plain (all-purpose) flour

1 tablespoon olive oil

2 stalks fresh rosemary

3 cloves garlic, unpeeled

½ cup (125ml) dry white wine

¾ cup (180ml) chicken stock

20g (¾ ounce) butter

4 rindless bacon slices (260g), chopped coarsely

2 small leeks (400g), sliced

1 stick celery (150g), trimmed, sliced thinly

2 sprigs fresh thyme

2 tablespoons plain (all-purpose) flour, extra

½ cup (125ml) dry white wine

1 cup (250ml) water

400g (12½ ounces) baby carrots, trimmed

1   Preheat oven to 180°C/350°F.

2   Toss chicken in flour; shake away excess flour.

3   Heat oil in a large flameproof baking dish; cook chicken until browned all over. Add rosemary, garlic, wine and stock; bring to the boil. Cover dish, bake 40 minutes or until chicken is cooked through. Strain pan juices and reserve.

4   Squeeze the garlic from skins, mash until smooth.

5   Melt butter in a large saucepan; cook bacon, leek, celery and thyme, stirring, until bacon is crisp and leek is soft.

6   Add extra flour; cook, stirring, 1 minute. Gradually stir in wine; bring to the boil. Add garlic, reserved pan juices and the water; bring to the boil. Add carrots and chicken; simmer, uncovered, 20 minutes or until carrots are tender and sauce is thickened.

nutritional count per serving
38.1g total fat
13.2g saturated fat
2621kJ (627 cal)
18.6g carbohydrate
40.3g protein
5.6g fibre

serving suggestion
Serve with mashed potato or cheesy mash (see page 174).

to freeze Pack into freezer-proof containers, leaving a 2.5cm (1 inch) space to allow for expansion. Seal, label and freeze for up to 3 months. Thaw overnight in the fridge. Reheat in a saucepan or microwave on medium power (50%) until heated through.

BRAISED RABBIT SAUCE WITH FETTUCCINE

prep + cook time 4 hours 15 minutes **serves** 6

⅓ cup (80ml) light olive oil

900g (1¾-pound) rabbit, cut into 8 pieces

1 medium red onion (170g), chopped finely

2 medium carrots (240g), chopped finely

1 medium parsnip (250g), chopped finely

1 stick celery (150g), trimmed, chopped finely

8 cloves garlic, chopped finely

800g (1½ pounds) canned crushed tomatoes

2 tablespoons tomato paste

1 cup (250ml) chicken stock

1 cup (250ml) dry red wine

2 teaspoons dried rigani

1 sprig fresh rosemary

1 cinnamon stick

600g (1¼ pounds) fettuccine pasta

2 tablespoons extra virgin olive oil

½ cup (40g) finely grated pecorino cheese

1 Preheat oven to 125°C/250°F.

2 Heat half the light olive oil in a 6-litre (24-cup) flameproof baking dish; cook rabbit, in batches, until browned. Remove from dish.

3 Heat remaining light olive oil in same dish; cook onion, carrot, parsnip and celery, covered, stirring occasionally, over low heat until soft. Add garlic, tomatoes, paste, stock, wine, herbs and cinnamon; bring to the boil. Return rabbit to dish, cover; cook, in oven, for 3½ hours or until rabbit is falling off the bone.

4 Remove rabbit from dish. When cool enough to handle, remove meat from bones; discard bones. Return meat to dish; season to taste. Cook, over heat; stirring, until hot.

5 Meanwhile, cook pasta in a large saucepan of boiling water until tender; drain. Toss pasta with extra virgin oil; season to taste.

6 Serve pasta topped with sauce and cheese.

nutritional count per serving
25g total fat
5.2g saturated fat
3164kJ (757 cal)
83.3g carbohydrate
38g protein
7.6g fibre

tips Other types of pasta, such as penne, also work well with this recipe. Dried rigani is dried Greek oregano available from delicatessens.

to freeze Complete the recipe to the end of step 4. Pack into freezer-proof containers, leaving a 2.5cm (1 inch) space to allow for expansion. Seal, label and freeze for up to 3 months. Thaw overnight in the fridge. Reheat in a saucepan, then continue cooking from step 5.

BEEF CARBONADE PIES

prep + cook time 3 hours 45 minutes **serves** 8

2kg (4 pounds) beef round steak, cut into
  2.5cm (1-inch) pieces

½ cup (75g) plain (all-purpose) flour

40g (1½ ounces) butter, melted

¼ cup (60ml) vegetable oil

4 medium brown onions (600g), sliced thickly

2 large carrots (360g), chopped coarsely

2 cloves garlic, crushed

2¾ cups (680ml) stout

2 tablespoons light brown sugar

¼ cup (60ml) cider vinegar

3 sprigs fresh thyme

1 bay leaf

2 sheets puff pastry

1 tablespoon milk

1 egg, beaten lightly

1 Coat beef in flour; shake off excess. Heat butter and 2 tablespoons of the oil in a large deep saucepan; cook beef, in batches, until browned all over. Remove from pan.

2 Heat remaining oil in same pan; cook onion, carrot and garlic, stirring, until onion softens. Return beef to pan with stout, sugar, vinegar, thyme and bay leaf; bring to the boil. Reduce heat; simmer, covered, for 1½ hours.

3 Uncover; simmer, stirring occasionally, for 1 hour or until beef is tender and sauce has thickened. Discard herbs.

4 Preheat oven to 220°C/425°F.

5 Spoon beef mixture into eight 1¼-cup (310ml) ovenproof dishes. Cut each pastry sheet into four rectangles; top dishes with one pastry piece. Brush pastry with combined milk and egg; place dishes on oven tray.

6 Bake pies for 15 minutes or until pastry is puffed and browned lightly.

nutritional count per serving
33.9g total fat
14.4g saturated fat
2930kJ (701 cal)
32.4g carbohydrate
58.2g protein
3.1g fibre

to freeze Complete the recipe to the end of step 3. Pack into freezer-proof containers, leaving a 2.5cm (1 inch) space to allow for expansion. Seal, label and freeze for up to 3 months. Thaw overnight in the fridge. Reheat in a saucepan or microwave on medium power (50%), then continue from step 4.

VEAL WITH ARTICHOKES, OLIVES AND LEMON

prep + cook time 3 hours **serves** 6

1 medium unpeeled lemon (140g), chopped coarsely

4 medium globe artichokes (800g)

1.2kg (2½ pounds) diced veal neck

¼ cup (35g) plain (all-purpose) flour

50g (1½ ounces) butter

¼ cup (60ml) olive oil

1 medium brown onion (150g), chopped finely

1 medium carrot (120g), chopped finely

2 cloves garlic, chopped finely

2 sprigs fresh marjoram

2 sprigs fresh oregano

1 cup (250ml) dry white wine

2 cups (500ml) chicken stock

1 cup (150g) pitted kalamata olives

2 teaspoons finely grated lemon rind

2 tablespoons lemon juice

2 tablespoons fresh oregano leaves

1 Place chopped lemon in a large bowl half-filled with cold water. Discard outer leaves from artichokes; cut tips from remaining leaves. Trim then peel the stalks. Quarter artichokes lengthways; using a teaspoon, remove and discard chokes. Place artichokes in the lemon water.

2 Preheat oven to 160°C/325°F.

3 Coat veal in flour; shake off excess. Heat butter and 2 tablespoons of the oil in a large flameproof baking dish; cook veal, in batches, until browned all over.

4 Heat remaining oil in same dish; cook onion, carrot, garlic and herb sprigs, stirring, until vegetables soften. Add wine; bring to the boil. Return veal to dish with stock; roast, covered, in oven for 1 hour.

5 Add artichokes; roast, covered, in oven for 30 minutes. Uncover; cook a further 30 minutes or until veal is tender. Stir in olives, rind and juice.

6 Divide stew among plates; top with oregano leaves.

nutritional count per serving
21.6g total fat
7.4g saturated fat
2040kJ (488 cal)
14.6g carbohydrate
50.2g protein
3.4g fibre

to freeze Complete the recipe up to the end of step 5. Pack into freezer-proof containers, leaving a 2.5cm (1 inch) space to allow for expansion. Seal, label and freeze for up to 3 months. Thaw overnight in the fridge. Reheat, covered, in a 180°C/350°F oven for 30 minutes or microwave on medium power (50%) until heated through.

LAMB NECK CHOP AND LENTIL STEW WITH KUMARA CARROT MASH

prep + cook time 2 hours **serves** 4

1 cup (200g) brown lentils

1 tablespoon vegetable oil

1.5kg (3 pounds) lamb neck chops

2 medium brown onions (300g), chopped coarsely

2 cloves garlic, crushed

4 rindless bacon slices (260g), chopped coarsely

1 teaspoon caraway seeds

2 teaspoons ground cumin

½ cup (125ml) dry red wine

⅓ cup (90g) tomato paste

2 cups (500ml) beef stock

425g (13½ ounces) canned diced tomatoes

½ cup coarsely chopped fresh coriander (cilantro)

KUMARA CARROT MASH

2 medium kumara (orange sweet potato) (800g), chopped coarsely

2 medium carrots (240g), chopped coarsely

1 teaspoon ground cumin

⅓ cup (80ml) buttermilk

1 Cook lentils in a large saucepan of boiling water, uncovered, for 15 minutes or until tender; drain.

2 Preheat oven to 180°C/350°F.

3 Meanwhile, heat oil in a large flameproof baking dish; cook lamb, in batches, until browned.

4 Cook onion, garlic and bacon in same pan, stirring, until onion is just browned and bacon is crisp. Add spices; cook, stirring, until fragrant. Add wine, paste, stock and tomatoes; bring to the boil. Return lamb to dish, stir in lentils; roast, covered, in oven for 1 hour 10 minutes.

5 Meanwhile, make kumara carrot mash.

6 Stir coriander into stew just before serving with mash.

KUMARA CARROT MASH Boil, steam or microwave kumara and carrot, separately, until tender; drain. Dry-fry cumin in a small frying pan until fragrant. Mash vegetables in a large bowl with cumin and buttermilk until smooth.

nutritional count per serving
47.9g total fat
19.6g saturated fat
3896kJ (932 cal)
44.2g carbohydrate
76.1g protein
9.9g fibre

to freeze Complete the recipe to the end of step 4. Pack into freezer-proof containers, leaving a 2.5cm (1 inch) space to allow for expansion. Seal, label and freeze for up to 3 months. Thaw overnight in the fridge. Reheat in a saucepan or microwave on medium power (50%) until heated through, then continue from step 5.

CHICKEN AND MERGUEZ CASSOULET

prep + cook time 3 hours (+ standing) serves 6

1½ cups (290g) lima beans

1 tablespoon vegetable oil

8 chicken thigh cutlets (1.3kg), halved

6 merguez sausages (480g)

1 large brown onion (200g), chopped coarsely

2 medium carrots (240g), cut into 1cm (½-inch) pieces

2 cloves garlic, chopped finely

4 sprigs fresh thyme

2 tablespoons tomato paste

1 teaspoon finely grated lemon rind

425g (13½ ounces) canned diced tomatoes

1 cup (250ml) chicken stock

1 cup (250ml) water

2 cups (140g) fresh breadcrumbs

1 Place beans in a medium bowl, cover with cold water; stand overnight. Drain. Rinse under cold water; drain. Cook beans in a large saucepan of boiling water, uncovered, 10 minutes; drain.

2 Heat oil in a large flameproof baking dish; cook chicken, in batches, until browned all over. Remove from pan.

3 Cook sausages, in batches, in same dish until browned all over. Drain on absorbent paper; halve sausages. Reserve 1 tablespoon of fat from dish; discard remainder.

4 Preheat oven to 160°C/325°F.

5 Heat reserved fat in same dish; cook onion, carrot, garlic and thyme, stirring, until onion softens. Add paste; cook, stirring, 2 minutes. Return chicken to dish with drained beans, rind, tomatoes, stock and the water; bring to the boil. Cover; cook in oven 40 minutes. Uncover; cook 1¼ hours or until liquid is almost absorbed and beans are tender.

6 Preheat grill (broiler).

7 Sprinkle cassoulet with breadcrumbs; place under hot grill until breadcrumbs are browned lightly.

nutritional count per serving
42.1g total fat
14.2g saturated fat
3469kJ (830 cal)
46.1g carbohydrate
60.6g protein
12.7g fibre

serving suggestion
Serve with couscous.

tip Ask the butcher to cut the chicken thigh cutlets in half for you.

to freeze Pack into freezer-proof containers, leaving a 2.5cm (1 inch) space to allow for expansion. Seal, label and freeze for up to 3 months. Thaw overnight in the fridge. Reheat, covered, in a 160°C/325°F oven for 30 minutes or microwave on medium power (50%) until heated through.

SLOW-ROASTED BEEF SHANKS

prep + cook time 2 hours 45 minutes **serves** 6

1 large beef shank (2.5kg), quartered crossways

2 tablespoons plain (all-purpose) flour

2 tablespoons olive oil

800g (1½ pounds) canned crushed tomatoes

½ cup (125ml) dry white wine

½ cup (125ml) beef stock

¼ cup (70g) tomato paste

¼ cup finely chopped fresh flat-leaf parsley

2 tablespoons finely chopped fresh lemon thyme

1 Preheat oven to 180°C/350°F.

2 Toss shank pieces in flour to coat; shake off excess. Heat oil in a large frying pan; cook shank pieces, in batches, until browned and almost crunchy all over.

3 Place tomatoes, wine, stock and paste in a deep 5-litre (20-cup) baking dish; stir to combine. Place shank pieces, one at a time, standing upright, in dish; roast, covered, for 2 hours or until tender.

4 Remove shanks from dish. When cool enough to handle, remove meat from bones. Discard bones; chop meat coarsely. Return meat to dish with tomato sauce; reheat if necessary. Season to taste.

5 Just before serving, stir in herbs.

nutritional count per serving
18.8g total fat
6.1g saturated fat
1701kJ (407 cal)
8.5g carbohydrate
46.4g protein
2.4g fibre

serving suggestion
Serve with cheesy mash (see page 174).

tip Ask the butcher to quarter the beef shank crossways so that the pieces will fit into the baking dish.

to freeze Complete the recipe up to the end of step 4. Pack into freezer-proof containers, leaving a 2.5cm (1 inch) space to allow for expansion. Seal, label and freeze for up to 3 months. Thaw overnight in the fridge. Reheat in a saucepan or microwave on medium power (50%) until heated through.

PASTITSIO

prep + cook time 2 hours 15 minutes **serves** 6

250g (8 ounces) macaroni pasta

2 eggs, beaten lightly

¾ cup (60g) coarsely grated kefalotyri cheese

2 tablespoons fresh breadcrumbs

MEAT SAUCE

2 tablespoons olive oil

2 medium brown onions (300g), chopped finely

750g (1½ pounds) minced (ground) lamb

410g (13 ounces) canned crushed tomatoes

⅓ cup (90g) tomato paste

½ cup (125ml) beef stock

¼ cup (60ml) dry white wine

½ teaspoon ground cinnamon

1 egg, beaten lightly

CHEESE SAUCE

90g (3 ounces) butter

½ cup (75g) plain (all-purpose) flour

3½ cups (875ml) milk

1 cup (80g) coarsely grated kefalotyri cheese

2 egg yolks

1 Preheat oven to 180°C/350°F. Oil a shallow 2.5-litre (10-cup) ovenproof dish.

2 Make meat sauce and cheese sauce.

3 Cook pasta in a large saucepan of boiling water until tender; drain. Combine hot pasta, egg and cheese in a large bowl. Spoon pasta into dish, gently pressing down to flatten the layer.

4 Top pasta evenly with meat sauce; pour cheese sauce on top, smooth the surface. Sprinkle with breadcrumbs.

5 Bake pastitsio 1 hour or until browned lightly. Stand 10 minutes before serving.

MEAT SAUCE Heat oil in a large saucepan; cook onion and lamb, stirring, until lamb is browned. Stir in tomato, paste, stock, wine and cinnamon; simmer, uncovered, 20 minutes or until mixture is thick. Cool; stir in egg.

CHEESE SAUCE Melt butter in a medium saucepan, add flour; cook, stirring, until mixture bubbles and thickens. Remove from heat; gradually stir in milk. Stir over heat until sauce boils and thickens; stir in cheese. Cool 5 minutes; stir in egg yolks.

nutritional count per serving
45.8g total fat
23.2g saturated fat
3440kJ (823 cal)
51.6g carbohydrate
48.4g protein
4g fibre

tip Kefalotyri cheese is a hard, salty cheese made from sheep and/or goat's milk. Its colour varies from white to yellow depending on the mixture of milk used in the process and its age. It is a great cheese for grating over pasta or salads, it can replace parmesan.

to freeze Seal, label and freeze for up to 3 months. Thaw overnight in the fridge. Reheat, covered, in a 180°C/350°F oven for 30 minutes or until heated through; remove cover, bake a further 10 minutes or until breadcrumbs are browned.

ASIAN-STYLE BRAISED PORK NECK

prep + cook time 2 hours 40 minutes **serve** 4

1 tablespoon peanut oil

1kg (2-pound) piece pork neck

2 cinnamon sticks

2 whole star anise

½ cup (125ml) soy sauce

½ cup (125ml) chinese rice wine

¼ cup (55g) firmly packed light brown sugar

5cm (2-inch) piece fresh ginger (25g), sliced thinly

4 cloves garlic, quartered

1 medium brown onion (150g), chopped coarsely

1 cup (250ml) water

1 Preheat oven to 160°C/325°F.

2 Heat oil in a medium deep flameproof baking dish; cook pork, uncovered, until browned all over. Remove from heat.

3 Add combined spices, sauce, wine, sugar, ginger, garlic, onion and the water to dish; turn pork to coat in mixture. Roast, uncovered, 2 hours or until pork is tender, turning every 20 minutes.

4 Remove pork; cover to keep warm. Strain braising liquid through muslin-lined strainer over a medium saucepan; bring to the boil. Reduce heat; simmer 5 minutes or until sauce thickens slightly.

5 Serve pork drizzled with sauce.

nutritional count per serving
29.6g total fat
8.4g saturated fat
2592kJ (620 cal)
22.1g carbohydrate
62.1g protein
10.4g fibre

serving suggestion
Serve with steamed gai lan in oyster sauce (see page 466).

to freeze Pack into freezer-proof containers, leaving a 2.5cm (1 inch) space to allow for expansion. Seal, label and freeze for up to 3 months. Thaw overnight in the fridge. Reheat in microwave on medium power (50%) until heated through.

SOUR PORK CURRY

prep + cook time 2 hours 45 minutes **serves** 4

1 tablespoon vegetable oil

1kg (2 pounds) pork neck

1 teaspoon shrimp paste

¼ cup coarsely chopped fresh coriander (cilantro) root and stem mixture

2cm (¾-inch) piece fresh galangal (10g), chopped finely

5 dried long red chillies, chopped finely

3 fresh long red chillies, chopped finely

2 tablespoons fish sauce

¾ cup (235g) tamarind concentrate

2 tablespoons caster (superfine) sugar

2 cups (500ml) chicken stock

1 litre (4 cups) water

½ cup fresh thai basil leaves, chopped coarsely

1 Heat oil in a large flameproof baking dish; cook pork, uncovered, until browned. Remove from dish.

2 Preheat oven to 160°C/325°F.

3 Add paste, coriander root and stem mixture, galangal and chillies to dish; cook, stirring, until fragrant. Add sauce, tamarind, sugar, stock and the water; bring to the boil. Return pork to dish, cover; roast 1 hour. Uncover; roast another 1 hour.

4 Remove pork from dish, cover; stand 10 minutes before slicing thickly. Stir basil into sauce; serve pork slices with sauce.

nutritional count per serving
9.3g total fat
2.1g saturated fat
1680kJ (402 cal)
18.3g carbohydrate
59.7g protein
1.5g fibre

tip Thai basil, also known as horapa, is available from greengrocers and Asian supermarkets.

to freeze Pack into freezer-proof containers, leaving a 2.5cm (1 inch) space to allow for expansion. Seal, label and freeze for up to 3 months. Thaw overnight in the fridge. Reheat in a saucepan or microwave on medium power (50%) until heated through.

PORK, CHICKEN AND BLACK-EYED BEAN CASSOULET

prep + cook time 3 hours (+ standing) **serves** 4

1 cup (200g) black-eyed beans

1 tablespoon olive oil

500g (1 pound) boned pork belly, rind removed, sliced thinly

8 chicken drumettes (640g)

4 thin pork sausages (320g)

1 medium brown onion (150g), chopped coarsely

1 stick celery (150g), trimmed, sliced thinly

1 small leek (200g), sliced thinly

1 teaspoon fresh thyme leaves

½ cup (125ml) dry white wine

400g (12½ ounces) canned diced tomatoes

2 cups (500ml) chicken stock

3 cups (210g) stale breadcrumbs

½ cup finely chopped fresh flat-leaf parsley

50g (1½ ounces) butter, melted

1 Place beans in a medium bowl, cover with cold water; stand 3 hours or overnight. Drain. Rinse under cold water; drain.

2 Preheat oven to 180°C/350°F.

3 Heat oil in a large flameproof baking dish; cook pork, chicken and sausages, in batches, until browned all over.

4 Cook onion, celery, leek and thyme in same dish, stirring, until onion softens. Add wine; cook, stirring, 5 minutes. Return pork, chicken and sausages to dish with tomatoes, stock and beans; bake, covered 40 minutes.

5 Uncover; sprinkle with combined breadcrumbs, parsley and butter. Bake, uncovered, 40 minutes or until meat is tender and top is lightly browned.

nutritional count per serving
65.2g total fat
25.3g saturated fat
4314kJ (1032 cal)
51.3g carbohydrate
57g protein
9.9g fibre

to freeze Pack into freezer-proof containers, leaving a 2.5cm (1 inch) space to allow for expansion. Seal, label and freeze for up to 3 months. Thaw overnight in the fridge. Reheat in a 180°C/350°F oven for 30 minutes or microwave on medium power (50%) until heated through.

DUCK LEGS WITH PANCETTA AND WHITE BEANS

prep + cook time 3 hours 40 minutes **serves** 6

⅓ cup (80ml) light olive oil

200g (6½ ounces) thinly sliced pancetta, chopped coarsely

1 large brown onion (200g), chopped finely

2 medium carrots (240g), chopped finely

1 stick celery (150g), trimmed, chopped finely

6 sprigs fresh thyme

6 duck marylands (1.8kg)

1 cup (250ml) dry red wine

1 cup (250ml) chicken stock

800g (1½ pounds) canned white beans, drained, rinsed

1 cup (70g) stale breadcrumbs

1 Preheat oven to 110°C/220°F.

2 Heat half the oil in a large frying pan; cook pancetta, stirring, until crisp. Transfer to a large baking dish.

3 Heat remaining oil in same pan; cook onion, carrot, celery and thyme, stirring, until soft. Transfer to dish; top with duck.

4 Bring wine and stock to the boil in a small saucepan; pour over duck. Cover dish with foil; roast, in oven, 2 hours. Remove from oven.

5 Increase oven to 125°C/250°F.

6 Remove foil from dish; stir beans into dish, sprinkle breadcrumbs on duck. Roast, uncovered, 1 hour or until duck is tender.

nutritional count per serving
80.5g total fat
23g saturated fat
3938kJ (942 cal)
14.6g carbohydrate
33.7g protein
3.9g fibre

serving suggestion
Serve with wilted spinach.

tip Duck marylands have the leg and thigh still connected in a single piece; the bones and skin remain intact.

to freeze Complete recipe to the end of step 4. Pack into a freezer-proof container, leaving a 2.5cm (1 inch) space to allow for expansion. Seal, label and freeze for up to 3 months. Thaw overnight in the fridge, then continue from step 5.

WALNUT AND FIG CAKE WITH BRANDY SYRUP

prep + cook time 1 hour 45 minutes **serves** 10

125g (4 ounces) butter

1 teaspoon finely grated lemon rind

¾ cup (165g) caster (superfine) sugar

2 eggs

1¾ cups (260g) self-raising flour

¾ cup (180ml) buttermilk

¾ cup (75g) coarsely chopped roasted walnuts

2 medium fresh figs (120g)

½ cup (60g) roasted walnut halves

BRANDY SYRUP

1 cup (220g) caster (superfine) sugar

⅓ cup (80ml) water

2 tablespoons lemon juice

1 tablespoon brandy

1 Preheat oven to 180°C/350°F. Grease a 14cm x 22.5cm (5½-inch x 10¼-inch) loaf pan; line base and two long sides with baking paper, extending the paper 5cm (2-inches) over long sides.

2 Beat butter, rind and sugar in a small bowl with an electric mixer until light and fluffy. Beat in eggs, one at a time. Transfer mixture to a large bowl; stir in sifted flour and buttermilk, then chopped walnuts. Spread mixture into pan; top with thickly sliced figs and walnut halves.

3 Bake cake 1¼ hours. Stand cake in pan 5 minutes before turning, top-side up, onto a wire rack over a tray; remove baking paper.

4 Meanwhile, make brandy syrup.

5 Pour hot syrup over hot cake. Place cake on a plate; pour excess syrup from tray into a jug.

6 Serve cake drizzled with remaining syrup.

BRANDY SYRUP Stir ingredients in a small saucepan, over heat, without boiling, until sugar dissolves. Bring to the boil; boil, uncovered, without stirring, 3 minutes.

nutritional count per serving
16.1g total fat
7.6g saturated fat
1686kJ (403 cal)
58.7g carbohydrate
5.9g protein
1.4g fibre

to freeze Wrap cake in two layers of plastic wrap. Seal, label and freeze for up to 1 month. Thaw overnight at room temperature. This cake will also keep in an airtight container at room temperature for 3 days or in the refrigerator for 1 week.

ALMOND CARROT CAKE

prep + cook time 1 hour 35 minutes **serves** 9

5 eggs, separated

1 teaspoon finely grated lemon rind

1¼ cups (275g) caster (superfine) sugar

2 cups (480g) coarsely grated carrot

2 cups (240g) ground almonds

½ cup (75g) self-raising flour

2 tablespoons roasted slivered almonds

CREAM CHEESE FROSTING

90g (3 ounces) packaged cream cheese, softened

90g (3 ounces) butter, softened

½ cup (80g) icing (confectioners') sugar

1 teaspoon lemon juice

1 Preheat oven to 180°C/350°F. Grease a deep 20cm (8-inch) square cake pan; line base with baking paper.

2 Beat egg yolks, rind and sugar in a small bowl with an electric mixer until thick and creamy. Transfer mixture to a large bowl; stir in carrot, ground almonds and sifted flour.

3 Beat egg whites in a small bowl with an electric mixer until soft peaks form; fold into carrot mixture, in two batches. Pour mixture into pan.

4 Bake cake 1¼ hours. Stand cake in pan 5 minutes; turn, top-side up, onto a wire rack to cool.

5 Meanwhile, make cream cheese frosting.

6 Spread cold cake with cream cheese frosting; top with slivered almonds.

CREAM CHEESE FROSTING Beat cream cheese and butter in a small bowl with an electric mixer until light and fluffy; gradually beat in icing sugar and juice.

nutritional count per serving
31.3g total fat
9.5g saturated fat
2199kJ (526 cal)
49.9g carbohydrate
11.9g protein
4.5g fibre

tip You will need about 4 medium carrots (480g) for the amount of grated carrot required in this recipe.

to freeze Complete the recipe to the end of step 4. Wrap cake in two layers of plastic wrap. Seal, label and freeze for up to 2 months. Thaw overnight at room temperature, then continue recipe from step 5.

ACCOMPANIMENTS

rice, couscous, grains & pulses

CLASSIC PULAO

prep + cook time 30 minutes (+ standing) **serves** 4

Soak 1⅓ cups basmati rice in a medium bowl of cold water for 20 minutes; drain. Melt 50g (1½ ounces) butter in a large saucepan; stir in 1 finely chopped brown onion and 2 crushed garlic cloves until onion softens. Stir in 1 cinnamon stick and 1 dried bay leaf; cook 2 minutes. Add rice; cook, stirring, 2 minutes. Add 2½ cups hot chicken stock and ⅓ cup sultanas; simmer, covered, 10 minutes or until rice is tender and liquid is absorbed. Sprinkle with ½ cup roasted unsalted cashews. Season to taste. Remove cinnamon before serving.

nutritional count per serving 20.6g total fat (8.8g saturated fat); 2128kJ (509 cal); 68.7g carbohydrate; 10.5g protein; 3g fibre

SPICED LENTILS

prep + cook time 20 minutes **serves** 4

Cook 1½ cups red lentils in a large saucepan of boiling water until tender; drain. Melt 25g (¾ ounce) butter in a large frying pan; cook 1 finely chopped small brown onion, 1 crushed garlic clove, ½ teaspoon ground cumin, ½ teaspoon ground coriander, ¼ teaspoon ground turmeric and ¼ teaspoon cayenne pepper, stirring, until onion softens. Add lentils, ½ cup chicken stock and 25g (¾ ounce) butter; cook, stirring, until hot. Remove from heat, stir in 2 tablespoons coarsely chopped fresh flat-leaf parsley. Season to taste.

nutritional count per serving 11.9g total fat (7g saturated fat); 1354kJ (324 cal); 29.9g carbohydrate; 18.9g protein; 10.8g fibre

SOFT POLENTA

prep + cook time 20 minutes serves 6

Boil 3 cups water and 2 cups vegetable stock in a
large saucepan. Gradually add 2 cups polenta, stirring
constantly. Reduce heat; simmer, stirring, 10 minutes
or until polenta thickens. Add 1 cup milk and ¼ cup
finely grated parmesan cheese; stir until cheese melts.
Season to taste.

nutritional count per serving 4.2g total fat (2.1g saturated fat);
1016kJ (243 cal); 41.7g carbohydrate; 8.2g protein; 1.6g fibre

TABBOULEH

prep time 30 minutes (+ refrigeration) serves 4

Place ¼ cup burghul in a shallow medium bowl. Halve
3 medium tomatoes; scoop pulp from tomato over
burghul. Chop tomato flesh finely; spread over burghul.
Cover; refrigerate 1 hour. Combine burghul mixture in
a large bowl with 3 cups coarsely chopped fresh flat-
leaf parsley, 3 finely chopped green onions (scallions),
½ cup coarsely chopped fresh mint, 1 crushed garlic
clove, ¼ cup lemon juice and ¼ cup olive oil. Season
to taste.

nutritional count per serving 14.2g total fat (2g saturated fat);
790kJ (189 cal); 9.4g carbohydrate; 3.6g protein; 5.9g fibre

WILD RICE SALAD WITH SPINACH AND FIGS

prep + cook time 15 minutes **serves** 8

Cook 2 cups wild rice blend in a large saucepan of boiling water until tender; drain. Rinse under cold water; drain. Place in a large bowl. Meanwhile, place 2 teaspoons finely grated orange rind, ½ cup orange juice, 2 tablespoons olive oil and 1 tablespoon white balsamic vinegar in a screw-top jar; shake well. Combine dressing, rice, ¾ cup coarsely chopped roasted pecans, ½ cup thinly sliced dried figs, 100g (3 ounces) baby spinach leaves and 2 thinly sliced green onions (scallions) in a large bowl. Season to taste.

nutritional count per serving 13g total fat (1.2g saturated fat); 1359kJ (325 cal); 44.8g carbohydrate; 5.1g protein; 3.6g fibre

PRESERVED LEMON COUSCOUS

prep time 15 minutes **serves** 4

Combine 1 cup couscous with 1 cup boiling water in a medium heatproof bowl, cover; stand 5 minutes or until water is absorbed, fluffing with fork occasionally. Stir in 1 teaspoon ground cumin, 2 tablespoons finely chopped preserved lemon rind, ½ cup raisins, 1 cup coarsely chopped fresh mint and ¼ cup lemon juice. Season to taste.

nutritional count per serving 0.7g total fat (0.1g saturated fat); 1066kJ (255 cal); 52.8g carbohydrate; 7.4g protein; 2.5g fibre

SPANISH RICE AND PEAS

prep + cook time 30 minutes **serves** 6

Combine 1½ cups water, 1½ cups chicken stock and ¼ cup olive oil in a medium saucepan; bring to the boil. Stir in 2 cups white medium-grain rice; cook, uncovered, without stirring, 10 minutes or until liquid has almost evaporated. Reduce heat; simmer, covered, 5 minutes. Meanwhile, trim and chop 4 green onions (scallions). Gently stir in onion and 1 cup frozen peas; simmer, covered, 5 minutes or until rice and peas are tender. Season to taste.

nutritional count per serving 9.8g total fat (1.6g saturated fat); 1437kJ (343 cal); 56.1g carbohydrate; 6.1g protein; 2.5g fibre

OLIVE AND PARSLEY COUSCOUS

prep + cook time 15 minutes **serves** 6

Bring 1½ cups vegetable stock to the boil in a medium saucepan. Remove from heat; stir in 1½ cups couscous and 30g (1 ounce) butter. Cover; stand 5 minutes or until liquid is absorbed, fluffing with fork occasionally. Stir in 1 cup pitted kalamata olives and ½ cup coarsely chopped fresh flat-leaf parsley. Season to taste.

nutritional count per serving 4.9g total fat (2.9g saturated fat); 1074kJ (257 cal); 45.5g carbohydrate; 6.8g protein; 1g fibre

SPECIAL OCCASION

FOR THE SLOW COOKER

Slow cookers are great for making no-fuss dishes when entertaining throughout the cooler months. Whether it is Portuguese-style chicken, a creamy mushroom risotto or a rich chocolate cake, the slow cooker can do it all.

MASSAMAN BEEF CURRY

prep + cook time 8 hours 45 minutes **serves** 6

2 tablespoons peanut oil

2 large brown onions (400g), cut into thin wedges

1kg (2 pounds) gravy beef, chopped coarsely

⅔ cup (200g) massaman curry paste

1 cup (250ml) coconut milk

1 cup (250ml) chicken stock

2 cinnamon sticks

2 dried bay leaves

3 medium potatoes (600g), chopped coarsely

½ cup (70g) roasted unsalted peanuts

2 tablespoons light brown sugar

1 tablespoon fish sauce

⅓ cup lightly packed fresh coriander (cilantro) leaves

1 lime, cut into wedges

1 Heat half the oil in a large frying pan; cook onion, stirring, 10 minutes or until browned lightly. Transfer to a 4.5-litre (18-cup) slow cooker.

2 Heat remaining oil in same pan; cook beef, in batches, until browned. Add paste; cook, stirring, 1 minute or until fragrant. Transfer to cooker.

3 Add coconut milk, stock, cinnamon, bay leaves, potato and nuts to cooker. Cook, covered, on low, 8 hours.

4 Discard cinnamon sticks. Stir in sugar and sauce. Serve topped with coriander leaves; accompany with lime wedges.

nutritional count per serving
48.3g total fat
16.6g saturated fat
3051kJ (730 cal)
25.9g carbohydrate
45.6g protein
7.5g fibre

tip You could use chuck steak in this recipe.

not suitable to freeze

braised asian-style beef ribs

BRAISED ASIAN-STYLE BEEF RIBS

prep + cook time 8 hours 30 minutes serves 6

2kg (4 pounds) racks beef short ribs

½ cup (190g) hoisin sauce

¼ cup (60ml) salt-reduced soy sauce

¼ cup (60ml) mirin

2 x 3cm (1¼-inch) strips orange rind

½ cup (90g) honey

5cm (2-inch) piece fresh ginger (25g), grated

3 cloves garlic, crushed

1 fresh long red chilli, sliced thinly

2 teaspoons sesame oil

1   Cut rib racks into pieces to fit into a 4.5-litre (18-cup) slow cooker; place ribs in cooker. Combine remaining ingredients in a large jug; pour sauce over ribs. Cook, covered, on low, 8 hours. Season to taste.

2   Cut ribs into serving-sized pieces; serve with sauce.

nutritional count per serving
15g total fat
5.7g saturated fat
1622kJ (388 cal)
25g carbohydrate
35.1g protein
3.8g fibre

tip Ask the butcher to cut the ribs for you so they will fit into your slow cooker.

not suitable to freeze

VEAL WITH BALSAMIC SAGE SAUCE

prep + cook time 6 hours 30 minutes serves 6

6 pieces veal osso buco (1.2kg)

2 tablespoons plain (all-purpose) flour

1 tablespoon olive oil

20g (¾ ounce) butter

2 cloves garlic, sliced thinly

2 tablespoons coarsely chopped fresh sage

½ cup (125ml) balsamic vinegar

1 cup (250ml) chicken stock

1   Trim excess fat from veal; toss in flour to coat, shake off excess. Heat oil and butter in a large frying pan; cook veal, in batches, until browned. Transfer to a 4.5-litre (18-cup) slow cooker.

2   Add garlic and sage to same pan; cook, stirring, until fragrant. Add vinegar; boil, uncovered, 2 minutes or until reduced by half. Stir in stock. Transfer to cooker.

3   Cook, covered, on low, 6 hours. Season to taste. Serve topped with some extra sage leaves.

(photograph page 324)

nutritional count per serving
9.8g total fat
3.7g saturated fat
945kJ (226 cal)
3.4g carbohydrate
30.1g protein
0.3g fibre

serving suggestion
Serve with mashed potato or soft polenta, and steamed green beans.

tips You could use veal forequarter chops in this recipe. Use regular balsamic vinegar, not an aged vinegar or glaze.

to freeze Pack into freezer-proof containers, leaving a 2.5cm (1 inch) space to allow for expansion. Seal, label and freeze for up to 3 months. Thaw overnight in the fridge. Reheat in a saucepan or microwave on medium power (50%) until heated through.

veal with balsamic sage sauce (recipe page 323)

red pork curry (recipe page 326)

RED PORK CURRY

prep + cook time 4 hours 30 minutes serves 4

1⅔ cups (410ml) coconut cream

1 cup (250ml) salt-reduced chicken stock

¼ cup (75g) red curry paste

2 tablespoons fish sauce

3 fresh kaffir lime leaves, shredded finely

1.5kg (3 pounds) rindless boneless pork belly,
chopped coarsely

2 large kumara (orange sweet potatoes) (1kg),
chopped coarsely

500g (1 pound) snake beans, chopped coarsely

1 cup loosely packed fresh thai basil leaves

2 fresh long red chillies, sliced thinly

1 fresh kaffir lime leaf, shredded finely, extra

1   Combine coconut cream, stock, paste, sauce and
lime leaves in a 4.5-litre (18-cup) slow cooker; add
pork and kumara. Cook, covered, on high, 4 hours.

2   Skim fat from surface. Stir in beans; cook, covered,
on high, 30 minutes. Season to taste.

3   Serve topped with basil, chilli and extra shredded
lime leaf.

(photograph page 325)

nutritional count per serving
21.9g total fat
12.1g saturated fat
1831kJ (438 cal)
18.9g carbohydrate
39.2g protein
5.1g fibre

serving suggestion
Serve with steamed rice.

tip Ask the butcher to chop
the pork belly for you.

to freeze Complete the
recipe to end of step 2.
Pack into freezer-proof
containers, leaving a 2.5cm
(1 inch) space to allow for
expansion. Seal, label and
freeze for up to 3 months.
Thaw overnight in the fridge.
Reheat in a saucepan or
microwave on medium
power (50%) until heated
through.

PORK AND GREEN OLIVE STEW

prep + cook time 8 hours 30 minutes serves 8

2 tablespoons olive oil

1.5kg (3 pounds) pork neck, chopped coarsely

1¼ cups (310ml) salt-reduced chicken stock

¾ cup (180ml) dry white wine

1 large brown onion (200g), chopped finely

4 cloves garlic, crushed

1 tablespoon coarsely chopped fresh rosemary

1.5kg (3 pounds) kipfler (fingerling) potatoes,
unpeeled, halved

½ cup (60g) seeded green olives

1   Heat oil in a large frying pan; cook pork, in batches,
until browned. Transfer to a 4.5-litre (18-cup)
slow cooker.

2   Add stock, wine, onion, garlic and rosemary to
cooker; stir to combine. Top with potato. Cook,
covered, on low, 8 hours. Skim fat from surface;
stir in olives. Season to taste.

nutritional count per serving   **not suitable to freeze**
10.9g total fat
3g saturated fat
1731kJ (414 cal)
28.5g carbohydrate
43.5g protein
4.4g fibre

serving suggestion
Serve with crusty bread.

PORK NECK WITH CIDER AND PEAR

prep + cook time 6 hours 30 minutes **serves** 4

1kg (2-pound) piece pork neck

185g (6 ounces) italian pork sausages

1 egg yolk

½ cup (70g) coarsely chopped pistachios

2 tablespoons coarsely chopped fresh sage

1 tablespoon olive oil

1 medium brown onion (150g), quartered

4 cloves garlic, halved

2 medium pears (460g), unpeeled, quartered

⅔ cup (160ml) alcoholic apple cider

6 fresh sage leaves

1 Place pork on board; slice through thickest part of pork horizontally, without cutting all the way through. Open pork out to form one large piece; trim pork.

2 Squeeze the filling from sausages into a small bowl, mix in egg yolk, nuts and chopped sage; season. Press sausage mixture along one long side of pork; roll pork to enclose filling. Tie pork with kitchen string at 2.5cm (1 inch) intervals.

3 Heat oil in a large frying pan; cook pork until browned all over. Remove from pan. Add onion and garlic to same pan; cook, stirring, until onion softens.

4 Place pears and onion mixture in a 4.5-litre (18-cup) slow cooker; top with pork then add cider and sage leaves. Cook, covered, on low, 6 hours.

5 Serve pork with pear mixture. Top with some extra sage leaves.

nutritional count per serving
45.3g total fat
13g saturated fat
3164kJ (757 cal)
19g carbohydrate
63g protein
5.6g fibre

serving suggestion
Serve with mashed potato and a radicchio salad.

tip Italian sausages are coarse pork sausages generally sold in plump links. They are usually flavoured with garlic and fennel seed or anise seed, and come in two styles – hot (flavoured with thai red chilli) and sweet (without the added heat). They are available from speciality butchers and delicatessens.

not suitable to freeze

PANANG LAMB CURRY

prep + cook time 4 hours 30 minutes **serves** 8

1.5kg (3 pounds) boneless lamb shoulder

1 tablespoon peanut oil

½ cup (150g) panang curry paste

2½ cups (625ml) coconut cream

2 tablespoons fish sauce

¼ cup (65g) grated palm sugar

2 tablespoons peanut butter

4 fresh kaffir lime leaves

225g (7 ounces) canned sliced bamboo shoots, drained, rinsed

1 small red capsicum (bell pepper) (150g), sliced thinly

200g (6½ ounces) green beans, trimmed, halved

½ cup loosely packed fresh coriander (cilantro) leaves

1 Cut lamb into 5cm (2-inch) pieces. Heat oil in a large frying pan; cook lamb, in batches, until browned. Transfer to a 4.5-litre (18-cup) slow cooker.

2 Cook paste in same pan, stirring, 1 minute or until fragrant. Add coconut cream, sauce, sugar, peanut butter and lime leaves; bring to the boil. Transfer to cooker.

3 Cook, covered, on low, 3½ hours. Add bamboo shoots, capsicum and beans to cooker; cook, covered, on low, 30 minutes or until vegetables are tender. Season to taste.

4 Serve curry topped with coriander.

nutritional count per serving
37.1g total fat
20.2g saturated fat
2347kJ (501 cal)
13.47g carbohydrate
42.3g protein
3.7g fibre

tips Panang curry has a distinct peanut flavour; the addition of peanut butter helps to bring out the flavour when using a bought paste. To reduce the fat content of this recipe, use coconut milk or light coconut milk, instead of the the coconut cream.

not suitable to freeze

LAMB STEW WITH ARTICHOKE AND PEAS

prep + cook time 7 hours **serves** 6

1.5kg (3 pounds) lamb shoulder chops

2 tablespoons plain (all-purpose) flour

2 tablespoons olive oil

12 fresh sage leaves

1 large brown onion (200g), chopped coarsely

2 sticks celery (300g), trimmed, chopped coarsely

1 large carrot (180g), chopped coarsely

4 cloves garlic, chopped finely

½ cup (125ml) dry white wine

1½ cups (375ml) chicken stock

1 tablespoon coarsely chopped fresh sage

½ cup (60g) frozen peas

360g (11½ ounces) small fresh globe artichokes, trimmed, halved, centre chokes removed

1 Trim excess fat from lamb. Toss lamb in flour to coat, shake off excess. Reserve excess flour.

2 Heat half the oil in a large frying pan; cook sage leaves until browned lightly and crisp. Drain on absorbent paper.

3 Cook lamb in same pan, in batches, until browned. Transfer to a 4.5-litre (18-cup) slow cooker. Sprinkle reserved excess flour over lamb.

4 Heat remaining oil in same pan; cook onion, celery and carrot, stirring, until softened. Add garlic; cook, stirring, until fragrant. Add wine; bring to the boil. Boil, uncovered, until liquid is almost evaporated. Stir onion mixture, stock and chopped sage into cooker. Cook, covered, on low, 6 hours.

5 Add peas and artichokes to cooker; cook, covered, 30 minutes. Season to taste. Serve topped with crisp sage leaves.

nutritional count per serving
14g total fat
4.5g saturated fat
1271kJ (304 cal)
8.9g carbohydrate
30.1g protein
4g fibre

tip You can also use lamb forequarter or chump chops for this recipe.

to freeze Complete the recipe to the end of step 4. Pack into freezer-proof containers, leaving a 2.5cm (1 inch) space to allow for expansion. Seal, label and freeze for up to 3 months. Thaw overnight in the fridge. Reheat in a saucepan, then continue from step 5.

CHICKEN, PORCINI AND BARLEY SOUP

prep + cook time 6 hours 30 minutes (+ standing) **serves** 4

20g (¾ ounce) dried porcini mushrooms

1 cup (250ml) boiling water

2 chicken marylands (700g)

1 medium brown onion (150g), chopped finely

2 cloves garlic, crushed

1 litre (4 cups) chicken stock

½ cup (100g) pearl barley

1 sprig fresh rosemary

1 sprig fresh thyme

1 medium parsnip (250g), chopped finely

1 small kumara (orange sweet potato) (250g), chopped finely

2 sticks celery (300g), trimmed, chopped finely

250g (8 ounces) swiss brown mushrooms, quartered

½ cup finely chopped fresh flat-leaf parsley

1 Place porcini mushrooms in a small heatproof bowl with the water; stand 15 minutes or until softened. Drain, reserve porcini and the soaking liquid.

2 Meanwhile, discard as much skin as possible from chicken. Place chicken, onion, garlic, stock, barley, rosemary, thyme, parsnip, kumara, celery, swiss brown mushrooms, porcini mushrooms and reserved soaking liquid into a 4.5-litre (18-cup) slow cooker. Cook, covered, on low, 6 hours.

3 Remove chicken from cooker. When cool enough to handle, remove meat from bone; shred coarsely. Discard bones. Return meat to cooker; season to taste. Serve topped with parsley.

nutritional count per serving
9.4g total fat
3g saturated fat
1488kJ (356 cal)
38.9g carbohydrate
29.2g protein
8.4g fibre

to freeze Pack into freezer-proof containers, leaving a 2.5cm (1 inch) space to allow for expansion. Seal, label and freeze for up to 3 months. Thaw overnight in the fridge. Reheat in a saucepan or microwave on medium power (50%) until heated through.

BUTTER CHICKEN

prep + cook time 4 hours 30 minutes (+ refrigeration) **serves** 6

12 chicken thigh cutlets (2.4kg), skin removed

2 tablespoons lemon juice

1 teaspoon chilli powder

¾ cup (210g) Greek-style yoghurt

5cm (2-inch) piece fresh ginger (25g), grated

2 teaspoons garam masala

45g (1½ ounces) butter

1 tablespoon vegetable oil

1 medium brown onion (150g), chopped finely

4 cloves garlic, crushed

1 teaspoon ground coriander

1 teaspoon ground cumin

1 teaspoon sweet paprika

2 tablespoons tomato paste

1⅔ cups (410g) canned tomato puree

⅔ cup (160ml) chicken stock

2 tablespoons honey

1 cinnamon stick

⅓ cup (80ml) pouring cream

⅓ cup (80g) ricotta cheese

½ cup loosely packed fresh coriander (cilantro) leaves

1 Combine chicken, juice and chilli powder in a large bowl. Cover; refrigerate 30 minutes.

2 Stir yoghurt, ginger and half the garam masala into chicken mixture.

3 Heat butter and oil in a large frying pan; cook chicken, in batches, until browned all over. Transfer to 4.5-litre (18-cup) slow cooker.

4 Cook onion and garlic in same pan, stirring, until onion softens. Add ground spices, paprika and remaining garam masala; cook, stirring, until fragrant. Remove from heat; stir in tomato paste, puree, stock, honey and cinnamon stick. Transfer to slow cooker. Cook, covered, on low, 4 hours.

5 Stir in cream; season to taste.

6 Serve topped with ricotta and coriander leaves.

nutritional count per serving
39.3g total fat
17g saturated fat
2750kJ (658 cal)
17.9g carbohydrate
57.8g protein
2.6g fibre

serving suggestion
Serve with steamed basmati rice and warm naan bread.

to freeze Complete the recipe to the end of step 4. Pack into freezer-proof containers, leaving a 2.5cm (1 inch) space to allow for expansion. Seal, label and freeze for up to 3 months. Thaw overnight in the fridge. Reheat in a saucepan or microwave on medium power (50%), then continue from step 5.

Soups, stews and curries are the types of dishes
that get better the next day after the flavours have had a
chance to develop. If you're planning on having a large
number of people over and you don't want to be a slave in the
kitchen on the day, it's worth cooking a large quantity
the day before and keeping it refrigerated.
Bring it to room temperature first then gently warm it
through on the stove, stirring occasionally to avoid
it catching on the bottom of the pan.

PORTUGUESE-STYLE CHICKEN

prep + cook time 6 hours 45 minutes **serves** 4

¼ cup (60ml) olive oil

¼ cup (70g) tomato paste

4 cloves garlic, quartered

2 tablespoons finely grated lemon rind

⅓ cup (80ml) lemon juice

4 fresh small red thai (serrano) chillies, chopped coarsely

1 tablespoon smoked paprika

½ cup firmly packed fresh oregano leaves

1.8kg (3¾-pound) whole chicken

1 medium lemon (140g), quartered

3 sprigs fresh lemon thyme

1 Blend or process 2 tablespoons of the oil, paste, garlic, rind, juice, chilli, paprika and oregano until smooth. Season to taste.

2 Rinse chicken under cold water; pat dry inside and out with absorbent paper. Place lemon quarters and thyme inside cavity of chicken; secure cavity with a fine skewer.

3 Make a pocket under skin of breast, drumsticks and thighs with fingers. Using disposable gloves, rub ¼ cup of the paste under skin. Tuck wing tips under chicken; tie legs together with kitchen string. Rub ¼ cup of paste all over chicken.

4 Heat remaining oil in a large frying pan; cook chicken until browned all over. Transfer to a 4.5-litre (18-cup) slow cooker. Cook, covered, on low, 6 hours.

5 Serve chicken cut into pieces with remaining paste.

nutritional count per serving
50g total fat
13.2g saturated fat
2688kJ (643 cal)
2.9g carbohydrate
45.8g protein
1.5g fibre

serving suggestion
Serve with potato chips or wedges, a green salad and lemon wedges.

tip Fresh chillies can burn your fingers, so wear disposable gloves when handling them.

not suitable to freeze

green olive and lemon chicken

GREEN OLIVE AND LEMON CHICKEN

prep + cook time 6 hours 20 minutes **serves** 4

15g (½ ounce) butter, softened

1 tablespoon olive oil

2 teaspoons finely grated lemon rind

3 cloves garlic, crushed

¼ cup (30g) pitted green olives, chopped finely

2 tablespoons finely chopped fresh
  flat-leaf parsley

1.5kg (3¼-pound) whole chicken

2 medium lemons (280g), quartered

1 Combine butter, oil, rind, garlic, olives and parsley in a medium bowl; season.

2 Rinse chicken under cold water; pat dry, inside and out, with absorbent paper. Use fingers to make a pocket between the breasts and skin; push half the butter mixture under skin. Rub remaining butter mixture all over chicken. Tuck wing tips under chicken; fill cavity with lemon, tie legs together with kitchen string. Trim skin around neck; secure neck flap to underside of chicken with small fine skewers.

3 Place chicken in a 4.5-litre (18-cup) slow cooker. Cook, covered, on low, 6 hours.

4 Cut chicken into quarters to serve.

nutritional count per serving
38.1g total fat
12.1g saturated fat
2086kJ (499 cal)
2g carbohydrate
37.7g protein
0.6g fibre

serving suggestion
Serve with roast potatoes
(see page 172) and steamed
vegetables.

tip Kitchen string is made
of a natural product such
as cotton or hemp so that it
neither affects the flavour
of the food it's tied around
nor melts when heated.

not suitable to freeze

SEAFOOD IN ROMESCO SAUCE

prep + cook time 4 hours 45 minutes **serves** 6

1kg (2 pounds) cleaned whole baby octopus

800g (1½ pounds) canned crushed tomatoes

4 cloves garlic, crushed

1 teaspoon dried chilli flakes

2 teaspoons smoked paprika

2 medium red capsicums (bell peppers) (400g),
  sliced thinly

2 tablespoons red wine vinegar

500g (1 pound) uncooked medium
  king prawns (shrimp)

500g (1 pound) cleaned mussels

½ cup (60g) ground almonds

½ cup coarsely chopped fresh flat-leaf parsley

⅓ cup coarsely chopped fresh oregano

1 Combine octopus, tomatoes, garlic, chilli flakes, paprika, capsicum and vinegar in a 4.5-litre (18-cup) slow cooker. Cook, covered, on low, 4 hours.

2 Shell and devein prawns, leaving tails intact. Add prawns, mussels and ground almonds to cooker; cook, covered, stirring occasionally, on high, 20 minutes or until prawns change colour and mussels open.

3 Serve topped with herbs.

(photograph page 344)

nutritional count per serving   **not suitable to freeze**
9.5g total fat
1.2g saturated fat
1509kJ (361 cal)
9.5g carbohydrate
57.1g protein
3.7g fibre

serving suggestion
Serve with steamed rice or
crusty bread.

seafood in romesco sauce (recipe on page 343)

greek-style lamb with potatoes (recipe page 346)

GREEK-STYLE LAMB WITH POTATOES

prep + cook time 8 hours 40 minutes serves 4

2 tablespoons olive oil

1kg (2 pounds) baby new potatoes

2kg (4-pound) lamb leg

2 sprigs fresh rosemary, chopped coarsely

2 tablespoons finely chopped fresh
   flat-leaf parsley

2 tablespoons finely chopped fresh oregano

3 cloves garlic, crushed

1 tablespoon finely grated lemon rind

2 tablespoons lemon juice

½ cup (125ml) beef stock

1   Heat half the oil in a large frying pan; cook potatoes until browned. Transfer to a 4.5-litre (18-cup) slow cooker.

2   Make small cuts in lamb at 2.5cm (1-inch) intervals; press rosemary into cuts. Combine parsley, oregano, garlic, rind, juice and remaining oil in a small bowl; rub mixture all over lamb, season.

3   Cook lamb in same heated pan until browned all over. Place lamb in cooker on top of potatoes; add stock. Cook, covered, on low, 8 hours.

4   Remove lamb and potatoes; cover lamb, stand 10 minutes before slicing.

5   Serve lamb with potatoes and sauce.

(photograph page 345)

nutritional count per serving
29.5g total fat
10.2g saturated fat
3206kJ (767 cal)
33.5g carbohydrate
88.4g protein
5.6g fibre

serving suggestion
Serve with a greek salad or steamed spinach.

not suitable to freeze
Lamb can be refrigerated, covered, overnight at the end of step 2.

CHICKEN WITH LEEKS AND ARTICHOKES

prep + cook time 6 hours 30 minutes serves 4

1.6kg (3¼-pound) whole chicken

1 medium lemon (140g), chopped coarsely

4 cloves unpeeled garlic

4 sprigs fresh tarragon

6 sprigs fresh flat-leaf parsley

45g (1½ ounces) butter

¾ cup (180ml) dry white wine

2 medium globe artichokes (400g), quartered

8 baby leeks (640g)

1 cup (250ml) chicken stock

1   Wash chicken under cold water; pat dry inside and out with absorbent paper. Place lemon, garlic and herbs in chicken cavity; season. Tuck wing tips under chicken; tie legs together with kitchen string.

2   Melt butter in a large frying pan; cook chicken until browned all over. Remove chicken. Add wine; bring to the boil.

3   Meanwhile, trim stems from artichokes; remove tough outer leaves. Place artichokes and leeks in a 4.5-litre (18-cup) slow cooker; add wine mixture and stock. Place chicken on vegetables. Cook, covered, on low, 6 hours.

4   Serve chicken with vegetables; drizzle with a little of the juices.

nutritional count per serving
42.2g total fat
16.3g saturated fat
2571kJ (615 cal)
5.6g carbohydrate
44.9g protein
4.2g fibre

serving suggestion
Serve with mashed potatoes and a green leafy salad.

tip Replace the baby leeks with 1 large leek (500g), sliced thickly.

not suitable to freeze

MOROCCAN-STYLE VEGETABLE STEW WITH HARISSA

prep + cook time 6 hours 45 minutes **serves** 4

1 medium red onion (170g), chopped coarsely

4 cloves garlic, quartered

2 teaspoons ground cumin

2 teaspoons ground coriander

2 teaspoons sweet paprika

1 fresh long red chilli, chopped finely

½ cup loosely packed fresh flat-leaf parsley leaves and
   stalks, chopped coarsely

1 cup loosely packed fresh coriander (cilantro) leaves
   and stalks, chopped coarsely

2 cups (500ml) vegetable stock

4 baby eggplant (240g), chopped coarsely

4 small zucchini (360g), chopped coarsely

2 small parsnips (240g), chopped coarsely

2 medium carrots (240g), halved lengthways,
   then halved crossways

¼ medium butternut pumpkin (500g), skin on,
   cut into 8 pieces

2 medium potatoes (400g), quartered

2 tablespoons honey

1 cup (280g) Greek-style yoghurt

2 tablespoons mild harissa sauce

⅓ cup loosely packed fresh coriander (cilantro) leaves,
   extra

1 Blend or process onion, garlic and spices until
   smooth. Combine paste with chilli, herbs and
   stock in a large jug.

2 Combine vegetables and stock mixture in a
   4.5-litre (18-cup) slow cooker. Cook, covered,
   on low, 6 hours. Stir in honey; season to taste.

3 Serve vegetables and sauce topped with yoghurt,
   harissa and extra coriander.

nutritional count per serving
12.2g total fat
5.3g saturated fat
1659kJ (397 cal)
52.1g carbohydrate
13.4g protein
11.9g fibre

serving suggestion
Serve with couscous.

not suitable to freeze

MUSHROOM RISOTTO

prep + cook time 2 hours 45 minutes **serves** 4

30g (1 ounce) butter

1 large brown onion (200g), chopped finely

½ cup (125ml) dry white wine

1 litre (4 cups) vegetable stock

2 cups (500ml) water

10g (½ ounce) dried porcini mushroom slices, torn

2 cups (400g) arborio rice

60g (2 ounces) butter, extra

300g (9½ ounces) button mushrooms, sliced thinly

200g (6½ ounces) swiss brown mushrooms, sliced thinly

2 cloves garlic, crushed

2 teaspoons finely chopped fresh thyme

1 cup (80g) finely grated parmesan cheese

1 Heat butter in a large frying pan; cook onion, stirring, until softened. Add wine; bring to the boil. Boil, uncovered, until liquid is almost evaporated. Add stock, the water and porcini; bring to the boil.

2 Place rice in a 4.5-litre (18-cup) slow cooker; stir in onion mixture. Cook, covered, on high, 1½ hours. Stir well.

3 Meanwhile, heat 20g (¾ ounce) of the extra butter in same pan; cook button mushrooms, stirring occasionally, until browned. Remove from pan. Heat another 20g (¾ ounce) butter in same pan; cook swiss brown mushrooms, stirring occasionally, until browned. Add garlic and thyme; cook, stirring, until fragrant.

4 Stir button mushrooms and swiss brown mushroom mixture into cooker. Cook, uncovered, on high, 20 minutes or until rice is tender.

5 Stir in cheese and remaining butter; season to taste. Serve immediately, topped with extra thyme and parmesan cheese.

nutritional count per serving
26.6g total fat
16.6g saturated fat
2947kJ (705 cal)
88.7g carbohydrate
20g protein
4.7g fibre

note This risotto has the texture of an oven-baked version rather than the creaminess of a traditional stirred risotto; it must be served immediately.

not suitable to freeze

RICH CHOCOLATE CAKE

prep + cook time 2 hours 30 minutes **serves** 12

180g (5½ ounces) dark (semi-sweet) chocolate,
  chopped coarsely

60g (2 ounces) butter, chopped coarsely

5 eggs, separated

1 tablespoon brandy

½ cup (60g) ground almonds

¼ cup (35g) plain (all-purpose) flour

⅓ cup (75g) caster (superfine) sugar

125g (4 ounces) fresh raspberries

CHOCOLATE GANACHE

½ cup (125ml) pouring cream

180g (5½ ounces) dark (semi-sweet) chocolate,
  chopped finely

1   Grease a 2-litre (8-cup) pudding steamer; line base
    with baking paper.

2   Stir chocolate and butter in a large saucepan over
    low heat until smooth. Remove from heat; cool
    10 minutes. Stir in egg yolks and brandy, then
    ground almonds and sifted flour.

3   Beat egg whites in a medium bowl with an electric
    mixer until soft peaks form. Add sugar; beat until
    sugar dissolves. Fold egg white mixture into chocolate
    mixture, in two batches. Spoon into steamer.

4   Place steamer, without lid, in a 4.5-litre (18-cup)
    slow cooker; pour enough boiling water into cooker
    to come halfway up the side of the steamer. Cook,
    covered, on high, 2 hours or until cake feels firm.

5   Remove steamer from cooker. Turn immediately
    onto a baking-paper-lined wire rack to cool.

6   Meanwhile, make chocolate ganache.

7   Spread cake with ganache; top with berries.

CHOCOLATE GANACHE Bring cream to the boil in a
small saucepan. Remove from heat; add chocolate,
stir until smooth. Stand at room temperature until
ganache is spreadable.

nutritional count per serving
22.7g total fat
14.8g saturated fat
1400kJ (335 cal)
26.7g carbohydrate
5.6g protein
2.5g fibre

serving suggestion
Serve with whipped cream
and/or ice-cream.

tip There is no need to cover
the pudding steamer with
foil or a lid because the cake
will be covered when the lid
is placed on the cooker.

to freeze Wrap cake in
two layers of plastic wrap.
Seal, label and freeze for up
to 3 months. Thaw overnight
in the fridge. Reheat in a
microwave on medium power
(50%) until heated through.

RHURBARB AND ORANGE COMPOTE

prep + cook time 4 hours (+ standing) **serves** 6

16 large trimmed stems rhubarb (1kg), chopped coarsely

1 teaspoon finely grated orange rind

2 large oranges (600g), peeled, sliced thickly

⅔ cup (150g) raw caster (superfine) sugar

¼ cup (60ml) cranberry juice

1 teaspoon ground ginger

1 teaspoon ground cinnamon

1 cup (80g) flaked almonds, roasted

CINNAMON YOGHURT CREAM

½ cup (125ml) thick (double) cream

½ cup (140g) Greek-style yoghurt

½ teaspoon cinnamon sugar

1 Grease a 4.5-litre (18-cup) slow cooker bowl.

2 Combine rhubarb, rind, orange, sugar, juice and spices in cooker. Cook, covered, on low, 3½ hours or until rhubarb is tender. Remove bowl from cooker. Stand 20 minutes before serving.

3 Meanwhile, make cinnamon yoghurt cream.

4 Divide rhubarb mixture into serving bowls; top with cinnamon yoghurt cream and nuts.

CINNAMON YOGHURT CREAM Combine ingredients in a small bowl.

nutritional count per serving   **not suitable to freeze**

20.5g total fat
8.8g saturated fat
1580kJ (378 cal)
37.7g carbohydrate
7.7g protein
6.3g fibre

FOR THE STOVE

There is nothing more comforting then the smell of something hearty cooking on the stove. Create magic in your kitchen with recipes that will draw your guests to the table. This chapter will help you cook crowd-pleasing dishes for all your family and friends.

MALAYSIAN LAMB CURRY

prep + cook time 1 hour 50 minutes **serves** 4

2 tablespoons garam masala

1 tablespoon ground cumin

1 tablespoon black mustard seeds

1 teaspoon ground turmeric

1kg (2 pounds) diced lamb shoulder

¼ cup (60ml) vegetable oil

2 medium brown onions (300g), sliced thinly

2 cloves garlic, crushed

3 dried long red chillies, chopped coarsely

2 long green chillies, chopped coarsely

400ml (12½ ounces) canned coconut cream

1 cup (250ml) beef stock

200g (6½ ounces) sugar snap peas, trimmed

½ cup loosely packed fresh coriander (cilantro) leaves

1 Combine spices with lamb in a large bowl.

2 Heat 2 tablespoons of the oil in a large saucepan; cook lamb mixture, in batches, until browned. Remove from pan.

3 Heat remaining oil in same pan; cook onion, garlic and chillies over low heat, stirring, until onion softens.

4 Return lamb to pan with coconut cream and stock; simmer, covered, 1 hour 20 minutes. Remove pan from heat; stir in peas. Serve curry topped with coriander.

nutritional count per serving
57.4g total fat
30g saturated fat
3390kJ (811 cal)
12.3g carbohydrate
58.4g protein
8.5g fibre

note This rich combination of spices cooked in coconut cream is classic Malaysian cooking, combining the country's Indian and Straits-Chinese influences. This recipe uses black mustard seeds (sometimes sold as brown mustard seeds), which are more pungent than the white (or yellow) seeds used in most prepared mustards.

not suitable to freeze

XACUTTI

prep + cook time 1 hour 35 minutes **serves** 4

1 cup (80g) desiccated coconut

½ teaspoon ground cinnamon

4 whole cloves

8 dried long red chillies

1 teaspoon ground turmeric

1 tablespoon poppy seeds

1 tablespoon cumin seeds

1 tablespoon fennel seeds

2 tablespoons coriander seeds

2 teaspoons black peppercorns

2 whole star anise

6 cloves garlic, quartered

2 tablespoons ghee

1 large brown onion (200g), chopped finely

1kg (2 pounds) diced beef rump

2 cups (500ml) water

2 cups (500ml) beef stock

2 tablespoons lime juice

1 Dry-fry coconut in a large frying pan over medium heat, stirring, until browned lightly. Remove from pan. Dry-fry cinnamon, cloves, chillies, turmeric, seeds, peppercorns and star anise in same pan, stirring, 1 minute or until fragrant.

2 Blend or process coconut, spice mixture and garlic until finely chopped.

3 Heat ghee in a large saucepan; cook onion, stirring, until onion softens. Add coconut spice mixture; cook, stirring, until fragrant. Add beef; cook, stirring, 2 minutes or until beef is coated with coconut spice mixture.

4 Add the water and stock; simmer, covered, 30 minutes, stirring occasionally. Uncover; cook 30 minutes or until beef is tender and sauce is thickened slightly. Remove pan from heat; stir in juice. Serve topped with a little sliced fresh chilli.

nutritional count per serving
38.2g total fat
23.8g saturated fat
2512kJ (600 cal)
5g carbohydrate
57.5g protein
5.2g fibre

to freeze Pack into freezer-proof containers, leaving a 2.5cm (1 inch) space to allow for expansion. Seal, label and freeze for up to 3 months. Thaw overnight in the fridge. Reheat in a saucepan or microwave on medium power (50%) until heated through.

CREAMY SEMI-DRIED TOMATO AND VEAL SOUP

prep + cook time 2 hours 30 minutes (+ cooling) **serves** 6

500g (1-pound) piece boneless veal shoulder

1 litre (4 cups) water

6 black peppercorns

1 bay leaf

60g (2 ounces) butter

1 medium brown onion (150g), chopped coarsely

1 clove garlic, crushed

⅓ cup (50g) plain (all-purpose) flour

6 large roma (egg) tomatoes (540g), chopped coarsely

2 tablespoons tomato paste

½ cup (125ml) pouring cream

⅓ cup (75g) drained semi-dried tomatoes, chopped finely

2 tablespoons finely shredded fresh basil

TOASTED CIABATTA WITH BASIL BUTTER

50g (1½ ounces) butter, softened

1 tablespoon finely chopped basil leaves

8 thick slices ciabatta (280g)

1 Place veal in a large saucepan with the water, peppercorns and bay leaf; bring to the boil. Reduce heat; simmer, covered, 1½ hours or until veal is tender.

2 Transfer veal to a medium bowl; using two forks, shred veal coarsely. Strain broth through muslin-lined sieve or colander into a large heatproof bowl; discard solids.

3 Melt butter in a large saucepan; cook onion and garlic, stirring, until onion softens. Add flour; cook, stirring, until mixture thickens and bubbles. Gradually stir in broth; stir over medium heat until soup boils and thickens slightly. Add fresh tomato and paste; return to the boil. Reduce heat; simmer, covered, 10 minutes. Cool 15 minutes.

4 Meanwhile, make toasted ciabatta with basil butter.

5 Blend or process soup, in batches, until smooth. Return soup to same cleaned pan, add cream; stir over medium heat until hot. Season to taste.

6 Serve soup topped with shredded veal, semi-dried tomato and basil; accompany with toasted ciabatta.

TOASTED CIABATTA WITH BASIL BUTTER Combine butter and basil in a small bowl. Toast ciabatta on both sides; spread with basil butter.

nutritional count per serving
28.2g total fat
16.6g saturated fat
2090kJ (500 cal)
33g carbohydrate
26.3g protein
5.4g fibre

to freeze Complete the recipe to the end of step 3. Pack into freezer-proof containers, leaving a 2.5cm (1 inch) space to allow for expansion. Seal, label and freeze for up to 3 months. Thaw overnight in the fridge. Reheat in a saucepan, then continue from step 4.

LAMB SHANK SOUP

prep + cook time 2 hours 40 minutes (+ standing & refrigeration) **serves** 4

1½ cups (300g) dried chickpeas (garbanzo beans)

1 tablespoon olive oil

1.5kg (3 pounds) french-trimmed lamb shanks

1 medium brown onion (150g), chopped finely

2 medium carrots (240g), chopped finely

2 sticks celery (300g), trimmed, sliced thinly

2 cloves garlic, crushed

1 teaspoon ground cumin

2 cups (500ml) chicken stock

1 litre (4 cups) water

8 large stalks silver beet (400g), chopped finely

¼ cup (60ml) lemon juice

1 Place chickpeas in a medium bowl, cover with water; stand overnight. Drain; rinse under cold water.

2 Meanwhile, heat oil in a large saucepan; cook lamb, in batches, until browned. Remove from pan.

3 Cook onion, carrot, celery, garlic and cumin in same pan, stirring, 5 minutes or until onion softens. Return lamb to pan with stock and the water; bring to the boil. Reduce heat; simmer, covered, 2 hours.

4 Remove pan from heat; when lamb is cool enough to handle, remove meat, chop coarsely. Refrigerate cooled soup mixture and lamb meat, covered separately, overnight.

5 Discard fat from surface of soup mixture. Place soup mixture, meat and chickpeas in a large saucepan; bring to the boil. Reduce heat; simmer, covered, 30 minutes. Add silver beet and juice; simmer, uncovered, until silver beet just wilts.

nutritional count per serving
28.2g total fat
9.9g saturated fat
2654kJ (635 cal)
35.7g carbohydrate
59.1g protein
15.6g fibre

serving suggesting
Serve with a warmed loaf of ciabatta.

to freeze Pack into freezer-proof containers, leaving a 2.5cm (1 inch) space to allow for expansion. Seal, label and freeze for up to 3 months. Thaw overnight in the fridge. Reheat in a saucepan or microwave on medium power (50%) until heated through.

MAPLE SYRUP PORK BELLY WITH PECANS

prep + cook time 2 hours 10 minutes **serves** 4

1kg (2 pounds) boneless pork belly, cut into four pieces

1 cup (250ml) pure maple syrup

3 cups (750ml) chicken stock

1 cinnamon stick

2 ancho chillies

6 whole cloves

2 cloves garlic, crushed

½ cup (125ml) soy sauce

½ cup (125ml) orange juice

1 tablespoon olive oil

750g (1½ pounds) silver beet, trimmed, sliced thinly

½ cup (60g) coarsely chopped roasted pecans

1 Combine pork, syrup, stock, cinnamon, chillies, cloves, garlic and soy in a saucepan large enough to hold pork in a single layer; bring to the boil. Reduce heat; simmer, covered, 1½ hours or until pork is tender, turning pork every 30 minutes. Remove pork; cover to keep warm.

2 Stir juice into braising liquid; bring to the boil. Reduce heat; simmer, uncovered, 5 minutes or until sauce thickens slightly. Strain sauce into a small bowl.

3 Meanwhile, heat oil in a large saucepan; cook silver beet, stirring, 5 minutes or until wilted.

4 Cut each pork piece into quarters. Divide silver beet among plates; top with pork, drizzle with sauce then top with nuts.

nutritional count per serving
67.2g total fat
18.9g saturated fat
4080kJ (976 cal)
62.3g carbohydrate
34.7g protein
4.1g fibre

serving suggesting
Serve with steamed basmati and wild rice blend.

tip Ancho chillies are a dried deep reddish brown chilli; you can purchase them from delicatessens or green grocers.

not suitable to freeze

NAVARIN OF LAMB

prep + cook time 1 hour 50 minutes **serves** 4

2 tablespoons olive oil

8 lamb noisettes (800g)

1 large brown onion (200g), sliced thickly

2 cloves garlic, crushed

2 tablespoons plain (all-purpose) flour

1 cup (250ml) water

3 cups (750ml) chicken stock

½ cup (125ml) dry red wine

400g (12½ ounces) canned diced tomatoes

¼ cup (70g) tomato paste

2 bay leaves

2 sprigs fresh rosemary

2 sticks celery (300g), trimmed, cut into
  5cm (2-inch) lengths

150g (4½ ounces) green beans, trimmed, halved

20 baby carrots (400g), trimmed

200g (6½ ounces) mushrooms

1 cup (120g) frozen peas

½ cup coarsely chopped fresh flat-leaf parsley

1   Heat oil in a large saucepan; cook lamb, in batches, until browned. Remove from pan.

2   Cook onion and garlic in same pan, stirring, until onion softens. Add flour; cook, stirring, until mixture bubbles and thickens. Gradually add the water, stock and wine; stir until mixture boils and thickens.

3   Return lamb to pan with tomatoes, paste, bay leaves and rosemary; bring to the boil. Reduce heat; simmer, covered, 30 minutes.

4   Add celery, beans, carrots and mushrooms to pan; simmer, covered, 30 minutes or until vegetables are tender. Add peas; simmer, uncovered, until peas are just tender.

5   Remove and discard toothpicks from lamb. Serve navarin topped with parsley.

nutritional count per serving
32.6g total fat
12.9g saturated fat
2913kJ (697 cal)
21.4g carbohydrate
69.3g protein
11g fibre

serving suggestion
Serve with creamy celeriac (celery root) mash.

tip Lamb noisettes are lamb sirloin chops with the bone removed and the "tail" wrapped around the meaty part of the chop and secured with a toothpick.

to freeze Complete the recipe to the end of step 3. Pack into freezer-proof containers, leaving a 2.5cm (1 inch) space to allow for expansion. Seal, label and freeze for up to 3 months. Thaw overnight in the fridge. Reheat in a saucepan, then continue from step 4.

LAMB AND QUINCE TAGINE WITH PISTACHIO COUSCOUS

prep + cook time 1 hour 50 minutes **serves** 4

45g (1½ ounces) butter

600g (1¼ pounds) diced lamb

1 medium red onion (170g), chopped coarsely

2 cloves garlic, crushed

1 cinnamon stick

2 teaspoons ground coriander

1 teaspoon ground cumin

1 teaspoon ground ginger

1 teaspoon dried chilli flakes

1½ cups (375ml) water

425g (13½ ounces) canned crushed tomatoes

2 medium quinces (600g), peeled, quartered

1 large zucchini (150g), chopped coarsely

2 tablespoons coarsely chopped fresh coriander (cilantro)

PISTACHIO COUSCOUS

1½ cups (300g) couscous

1 cup (250ml) boiling water

20g (¾ ounce) butter

½ cup finely chopped fresh coriander (cilantro)

¼ cup (35g) roasted unsalted shelled pistachios, chopped coarsely

1 Melt butter in a tagine or large saucepan; cook lamb, in batches, until browned. Remove from tagine.

2 Cook onion in same tagine, stirring, until soft. Add garlic, spices and chilli; cook, stirring, 1 minute or until fragrant.

3 Return lamb to tagine with the water, tomatoes and quince; bring to the boil. Reduce heat; simmer, covered, 30 minutes. Uncover; simmer, stirring occasionally, 1 hour or until quince is tender and sauce has thickened slightly.

4 Add zucchini; cook, stirring, 10 minutes or until zucchini is tender, season to taste.

5 Meanwhile, make pistachio couscous.

6 Sprinkle tagine with coriander; serve with couscous.

PISTACHIO COUSCOUS Combine couscous, the water and butter in a large heatproof bowl, cover; stand 5 minutes or until liquid is absorbed, fluffing with fork occasionally. Stir in coriander and nuts.

nutritional count per serving
31g total fat
14.7g saturated fat
3214kJ (769 cal)
76.7g carbohydrate
45.4g protein
12.3g fibre

to freeze Complete the recipe to the end of step 3. Pack into freezer-proof containers, leaving a 2.5cm (1 inch) space to allow for expansion. Seal, label and freeze for up to 3 months. Thaw overnight in the fridge. Reheat in a saucepan, then continue from step 4.

ROGAN JOSH

prep + cook time 2 hours 20 minutes **serves** 4

1kg (2 pounds) boned leg of lamb, trimmed

2 teaspoons ground cardamom

2 teaspoons ground cumin

2 teaspoons ground coriander

2 tablespoons oil

2 medium brown onions (300g), sliced thinly

4cm (1½-inch) piece fresh ginger (20g), grated

4 cloves garlic, crushed

2 teaspoons sweet paprika

½ teaspoon cayenne pepper

½ cup (125ml) beef stock

425g (13½ ounces) canned crushed tomatoes

2 bay leaves

2 cinnamon sticks

¾ cup (210g) yoghurt

¾ cup (110g) roasted slivered almonds

1 fresh long red chilli, sliced thinly

1 Cut lamb into 3cm (1¼-inch) pieces. Combine lamb and ground spices in a medium bowl.

2 Heat half the oil in a large deep saucepan; cook lamb mixture, in batches, until browned all over. Remove from pan.

3 Heat remaining oil in same pan; cook onion, ginger, garlic, paprika and cayenne over low heat, stirring, until onion softens.

4 Return lamb to pan with stock, tomatoes, bay leaves and cinnamon. Add yoghurt, 1 tablespoon at a time, stirring well between each addition; bring to the boil. Reduce heat; simmer, covered, 1½ hours or until lamb is tender.

5 Top lamb with nuts and chilli off the heat.

nutritional count per serving
33.8g total fat
6.4g saturated fat
2617kJ (626 cal)
12.2g carbohydrate
65.7g protein
5.3g fibre

serving suggestion
Serve with naan bread,
yoghurt and steamed rice.

not suitable to freeze

MINESTRONE

prep + cook time 4 hours (+ refrigeration) **serves** 6

1 ham hock (1kg)

1 medium brown onion (150g), quartered

1 stick celery (150g), trimmed, chopped coarsely

1 teaspoon black peppercorns

1 bay leaf

4 litres (16 cups) water

1 tablespoon olive oil

1 large carrot (180g), chopped finely

2 sticks celery (200g), trimmed, chopped finely, extra

3 cloves garlic, crushed

¼ cup (70g) tomato paste

2 large tomatoes (440g), chopped finely

1 small leek (200g), sliced thinly

1 cup (100g) small pasta shells

420g (13½ ounces) canned white beans,
  drained, rinsed

½ cup coarsely chopped fresh flat-leaf parsley

½ cup coarsely chopped fresh basil

½ cup (40g) flaked parmesan cheese

1 Preheat oven to 220°C/425°F.

2 Roast ham hock and onion in a medium baking dish for 30 minutes.

3 Place hock and onion in a large saucepan with celery, peppercorns, bay leaf and the water; bring to the boil. Reduce heat; simmer, uncovered, 2 hours.

4 Remove hock from broth. Strain broth through a muslin-lined sieve or colander into a large heatproof bowl; discard solids. Allow broth to cool. Cover; refrigerate until cold.

5 Remove ham from hock; shred coarsely. Discard bone, fat and skin.

6 Meanwhile, heat oil in a large saucepan; cook carrot and extra celery, stirring, 2 minutes. Add ham, garlic, paste and tomato; cook, stirring, 2 minutes.

7 Discard fat from surface of broth. Pour broth into a large measuring jug; add enough water to make 2 litres (8 cups). Add broth to pan; bring to the boil. Reduce heat; simmer, covered, 20 minutes.

8 Add leek, pasta and beans to pan; bring to the boil. Reduce heat; simmer, uncovered, until pasta is tender. Remove from heat; stir in herbs.

9 Serve bowls of soup topped with cheese.

nutritional count per serving
7.2g total fat
2.4g saturated fat
865kJ (207 cal)
19.6g carbohydrate
12.7g protein
6.1g fibre

tip Make the broth a day ahead so that it chills long enough for the fat to solidify on top. Skim away the fat before reheating the broth; continue with the recipe.

not suitable to freeze

chicken tagine with dates and honey

CHICKEN TAGINE WITH DATES AND HONEY

prep + cook time 2 hours **serves** 4

1kg (2 pounds) chicken thigh fillets

2 tablespoons olive oil

2 medium brown onions (300g), sliced thinly

4 cloves garlic, crushed

1 teaspoon cumin seeds

1 teaspoon ground coriander

1 teaspoon ground ginger

1 teaspoon ground turmeric

1 teaspoon ground cinnamon

½ teaspoon chilli powder

¼ teaspoon ground nutmeg

1½ cups (375ml) chicken stock

1 cup (250ml) water

½ cup (85g) seedless dates, halved

¼ cup (90g) honey

½ cup (80g) blanched almonds, roasted

1 tablespoon chopped fresh coriander (cilantro)

1 Cut chicken into 3cm (1¼-inch) strips. Heat half the oil in a medium saucepan; cook chicken, in batches, stirring, until browned. Drain.

2 Heat remaining oil in same pan; cook onion, garlic and spices, stirring, until onion is soft.

3 Return chicken to pan with stock and the water; simmer, covered, 1 hour. Remove lid, simmer 30 minutes or until mixture is thickened slightly and chicken is tender.

4 Stir in dates, honey and nuts; top with coriander.

nutritional count per serving
38.7g total fat
7.7g saturated fat
2888kJ (691 cal)
31.2g carbohydrate
53.1g protein
4.2g fibre

to freeze Complete the recipe to the end of step 3. Pack into freezer-proof containers, leaving a 2.5cm (1 inch) space to allow for expansion. Seal, label and freeze for up to 3 months. Thaw overnight in the fridge. Reheat in a saucepan, then continue from step 4.

SPICED CORIANDER, LENTIL AND BARLEY SOUP

prep + cook time 1 hour 30 minutes (+ cooling) **serves** 4

1 tablespoon coriander seeds

1 tablespoon cumin seeds

1 tablespoon ghee (clarified butter)

6 cloves garlic, crushed

2 fresh small red thai (serrano) chillies, chopped finely

1¼ cups (250g) soup mix

1 litre (4 cups) chicken stock

3½ cups (875ml) water

1 cup coarsely chopped fresh coriander (cilantro)

⅓ cup (95g) Greek-style yoghurt

1 tablespoon mango chutney

1 Dry-fry seeds in large saucepan, stirring, until fragrant. Using pestle and mortar, crush seeds.

2 Melt ghee in same pan; cook crushed seeds, garlic and chilli, stirring, 5 minutes.

3 Add soup mix, stock and the water; bring to the boil. Reduce heat; simmer, covered, stirring occasionally, 1 hour. Cool 15 minutes.

4 Blend or process half the soup, in batches, until smooth. Return pureed soup to pan with unprocessed soup; stir over medium heat until hot. Remove from heat; stir in coriander.

5 Serve soup topped with yoghurt and chutney.

(photograph page 380)

nutritional count per serving
7.9g total fat
4.6g saturated fat
1350kJ (323 cal)
49.7g carbohydrate
11.4g protein
3g fibre

tip Soup mix is a blend of dried pulses and grains, available from supermarkets.

to freeze Complete the recipe to the end of step 4. Pour into freezer-proof containers, leaving a 2.5cm (1 inch) space to allow for expansion. Seal, label and freeze for up to 3 months. Thaw overnight in the fridge. Reheat in a large saucepan until heated through.

spiced coriander, lentil and barley soup (recipe page 379)

mixed dhal (recipe page 382)

MIXED DHAL

prep + cook time 1 hour 25 minutes **serves** 4

2 tablespoons ghee

1 medium brown onion (150g), chopped finely

2 cloves garlic, crushed

4cm (1½-inch) piece fresh ginger (20g), grated

1½ tablespoons black mustard seeds

1 long green chilli, chopped finely

1 tablespoon ground cumin

1 tablespoon ground coriander

2 teaspoons ground turmeric

½ cup (100g) brown lentils

⅓ cup (65g) red lentils

⅓ cup (85g) yellow split peas

⅓ cup (85g) green split peas

400g (12½ ounces) canned crushed tomatoes

2 cups (500ml) vegetable stock

1½ cups (375ml) water

140ml (4½ ounces) canned coconut cream

1 Heat ghee in a large saucepan; cook onion, garlic and ginger, stirring, until onion softens. Add seeds, chilli and spices; cook, stirring, until fragrant.

2 Add lentils and peas to pan. Stir in tomatoes, stock and the water; simmer, covered, stirring occasionally, 1 hour or until lentils are tender.

3 Just before serving, add coconut cream; stir over low heat until dhal is heated through.

(photograph page 381)

nutritional count per serving
18.4g total fat
12.5g saturated fat
1898kJ (454 cal)
42.6g carbohydrate
23.3g protein
12.7g fibre

tip Dhal is best made a day ahead to develop its flavour. Cover, refrigerate overnight. Reheat in a saucepan or microwave on medium power (50%) until heated through.

not suitable to freeze

PORK WITH BEANS AND BEER

prep + cook time 2 hours 40 minutes **serves** 8

3 cloves garlic, crushed

½ teaspoon freshly ground black pepper

1.8kg (3½ pounds) pork neck

1 tablespoon olive oil

3 rindless bacon slices (195g), chopped finely

2 medium brown onions (300g), sliced thinly

2 teaspoons caraway seeds

1½ cups (375ml) beer

1 cup (200g) dried haricot beans

1½ cups (375ml) chicken stock

¼ small (300g) white cabbage, shredded finely

1 Rub combined garlic and pepper all over pork. Secure pork with kitchen string at 2cm (¾-inch) intervals to make an even shape.

2 Heat oil in a large flameproof baking dish; cook pork until browned all over. Remove from dish.

3 Cook bacon, onion and seeds in same dish, stirring, until onion is soft and bacon is browned lightly.

4 Return pork to dish with beer, beans and stock; simmer, covered, 2 hours or until beans and pork are tender. Remove pork from dish. Add cabbage; cook, stirring, until just wilted.

5 Serve pork with bean mixture.

nutritional count per serving   **not suitable to freeze**
24.4g total fat
7.8g saturated fat
2261kJ (541 cal)
13.9g carbohydrate
59.8g protein
6.7g fibre

pork with beans and beer

DRUNKEN DUCK

prep + cook time 2 hours 45 minutes **serves** 4

1 whole duck (2kg)

1 tablespoon vegetable oil

1 medium brown onion (150g), chopped coarsely

2 cloves garlic, crushed

1 fresh small red thai (serrano) chilli, chopped finely

4cm (1½-inch) piece fresh ginger (20g), grated

2 cups (500ml) chinese cooking wine (shao hsing)

1 cup (250ml) water

1 tablespoon dark soy sauce

½ teaspoon five-spice powder

15g (½ ounce) sliced dried shiitake mushrooms

4 green onions (scallions), sliced thinly

1 Discard neck from duck. Rinse duck under cold water; pat dry inside and out with absorbent paper. Heat oil in a large saucepan; cook duck until browned all over. Remove from pan.

2 Reserve 1 tablespoon of the pan juices; discard remainder. Heat reserved juices in same pan, add brown onion, garlic, chilli and ginger; cook, stirring, until onion softens. Return duck to pan with wine, the water, sauce, five-spice and mushrooms; bring to the boil. Reduce heat; simmer, covered, 2 hours, turning duck occasionally.

3 Carefully remove duck from pan; cut into four pieces. Divide duck between serving bowls; drizzle with pan liquid, sprinkle with green onion.

nutritional count per serving   **not suitable to freeze**
20.5g total fat
6g saturated fat
953kJ (228 cal)
1.2g carbohydrate
7.2g protein
0.2g fibre

COQ AU VIN

prep + cook time 1 hour 30 minutes **serves** 4

800g (1½ pounds) spring onions

¼ cup (60ml) olive oil

6 rindless bacon slices (390g), chopped coarsely

2 cloves garlic, crushed

8 chicken thigh fillets (880g)

¼ cup (35g) plain (all-purpose) flour

2 cups (500ml) dry red wine

1½ cups (375ml) chicken stock

2 tablespoons tomato paste

3 bay leaves

4 sprigs fresh thyme

2 sprigs fresh rosemary

300g (9½ ounces) button mushrooms

1 Trim green ends from onions, leaving about 4cm (1½ inches) of stem attached; trim roots. Heat 1 tablespoon of the oil in a large frying pan; cook onions, stirring, until browned all over. Remove from pan.

2 Add bacon and garlic to pan; cook, stirring, until bacon is crisp. Remove from pan.

3 Coat chicken in flour; shake off excess. Heat remaining oil in same pan; cook chicken, in batches, until browned all over. Drain on absorbent paper.

4 Return chicken to pan with wine, stock, paste, bay leaves, herbs, onions and bacon mixture. Bring to the boil; reduce heat, simmer, uncovered, 35 minutes or until chicken is tender and sauce has thickened slightly.

5 Add mushrooms; simmer, uncovered, until mushrooms are tender.

nutritional count per serving
43.6g total fat
11.8g saturated fat
3428kJ (820 cal)
16.3g carbohydrate
67.8g protein
6.4g fibre

serving suggestion
Serve with mashed potato or crusty bread.

to freeze Complete recipe to the end of step 4. Pack into freezer-proof containers, leaving a 2.5cm (1 inch) space to allow for expansion. Seal, label and freeze for up to 3 months. Thaw overnight in the fridge. Reheat in a saucepan, adding a little stock or water if necessary, then continue from step 5.

SPRING VEGETABLE BROTH WITH CHEESE-FILLED ZUCCHINI FLOWERS

prep + cook time 2 hours **serves** 4

2.5 litres (10 cups) water

3 medium pontiac potatoes (600g), unpeeled, halved

2 medium tomatoes (300g), quartered

2 medium carrots (240g), chopped coarsely

2 stalks celery (200g), trimmed, chopped coarsely

1 large brown onion (200g), chopped coarsely

100g (3 ounces) mushrooms, halved

2 cloves garlic, unpeeled, bruised

8 black peppercorns

1 bay leaf

2 sprigs fresh flat-leaf parsley

2 sprigs fresh dill

12 baby zucchini with flowers attached (240g)

170g (5½ ounces) asparagus, chopped coarsely

150g (4½ ounces) sugar snap peas, halved diagonally

CHEESE-FILLED ZUCCHINI FLOWERS

150g (4½ ounces) soft goat's cheese

1 teaspoon finely grated lemon rind

1 tablespoon lemon juice

1 tablespoon finely chopped fresh dill

1 Place the water in a large saucepan with potato, tomato, carrot, celery, onion, mushrooms, garlic, peppercorns, bay leaf, parsley and dill; bring to the boil. Reduce heat; simmer, uncovered, 1½ hours. Strain broth through muslin-lined sieve or colander into a large heatproof bowl. Discard solids.

2 Meanwhile, separate flowers from each zucchini; reserve flowers for cheese-filled zucchini flowers. Chop zucchini coarsely; reserve for broth.

3 Make cheese-filled zucchini flowers.

4 Return broth to same cleaned pan; bring to the boil. Remove pan from heat; add reserved zucchini, asparagus and peas.

5 Serve bowls of soup topped with zucchini flowers.

CHEESE-FILLED ZUCCHINI FLOWERS Combine ingredients in a small bowl. Discard stamens from reserved zucchini flowers; fill flowers with cheese mixture, twist petal tops to enclose filling.

nutritional count per serving   **not suitable to freeze**
6.7g total fat
3.9g saturated fat
1104kJ (264 cal)
30.9g carbohydrate
14.6g protein
10.5g fibre

QUINCE AND CHICKEN TAGINE

prep + cook time 2 hours **serves** 4

2 medium quinces (700g), peeled, cored,
  cut into wedges

40g (1½ ounces) butter

⅓ cup (115g) honey

3 cups (750ml) water

2 teaspoons orange flower water

2 teaspoons olive oil

4 chicken drumsticks (600g)

4 chicken thigh cutlets (800g), skin removed

1 large brown onion (200g), chopped coarsely

3 cloves garlic, crushed

1 teaspoon ground cumin

1 teaspoon ground ginger

pinch saffron threads

2 cups (500ml) chicken stock

2 large zucchini (300g), chopped coarsely

¼ cup coarsely chopped fresh coriander (cilantro)

1 Place quinces, butter, honey, the water and orange flower water in a medium saucepan; bring to the boil. Reduce heat; simmer, covered, 1 hour, stirring occasionally. Remove lid, cook, stirring occasionally, 45 minutes or until quince is red in colour.

2 Meanwhile, heat oil in a large frying pan; cook chicken, in batches, until browned. Remove from pan.

3 Cook onion, garlic and spices in same pan, stirring, until onion softens. Return chicken to pan, then add stock; bring to the boil. Reduce heat; simmer, covered, 20 minutes. Remove lid; simmer, 20 minutes or until chicken is cooked though. Add zucchini; cook, uncovered, 10 minutes or until zucchini is tender. Stir in quince and ½ cup of the quince syrup.

4 Serve tagine topped with coriander.

nutritional count per serving
32.1g total fat
12.2g saturated fat
2780kJ (665 cal)
42.1g carbohydrate
46.7g protein
11.4g fibre

serving suggestion
Serve with couscous.

not suitable to freeze

CREAMY CRAB AND TOMATO BISQUE

prep + cook time 2 hours 20 minutes **serves** 4

4 uncooked medium blue swimmer crabs (1.3kg)

60g (2 ounces) butter

1 medium brown onion (150g), chopped coarsely

1 medium carrot (120g), chopped coarsely

1 medium leek (350g), chopped coarsely

2 cloves garlic, crushed

1 tablespoon tomato paste

2 tablespoons brandy

1 cup (250ml) dry white wine

1.25 litres (5 cups) fish stock

1 bay leaf

2 sprigs fresh thyme

2 medium tomatoes (300g), chopped finely

20g (¾ ounces) butter, extra

1 tablespoon plain (all-purpose) flour

½ cup (125ml) pouring cream

1 Slide knife under top of crab shells at back, lever off and discard. Discard gills; rinse crabs under cold water. Using cleaver or heavy knife, chop each body into quarters.

2 Melt butter in a large saucepan; cook onion, carrot, leek and garlic, stirring, until vegetables soften. Add crab, in batches; cook, stirring, until changed in colour.

3 Add paste to pan; cook, stirring, 2 minutes. Return crab to pan with brandy; stir over heat 2 minutes or until alcohol evaporates.

4 Add wine, stock, bay leaf, thyme and tomato; bring to the boil. Reduce heat; simmer, uncovered, 45 minutes.

5 Meanwhile, using back of teaspoon, work extra butter into flour in a small bowl.

6 Strain soup through muslin-lined sieve or colander into a large heatproof bowl; extract as much meat as possible from crab, add to soup. Discard shells, claws and other solids.

7 Return soup to same cleaned pan; bring to the boil. Stir in flour mixture and cream; stir until soup boils and thickens slightly.

nutritional count per serving
32g total fat
20.1g saturated fat
2152kJ (515 cal)
13.1g carbohydrate
27.1g protein
4.4g fibre

tip Making your own fish stock will enhance the flavour of this dish – see page 471 for the recipe.

not suitable to freeze

SMOKY OCTOPUS STEW WITH RED WINE AND OLIVES

prep + cook time 1 hour 30 minutes **serves** 4

1kg (2 pounds) cleaned baby octopus

2 bay leaves

2 tablespoons olive oil

1 large brown onion (200g), sliced thinly

2 cloves garlic, crushed

1½ teaspoons smoked paprika

5 medium tomatoes (750g), peeled, chopped coarsely

⅓ cup (50g) drained sun-dried tomatoes,
  chopped coarsely

2 tablespoons tomato paste

¾ cup (180ml) dry red wine

¼ cup (60ml) water

1¼ cups (200g) seeded kalamata olives

2 tablespoons coarsely chopped fresh flat-leaf parsley

1 Cut heads from octopus; cut tentacles into two pieces.

2 Place octopus and bay leaves in a large saucepan of water; bring to the boil. Reduce heat; simmer, covered, 30 minutes or until octopus is just tender. Drain; discard bay leaves.

3 Heat oil in same cleaned pan; cook onion and garlic, stirring, until onion softens. Add paprika, fresh and sun-dried tomatoes, paste, wine, the water and octopus; bring to the boil. Reduce heat; simmer, covered, 30 minutes. Stir in olives.

4 Serve stew topped with parsley.

nutritional count per serving
15.1g total fat
2.4g saturated fat
2169kJ (519 cal)
23.8g carbohydrates
63.6g protein
5.7g fibre

serving suggestion
Serve with sourdough bread.

not suitable to freeze

VIETNAMESE BEEF PHO

prep + cook time 1 hour 40 minutes **serves** 6

2 litres (8 cups) water

1 litre (4 cups) beef stock

1kg (2 pounds) chuck steak

2 whole star anise

8cm (3¼-inch) piece fresh ginger (40g), grated

⅓ cup (80ml) japanese soy sauce

200g (6½ ounces) bean thread noodles

1½ cups (120g) bean sprouts

⅓ cup loosely packed fresh mint leaves

¼ cup loosely packed fresh coriander (cilantro) leaves

4 green onions (scallions), sliced thinly

2 fresh long red chillies, sliced thinly

¼ cup (60ml) fish sauce

1 medium lemon (140g), cut into six wedges

1 Place the water and stock in a large saucepan with beef, star anise, ginger and soy sauce; bring to the boil. Reduce heat; simmer, covered, 30 minutes. Uncover, simmer 30 minutes or until beef is tender.

2 Meanwhile, place noodles in medium heatproof bowl, cover with boiling water; stand until just tender, drain. Combine sprouts, mint, coriander, onion and chilli in medium bowl.

3 Remove beef from pan. Strain broth through muslin-lined sieve or colander into large heatproof bowl; discard solids. When beef is cool enough to handle, remove and discard fat and sinew. Slice beef thinly, return to same cleaned pan with broth; bring to the boil. Stir in fish sauce.

4 Divide noodles among soup bowls; ladle hot beef broth into bowls, top with sprout mixture, serve with lemon.

nutritional count per serving
8g total fat
3.3g saturated fat
1166kJ (279 cal)
11.8g carbohydrate
38.3g protein
2.4g fibre

tips Large bowls of pho are a breakfast favourite throughout Vietnam, but we like to eat it any time of the day. Round steak, skirt steak and gravy beef are also suitable for this recipe, but the cooking times will change depending on which cut is used.

not suitable to freeze

POACHED PEARS AND QUINCE WITH ALMOND CRUMBLE

prep + cook time 2 hours 30 minutes **serves** 6

3 cups (660g) caster (superfine) sugar

3 cups (750ml) water

3 medium quinces (1kg), peeled, quartered, cored

2 strips lemon rind

3 medium pears (700g), peeled, halved, cored

2 tablespoons lemon juice, approximately

ALMOND CRUMBLE

½ cup (75g) plain (all-purpose) flour

75g (2½ ounces) butter, chopped

⅓ cup (75g) firmly packed light brown sugar

1 teaspoon ground cinnamon

½ cup (80g) coarsely chopped almond kernels

1 Stir sugar and the water in a large saucepan over low heat until sugar dissolves. Add quince and rind; bring to the boil. Reduce heat; simmer, covered, 1¾ hours or until quince is tender and rosy pink.

2 Meanwhile, make almond crumble.

3 Remove quince from syrup with a slotted spoon. Add pear to same syrup; bring to the boil. Reduce heat, simmer, uncovered, 10 minutes or until pears are tender. Remove with slotted spoon.

4 Boil syrup, uncovered, until reduced to 2 cups. Adjust the sweetness of the syrup with enough juice to taste.

5 Serve fruit drizzled with a little syrup and topped with almond crumble.

ALMOND CRUMBLE Preheat oven to 160°C/325°F. Sift flour into a medium bowl; rub in butter. Add sugar, cinnamon and almonds; mix well. Place mixture on oven tray; bake 30 minutes or until browned and crisp, turning occasionally with an egg slicer to retain large pieces.

nutritional count per serving
17.9g total fat
7.3g saturated fat
3299kJ (788 cal)
154.6g carbohydrate
4.7g protein
4.5g fibre

serving suggestion
Serve with custard, cream or ice-cream.

tip The poached fruit and almond crumble can be prepared several hours ahead. Reheat the fruit in the syrup before serving.

not suitable to freeze

FOR THE OVEN

Entertaining will be a breeze with these flavoursome recipes. Impress your guests with a mustard-crusted rack of veal, or a roasted chicken with gremolata all cooked slowly in your oven ensuring you cook tender and juicy meals every time.

STICKY QUINCE ROASTED LAMB

prep + cook time 1 hours 15 minutes (+ refrigeration) **serves** 4

1.2kg (2½-pound) butterflied leg of lamb

2 teaspoons fennel seeds

2 teaspoons sweet paprika

2 cloves garlic, crushed

¼ cup (60ml) red wine vinegar

¼ cup (60ml) olive oil

2 medium fennel bulbs (600g), trimmed,
 cut into wedges

2 medium red onions (340g), cut into wedges

¼ cup (80g) quince paste

1 medium lemon (140g), cut into wedges

1 Combine lamb, seeds, paprika, garlic, vinegar and 2 tablespoons of the oil in a large bowl. Cover; refrigerate 15 minutes.

2 Preheat oven to 240°C/475°F.

3 Combine fennel, onion and remaining oil in a large baking dish. Place lamb on vegetables; season. Roast, uncovered, 20 minutes.

4 Meanwhile, stir quince paste in a small saucepan over low heat until warmed.

5 Remove dish from oven; brush warm paste over lamb. Roast, uncovered, 20 minutes or until lamb is cooked as desired. Remove lamb from dish. Cover, stand 15 minutes.

6 Meanwhile, return vegetables to oven for another 15 minutes or until tender.

7 Serve lamb with vegetables and lemon wedges.

nutritional count per serving
31.9g total fat
10.6g saturated fat
2537kJ (607 cal)
15.6g carbohydrate
68g protein
4.3g fibre

serving suggestion
Serve with a baby spinach leaf salad.

tips You can also marinate the lamb in a large resealable plastic bag. Quince paste can be warmed in a microwave-safe jug in a microwave oven. Quince paste is available from delicatessens and most major supermarkets.

not suitable to freeze

BEEF RIB ROAST WITH ROASTED BEETROOT AND POTATOES PUREE

prep + cook time 2 hours (+ standing) **serves** 4

2kg (2 pounds) beef standing rib roast

¼ cup (60ml) olive oil

sea salt flakes

2 teaspoons cracked pepper

600g (1¼ pounds) small beetroot, scrubbed, trimmed

1kg (2 pounds) sebago potatoes

40g (1½ ounces) butter, chopped

⅔ cup (160ml) milk, warmed

⅓ cup (80ml) pouring cream, warmed

¼ cup finely grated fresh horseradish

1 Preheat oven to 220°C/425°F.

2 Tie beef with kitchen string at 2cm (¾-inch) intervals. Brush beef with 1 tablespoon of the oil; sprinkle with salt and pepper. Toss beetroot in remaining oil; add to dish. Roast, uncovered, 20 minutes.

3 Reduce oven to 180°C/325°F; roast beef and beetroot, uncovered, further 1 hour or until beef is cooked as desired and beetroot are tender. Remove beef from dish; cover, stand 20 minutes. Continue roasting beetroot further 15 minutes or until tender.

4 Meanwhile, boil, steam or microwave potatoes until tender; drain. Mash potatoes; push through a sieve or mouli into a large bowl. Stir in butter then gradually beat in warmed milk and cream.

5 Serve beef with roasted beetroot, potato puree and horseradish.

nutritional count per serving   **not suitable to freeze**

59g total fat

25.6g saturated fat

4644kJ (1111 cal)

39.9g carbohydrate

101.8g protein

7.3g fibre

BRAISED BEEF IN GINGER BROTH

prep + cook time 7 hours 15 minutes **serves** 4

1kg (2 pounds) beef brisket

30g (1 ounce) fresh shiitake mushrooms, sliced

30g (1 ounce) oyster mushrooms, sliced

30g (1 ounce) enoki mushrooms, sliced

1 tablespoon light soy sauce

¼ teaspoon sesame oil

3cm (1¼-inch) piece fresh ginger (15g), grated

GINGER BROTH

100g (3-ounce) bunch coriander (cilantro) with
  roots attached

10cm (4-inch) piece fresh ginger (50g), sliced thinly

1 stalk celery (100g), trimmed, chopped coarsely

1 medium carrot (120g), chopped coarsely

1 large red onion (300g), chopped coarsley

3 cloves garlic, chopped

5 green onions (scallions), chopped

3.5 litres (14 cups) water

1 Make ginger broth.

2 Preheat oven to 140°C/285°F.

3 Add beef to broth; cook, covered, in oven, 6 hours.

4 Remove beef from broth; cover to keep warm.
Add mushrooms to broth; simmer, uncovered,
5 minutes or until mushrooms are tender.
Stir in sauce and oil.

5 Slice beef thinly; divide beef between bowls.
Ladle broth into bowls. Serve topped with ginger
and reserved coriander leaves.

GINGER BROTH Wash coriander; chop roots and
stems coarsely, reserve leaves (to sprinkle over
broth before serving). Combine ingredients (except
coriander leaves) in large deep flameproof dish;
bring to the boil. Reduce heat; simmer, uncovered,
1 hour. Using slotted spoon, discard solids.

nutritional count per serving
15.5g total fat
6.3g saturated fat
1722kJ (412 cal)
8.7g carbohydrate
56.6g protein
5.1g fibre

tip The ginger broth can
be made ahead and kept,
covered, for several days
in the fridge.

to freeze Pour ginger broth
to into freezer-proof
containers, leaving a 2.5cm
(1 inch) space to allow for
expansion. Seal, label and
freeze for up to 6 months.
Thaw overnight in the fridge.
Reheat in a large saucepan.

SIRLOIN ROAST WITH HERB STUFFING

prep + cook time 1 hour 50 minutes **serves** 8

2.5kg (5-pound) boneless beef sirloin roast

2 tablespoons olive oil

2 tablespoons plain (all-purpose) flour

⅓ cup (80ml) dry red wine

1½ cups (375ml) beef stock

HERB STUFFING

45g (1½ ounces) butter

2 rindless bacon slices (130g), chopped finely

1 medium brown onion (150g), chopped finely

1 clove garlic, crushed

1½ cups (105g) stale breadcrumbs

½ cup (40g) coarsely grated parmesan cheese

1 egg

1 tablespoon wholegrain mustard

2 tablespoons finely chopped fresh oregano

2 tablespoons finely chopped fresh flat-leaf parsley

2 teaspoons finely grated lemon rind

1   Make herb stuffing.

2   Preheat oven to 220°C/425°F.

3   Cut between fat and meat of beef, making a pocket for stuffing; trim and discard a little of the fat. Spoon stuffing into pocket; lay fat over stuffing to enclose. Tie beef with kitchen string at 2cm (¾-inch) intervals; place beef on wire rack over shallow large baking dish. Drizzle with oil.

4   Roast beef, uncovered, 1½ hours. Remove beef from dish; cover with foil, stand 10 minutes. Slice beef thinly.

5   Reserve 2 tablespoons of beef juices in baking dish; place over heat. Add flour; cook, stirring, until mixture thickens and bubbles. Gradually add wine and stock, stirring, until gravy boils and thickens slightly.

6   Serve beef with gravy.

HERB STUFFING   Melt butter in a medium frying pan; cook bacon, onion and garlic, stirring, until onion softens. Cool. Combine bacon mixture with remaining ingredients in a medium bowl.

nutritional count per serving
32.9g total fat
14g saturated fat
2700kJ (646 cal)
12.6g carbohydrate
73g protein
1.1g fibre

serving suggestion
Serve with roast potatoes
(see page 172) and pumpkin.

not suitable to freeze

BRAISED BEEF CHEEKS IN RED WINE

prep + cook time 3 hours 30 minutes **serves** 4

2 tablespoons olive oil

1.6kg (3¼ pounds) beef cheeks, trimmed

1 medium brown onion (150g), chopped coarsely

1 medium carrot (120g), chopped coarsely

3 cups (750ml) dry red wine

¼ cup (60ml) red wine vinegar

800g (1½ pounds) canned whole tomatoes

¼ cup (55g) firmly packed light brown sugar

6 black peppercorns

2 sprigs fresh rosemary

2 tablespoons fresh oregano leaves

1 large fennel bulb (550g), cut into thin wedges

400g (12½ ounces) spring onions, trimmed, halved

200g (6½ ounces) swiss brown mushrooms

1   Preheat oven to 160°C/325°F.

2   Heat half the oil in a large flameproof baking dish; cook beef over heat, in batches, until browned all over. Remove from dish.

3   Heat remaining oil in same dish; cook brown onion and carrot, stirring, until onion softens. Return beef to dish with wine, vinegar, tomatoes, sugar, peppercorns, herbs and fennel; bring to the boil. Cook, covered, in oven for 2 hours.

4   Stir in spring onion and mushrooms; cook, uncovered, in oven a further 45 minutes or until beef is tender.

nutritional count per serving
41.5g total fat
14.9g saturated fat
4147kJ (992 cal)
29.2g carbohydrate
89.9g protein
8.9g fibre

serving suggestion
Serve with soft polenta
(see page 313).

to freeze Complete the recipe to the end of step 3. Pack into freezer-proof containers, leaving a 2.5cm (1 inch) space to allow for expansion. Seal, label and freeze for up to 3 months. Thaw overnight in the fridge. Reheat in a saucepan, adding a little stock or water if necessary, then continue from step 4.

BRAISED OXTAIL WITH ORANGE GREMOLATA

prep + cook time 3 hours 35 minutes **serves** 4

1.5kg (3 pounds) oxtails

2 tablespoons plain (all-purpose) flour

2 tablespoons olive oil

1 medium brown onion (150g), chopped coarsely

2 cloves garlic, crushed

½ cup (125ml) sweet sherry

400g (12½ ounces) canned crushed tomatoes

1 cup (250ml) beef stock

1 cup (250ml) water

4 sprigs fresh thyme

2 bay leaves

10cm (4-inch) strip orange rind

4 medium tomatoes (600g), chopped coarsely

ORANGE GREMOLATA

¼ cup finely chopped fresh flat-leaf parsley

1 tablespoon finely grated orange rind

1 clove garlic, crushed

1   Preheat oven to 160°C/325°F.

2   Cut oxtail into 5cm (2-inch) pieces. Coat oxtail in flour; shake off excess. Heat half the oil in a large flameproof baking dish; cook oxtail, in batches, until browned all over. Remove from dish.

3   Heat remaining oil in same dish; cook onion and garlic, stirring, until onion softens. Return oxtail to dish with sherry, canned tomatoes, stock, the water, herbs and rind. Cook, covered, in the oven, for 3 hours or until oxtail is tender. Stir in fresh tomato.

4   Meanwhile, make orange gremolata.

5   Serve oxtail topped with gremolata.

ORANGE GREMOLATA Combine ingredients in a small bowl.

nutritional count per serving
110.2g total fat
40g saturated fat
5656kJ (1353 cal)
15.8g carbohydrate
69.5g protein
4.1g fibre

serving suggestion
Serve with cheesy mash (see page 174).

to freeze Complete the recipe to the end of step 3. Pack into freezer-proof containers, leaving a 2.5cm (1 inch) space to allow for expansion. Seal, label and freeze for up to 3 months. Thaw overnight in the fridge. Reheat in a saucepan, adding a little stock or water if necessary, then continue from step 4.

OSSO BUCO

prep + cook time 2 hours **serves** 6

6 pieces veal osso buco (1.8kg)

½ cup (75g) plain (all-purpose) flour

40g (1½ ounces) butter

2 tablespoons olive oil

3 sticks celery (450g), trimmed, chopped coarsely

6 drained anchovy fillets, chopped coarsely

¾ cup (180ml) dry white wine

800g (1½ pounds) canned diced tomatoes

½ cup (125ml) chicken stock

5 cloves garlic, crushed

10 fresh thyme sprigs

3 bay leaves

GREMOLATA

½ cup finely chopped fresh flat-leaf parsley

2 cloves garlic, chopped finely

1 teaspoon finely grated lemon rind

1   Preheat oven to 160°C/325°F.

2   Coat veal in flour, shake off any excess. Heat butter and oil in large frying pan; cook veal, in batches, until browned both sides. Transfer veal to large ovenproof dish.

3   Cook celery and anchovy in same pan, stirring, until celery softens. Add wine; bring to the boil. Stir in tomatoes, stock, garlic, thyme and bay leaves; return to the boil.

4   Pour tomato mixture over veal; cook, covered, in oven about 1½ hours or until veal starts to fall away from the bone.

5   Meanwhile, make gremolata.

6   Serve osso buco sprinkled with gremolata.

GREMOLATA Combine ingredients in a small bowl.

nutritional count per serving
13.2g total fat
4.8g saturated fat
1626kJ (389 cal)
14.4g carbohydrate
46.1g protein
3.8g fibre

serving suggestion
Serve with soft polenta (see page 313).

note Osso buco originates from Milan and is traditionally served with risotto alla milanese (saffron risotto).

to freeze Comple the recipe to the end of step 4. Pack into freezer-proof containers, leaving a 2.5cm (1 inch) space to allow for expansion. Seal, label and freeze for up to 3 months. Thaw overnight in the fridge. Reheat in a saucepan, adding a little stock or water if necessary, then continue from step 5.

BRAISED VEAL SHOULDER WITH WHITE BEANS

prep + cook time 1 hour 40 minutes **serves** 6

¼ cup (60ml) olive oil

1.2kg (2½-pound) boned veal shoulder, rolled, tied

2 medium brown onions (300g), sliced thickly

3 cloves garlic, crushed

½ cup (125ml) dry red wine

1 cinnamon stick

2 bay leaves

2 sprigs rosemary

½ cup (60g) pitted green olives

800g (1½ pounds) canned crushed tomatoes

2 medium carrots (240g), chopped coarsely

½ cup (60g) frozen peas

400g (12½ ounces) canned white beans, drained, rinsed

1 Preheat oven to 200°C/400°F.

2 Heat 2 tablespoons of the oil in a large flameproof dish; cook veal, turning frequently, until browned. Remove from dish.

3 Heat remaining oil in same dish; cook onion and garlic, stirring, until onion softens. Add wine, cinnamon, bay leaves, rosemary, olives and tomatoes; bring to the boil.

4 Return veal to dish; cover. Transfer to oven; cook, 30 minutes. Turn veal and stir tomato mixture. Add carrots; cook, covered, 30 minutes.

5 Remove veal from dish; cover to keep warm. Add peas and beans to dish; cook, covered, 10 minutes.

6 Serve veal with beans and vegetables.

nutritional count per serving
14.7g total fat
2.8g saturated fat
1697kJ (406 cal)
12.7g carbohydrate
49.2g protein
5.4g fibre

serving suggestion
Serve with roast potatoes (see page 172).

tips Ask the butcher to bone, roll and tie the meat for you. Many varieties of white beans are available canned, among them great northern, navy, cannellini, butter and haricot beans; any of these would be suitable for this recipe. Drain beans then rinse them well under cold water before using.

not suitable to freeze

MUSTARD-CRUSTED RACK OF VEAL

prep + cook time 1 hour **serves** 4

2 tablespoons wholegrain mustard

3 green onions (scallions), chopped finely

1 tablespoon finely chopped fresh rosemary

2 cloves garlic, crushed

2 tablespoons olive oil

1 x 8 cutlet veal rack (1kg)

2 small kumara (orange sweet potato) (500g), chopped coarsely

20g (¾ ounce) butter

⅓ cup (80ml) pouring cream

1 large brown onion (200g), sliced thinly

400g (12½ ounces) button mushrooms, sliced thinly

1 tablespoon plain (all-purpose) flour

¼ cup (60ml) dry white wine

¾ cup (180ml) chicken stock

¼ cup coarsely chopped fresh flat-leaf parsley

1 Preheat oven to 200°C/400°F.

2 Combine mustard, green onion, rosemary, half the garlic and half the oil in a small jug. Place veal on a wire rack over a large shallow flameproof baking dish; coat veal all over with mustard mixture. Roast, uncovered, 30 minutes or until browned all over and cooked as desired. Cover to keep warm.

3 Meanwhile, boil, steam or microwave kumara until tender; drain. Mash kumara in a large bowl with butter and half the cream until smooth.

4 Heat remaining oil in same flameproof dish; cook brown onion and remaining garlic, stirring, until onion softens. Add mushrooms; cook, stirring, 5 minutes or until just tender. Add flour; cook, stirring, until mixture thickens and bubbles. Gradually stir in wine and stock; stir until sauce boils and thickens. Add remaining cream and parsley; stir until heated through.

5 Serve veal with mushroom sauce and kumara mash.

nutritional count per serving   **not suitable to freeze**
28.6g total fat
12g saturated fat
2416kJ (578 cal)
22.4g carbohydrate
52.9g protein
5.9g fibre

VEAL SHIN ON MUSHROOM RAGU

prep + cook time 2 hours 30 minutes **serves** 4

40g (1½ ounces) butter

4 pieces veal osso buco (1kg)

2 cloves garlic, crushed

1 tablespoon fresh rosemary leaves

½ cup (125ml) port

1 cup (250ml) beef stock

MUSHROOM RAGU

40g (1½ ounces) butter

2 cloves garlic, crushed

1 large flat mushroom (100g), sliced thickly

200g (6½ ounces) swiss brown mushrooms, trimmed

200g (6½ ounces) shiitake mushrooms, sliced thickly

1 medium red capsicum (bell pepper) (200g),
   sliced thickly

1 medium green capsicum (bell pepper) (200g),
   sliced thickly

½ cup (125ml) beef stock

2 tablespoons port

1 Preheat oven to 160°C/350°F.

2 Melt butter in a medium flameproof baking dish; cook veal, uncovered, until browned both sides. Add garlic, rosemary, port and stock; cook, covered, in oven 2¼ hours.

3 Meanwhile, make mushroom ragu.

4 Serve veal on ragu.

MUSHROOM RAGU Heat butter in a large frying pan; cook garlic, mushrooms and capsicums, stirring, until vegetables are browned lightly and tender. Stir in stock and port; cook, covered, 30 minutes.

nutritional count per serving
17.9g total fat
11.1g saturated fat
1743kJ (417 cal)
9.4g carbohydrate
42.3g protein
4.5g fibre

serving suggestion
Serve with soft polenta
(see page 313).

not suitable to freeze

TRADITIONAL ROAST DINNER

prep + cook time 1 hour 40 minutes **serves** 6

2kg (4-pound) lamb leg

3 sprigs fresh rosemary, chopped coarsely

½ teaspoon sweet paprika

1kg (2 pounds) potatoes, chopped coarsely

500g (1-pound) piece pumpkin, chopped coarsely

3 small brown onions (240g), halved

2 tablespoons olive oil

2 tablespoons plain (all-purpose) flour

1 cup (250ml) chicken stock

¼ cup (60ml) dry red wine

CAULIFLOWER MORNAY

1 small cauliflower (1kg), cut into florets

50g (1½ ounces) butter

¼ cup (35g) plain (all-purpose) flour

2 cups (500ml) milk

¾ cup (90g) coarsely grated cheddar cheese

1 Preheat oven to 200°C/400°F.

2 Place lamb in a large oiled baking dish; using a sharp knife, score skin at 2cm (¾-inch) intervals, sprinkle with rosemary and paprika. Roast lamb, uncovered, 15 minutes.

3 Reduce oven to 180°C/350°F; roast lamb, uncovered, 45 minutes or until cooked as desired.

4 Meanwhile, place potato, pumpkin and onion, in single layer, in large shallow baking dish; drizzle with oil. Roast, uncovered, for the last 45 minutes of lamb cooking time.

5 Make cauliflower mornay.

6 Remove lamb and vegetables from oven; cover to keep warm. Strain pan juices from lamb into medium jug. Return ¼ cup of the pan juices to flameproof dish over medium heat, add flour; cook, stirring, about 5 minutes or until mixture bubbles and browns. Gradually add stock and wine; cook over high heat, stirring, until gravy boils and thickens.

7 Strain gravy; serve with sliced lamb, roasted vegetables and cauliflower mornay.

CAULIFLOWER MORNAY Boil, steam or microwave cauliflower until tender; drain. Melt butter in medium saucepan, add flour; cook, stirring, until mixture bubbles and thickens. Gradually add milk; cook, stirring, until mixture boils and thickens. Stir in half of the cheese. Preheat grill (broiler). Place cauliflower in 1.5-litre (6-cup) shallow flameproof dish; pour mornay sauce over cauliflower, sprinkle with remaining cheese. Place under preheated grill about 10 minutes or until browned lightly.

nutritional count per serving   **not suitable to freeze**
35.6g total fat
17g saturated fat
3244kJ (776 cal)
40.5g carbohydrate
71.9g protein
7g fibre

MOROCCAN-SPICED LAMB SHOULDER

prep + cook time 3 hours 30 minutes **serves** 4

2 teaspoons fennel seeds

1 teaspoon ground cinnamon

1 teaspoon ground ginger

1 teaspoon ground cumin

¼ teaspoon chilli powder

2 tablespoons olive oil

1.2kg (2½-pound) lamb shoulder, shank intact

2 cloves garlic, sliced thinly

6 baby brown onions (150g)

375g (12 ounces) baby carrots, trimmed

1 cup (250ml) water

1 Preheat oven to 180°C/350°F.

2 Dry-fry seeds and spices in a small frying pan until fragrant. Combine spice mixture with half the oil in a small bowl.

3 Using a sharp knife, score lamb at 2.5cm (1-inch) intervals; push garlic into cuts. Rub spice mixture all over lamb; season.

4 Heat remaining oil in a large flameproof dish; cook lamb, turning, until browned all over. Remove from dish.

5 Meanwhile, peel onions, leaving root ends intact. Add onions to dish; cook, stirring, until browned.

6 Add carrots and the water to dish, bring to the boil; place lamb on vegetables, cover loosely with foil. Roast 1½ hours.

7 Reduce oven to 160°C/325°F.

8 Remove foil from lamb; roast a further 1½ hours or until lamb is tender. Cover lamb; stand 10 minutes, then slice thinly. Strain pan juices into a small heatproof jug.

9 Serve lamb with onions, carrots and pan juices.

nutritional count per serving
21.9g total fat
7.3g saturated fat
1722kJ (412 cal)
6.5g carbohydrate
45.7g protein
3.1g fibre

serving suggestion
Serve with garlicky beans
with pine nuts (see page 466)
and roast baby potatoes.

not suitable to freeze

PISTACHIO, PANCETTA AND FIG-STUFFED LAMB

prep + cook time 3 hours **serves** 6

2 slices pancetta (30g), chopped finely

2 dried figs (30g), chopped finely

⅓ cup (45g) roasted unsalted shelled pistachios, chopped finely

⅓ cup (25g) panko (japanese breadcrumbs)

2 tablespoons olive oil

1.5kg (3-pound) boneless lamb forequarter

1 medium lemon (140g), halved

1 large red capsicum (bell pepper) (350g), chopped coarsely

1 large tomato (220g), chopped coaresly

400g (12½ ounces) canned crushed tomatoes

¼ cup loosely packed fresh oregano leaves

1 tablespoon olive oil, extra

1 teaspoon dried oregano

250g (8 ounces) haloumi cheese, sliced thickly

1 cup (280g) Greek-style yoghurt

½ cup finely chopped fresh mint

1 Preheat oven to 180°C/350°F.

2 Combine pancetta, figs, nuts, panko and oil in a small bowl; season.

3 Open lamb out, skin-side down, onto a board. Top with pancetta mixture. Roll lamb to enclose filling; tie with kitchen string at 2cm (¾-inch) intervals to secure.

4 Coarsely chop one lemon half. Combine chopped lemon with capsicum, fresh and canned tomatoes, and fresh oregano in a large casserole dish; season.

5 Add lamb to dish; rub with extra oil, sprinkle with dried oregano. Place cheese around lamb.

6 Cook lamb, covered, in oven, 1¾ hours. Uncover; cook a further 30 minutes or until lamb is cooked as desired.

7 Meanwhile, juice remaining lemon half; combine juice with yoghurt and mint in a small bowl.

8 Serve lamb with capsicum sauce, cheese and mint yoghurt.

nutritional count per serving
40.1g total fat
16.3g saturated fat
2939kJ (703 cal)
16.4g carbohydrate
66.7g protein
3.8g fibre

tip Panko is available from most supermarkets, where other packaged breadcrumbs are shelved.

not suitable to freeze

CIDER ROASTED PORK BELLY

prep + cook time 3 hours 45 minutes **serves** 4

1.5kg (3-pound) piece pork belly, rind on

2 tablespoons finely chopped fresh rosemary

1 tablespoon sea salt flakes

1⅓ cups (330ml) apple cider

4 medium parsnips (1kg), quartered

4 cloves garlic, peeled

1½ cups (375ml) salt-reduced chicken or
vegetable stock

2 medium green-skinned apples (300g),
unpeeled, quartered

800g (1½ pounds) canned brown lentils,
drained, rinsed

1 Preheat oven to 240°C/475°F.

2 Using a sharp knife, score pork rind in a criss-cross pattern. Place pork, rind-side up, in a large baking dish. Combine rosemary and salt in a small bowl; rub over pork. Roast pork, uncovered, 20 minutes or until the rind starts to blister and crackle.

3 Reduce oven to 160°C/325°F. Add cider to dish; roast, uncovered, 1¼ hours.

4 Add parsnips, garlic and stock to dish; roast a further 45 minutes.

5 Add apple and lentils to dish; roast 30 minutes or until apple is tender. Season to taste.

nutritional count per serving
57.8g total fat
19.5g saturated fat
4065kJ (972 cal)
46.1g carbohydrate
57.6g protein
10.3g fibre

serving suggestion
Serve with a green salad.

tip To get crispy crackling, the pork rind needs to be really dry: leave the pork rind uncovered in the fridge overnight; cover the pork flesh with plastic wrap to stop it drying out.

not suitable to freeze

SLOW-ROASTED HONEY AND SOY PORK NECK

prep + cook time 2 hours 35 minutes **serves** 4

1 tablespoon peanut oil

1kg (2-pound) piece pork neck

1 large brown onion (200g), sliced thinly

2 cloves garlic, sliced thinly

4cm (1½-inch) piece fresh ginger (20g), sliced thinly

1 cinnamon stick

2 whole star anise

½ cup (125ml) salt-reduced soy sauce

½ cup (125ml) chinese cooking wine (shao hsing)

¼ cup (90g) honey

1 cup (250ml) water

450g (14½ ounces) baby buk choy, trimmed, leaves separated

1 Preheat oven to 160°C/325°F.

2 Heat oil in a large flameproof baking dish; cook pork, turning occasionally, until browned. Remove from dish.

3 Cook onion, garlic and ginger in same dish until onion softens. Remove from heat. Stir in cinnamon, star anise, sauce, cooking wine, honey and the water.

4 Return pork to dish, turn to coat in spice mixture. Cover dish; cook in oven, 1 hour. Uncover; cook another 1 hour or until sauce thickens slightly. Remove pork from dish, cover; stand 10 minutes before slicing.

5 Add buk choy to dish; cook, stirring, 5 minutes or until just tender.

6 Serve pork with buk choy and sauce.

nutritional count per serving
30.6g total fat
9.8g saturated fat
2621kJ (627 cal)
5.9g carbohydrate
76.4g protein
2.5g fibre

serving suggestion
Serve with steamed rice.

to freeze Complete the recipe to the end of step 4. Pack into freezer-proof containers, leaving a 2.5cm (1 inch) space to allow for expansion. Seal, label and freeze for up to 3 months. Thaw overnight in the fridge. Reheat in the oven or a microwave on medium power (50%) until heated through, then continue from step 5.

ITALIAN BRAISED PORK

prep + cook time 3 hours 15 minutes **serves** 6

2 tablespoons olive oil

1.5kg (3 pounds) pork shoulder, rolled and tied

2 cloves garlic, crushed

1 medium brown onion (150g), chopped coarsely

½ small fennel bulb (100g), chopped coarsely

8 slices hot pancetta (120g), chopped coarsely

1 tablespoon tomato paste

½ cup (125ml) dry white wine

400g (12½ ounces) canned whole tomatoes

1 cup (250ml) chicken stock

1 cup (250ml) water

2 sprigs fresh rosemary

2 large fennel bulbs (1kg), halved, sliced thickly

SPICE RUB

1 teaspoon fennel seeds

2 teaspoons dried oregano

½ teaspoon cayenne pepper

1 tablespoon sea salt

1 tablespoon cracked black pepper

2 teaspoons olive oil

1   Preheat oven to 180°C/400°F.

2   Heat oil in a large flameproof baking dish; cook pork, over heat, until browned all over.

3   Meanwhile, make spice rub.

4   Remove pork from dish; discard all but 1 tablespoon of the oil in the dish. Cook garlic, onion, chopped fennel and pancetta in same dish, stirring, until onion softens. Add paste; cook, stirring, 2 minutes.

5   Rub pork with spice rub; return pork to dish with wine, tomatoes, stock, the water and rosemary; bring to the boil.

6   Cook pork, covered, in oven, for 1 hour. Add sliced fennel; cook, covered, another 1 hour. Remove pork from dish; discard rind. Cover to keep warm.

7   Cook braising liquid in dish over medium heat, uncovered, until thickened slightly. Return pork to dish; serve pork with sauce.

SPICE RUB Combine ingredients in a small bowl.

nutritional count per serving
32.8g total fat
10.7g saturated fat
2525kJ (604 cal)
7.5g carbohydrate
66.5g protein
4.6g fibre

serving suggestion
Serve with mashed potatoes
or soft polenta (see page 313).

not suitable to freeze

leg of lamb on lemon-scented potatoes

LEG OF LAMB ON LEMON-SCENTED POTATOES

prep + cook time 1 hour 40 minutes **serves** 6

4 slices pancetta (60g), chopped finely

2 cloves garlic, crushed

1 tablespoon finely chopped fresh rosemary

1 tablespoon finely grated lemon rind

1.2kg (2½-pound) easy-carve leg of lamb

6 medium potatoes (1.2kg), sliced thinly

¼ cup (60ml) lemon juice

1 cup (250ml) chicken stock

25g (¾ ounce) butter, chopped coarsely

1 medium lemon (140g), cut into wedges

1 Preheat oven to 220°C/425°F.

2 Combine pancetta, garlic, rosemary and rind in a small bowl.

3 Using a sharp knife, pierce lamb all over; press pancetta mixture into cuts.

4 Place potato in a large baking dish; drizzle with juice and stock, dot with butter. Season.

5 Place lamb on potatoes; roast 20 minutes. Reduce oven to 180°C/350°F; roast 1 hour or until lamb is cooked as desired. Cover lamb, stand 10 minutes.

6 Serve lamb with potatoes and lemon wedges.

nutritional count per serving　　**not suitable to freeze**
12.4g total fat
6.1g saturated fat
1547kJ (370 cal)
23.3g carbohydrate
39.3g protein
3.3g fibre

HERB AND OLIVE FISH FILLETS ON POTATO

prep + cook time 1 hour 35 minutes **serves** 4

750g (1½ pounds) desiree potatoes, sliced thinly

4 cloves garlic, crushed

¾ cup coarsely chopped fresh flat-leaf parsley

¼ cup (60ml) extra virgin olive oil

4 x 200g (6½-ounce) gemfish fillets

4 drained anchovy fillets, chopped finely

12 pitted black olives, halved

1 tablespoon chopped fresh basil

1 Preheat oven to 200°C/400°F.

2 Combine potatoes, garlic, ⅔ cup of the parsley and 2 tablespoons of the oil in a medium bowl. Layer potatoes in a baking dish.

3 Bake potatoes, uncovered, 50 minutes or until potato is almost tender. Place fish on potato; bake further 15 minutes.

4 Meanwhile, combine anchovies, olives, remaining parsley, basil and remaining oil in a small bowl.

5 Sprinkle anchovy mixture on fish; bake further 5 minutes or until fish is just cooked through. Serve with lemon wedges, if you like.

(photograph page 438)

nutritional count per serving　　**not suitable to freeze**
28.8g total fat
6.8g saturated fat
2220kJ (531 cal)
22.3g carbohydrate
44.3g protein
3.6g fibre

herb and olive fish fillets on potato (recipe page 437)

Seafood can be a great alternative to meat if you want a lighter option for special-occasion entertaining in winter. Serve with seasonal root vegetables that require a little slow cooking in the oven to maximise their flavour. Because seafood takes hardly any time to cook, it can simply be added to the vegetables during the last stages of cooking to ensure you have a complete meal that's ready at the same time.

TWICE-COOKED ASIAN PORK BELLY WITH STEAMED GINGER RICE

prep + cook time 3 hours 45 minutes (+ standing) **serves** 4

1kg (2-pound) pork belly, rind on

2 whole star anise

1 cinnamon stick

1 tablespoon olive oil

1 teaspoon five-spice powder

1 teaspoon coarse cooking salt (kosher salt)

¼ cup (60ml) japanese soy sauce

2 tablespoons lemon juice

2 teaspoons sesame oil

2 tablespoons fresh coriander (cilantro) leaves

2 tablespoons fresh mint leaves

STEAMED GINGER RICE

1 tablespoon olive oil

6 green onions (scallions), sliced thinly

2.5cm (1-inch) piece fresh ginger (15g), grated

1½ cups (300g) basmati rice

2 cups (500ml) chicken stock

2 tablespoons finely chopped fresh
   coriander (cilantro)

2 tablespoons finely chopped fresh mint

1   Using a sharp knife, score pork rind at 1cm (½-inch) intervals. Place pork in a large saucepan with star anise and cinnamon; cover with cold water. Bring to the boil, skimming scum from surface. Reduce heat; simmer gently, covered loosely, 1 hour.

2   Drain pork; place on an oven tray, top with baking paper and another tray. Weight with heavy cans; stand 2 hours or until pork is uniform in thickness.

3   Preheat oven to 220°C/425°F.

4   Combine olive oil, five-spice and salt in a small bowl; rub all over pork rind. Place pork on a wire rack over a large baking dish; pour enough water into dish to come 2cm (¾ inch) up sides of dish without touching pork. Roast pork, uncovered, 30 minutes.

5   Reduce oven to 125°C/250°F; roast pork further 2 hours or until tender and crackling is crisp.

6   Meanwhile, make steamed ginger rice.

7   Combine sauce, juice and sesame oil in a small bowl.

8   Cut pork into 12 pieces; serve with rice, drizzle with soy dressing and top with herbs.

STEAMED GINGER RICE Heat oil in a medium saucepan; cook onion, stirring, until softened. Add ginger and rice; stir to coat in oil. Add stock; bring to the boil. Reduce heat; simmer, covered, over low heat, 10 minutes. Remove from heat; stand, covered, 5 minutes. Fluff rice with fork; stir in herbs, season to taste.

nutritional count per serving
24.8g total fat
6.4g saturated fat
3005kJ (719 cal)
62.7g carbohydrate
60.1g protein
1.1g fibre

serving suggestion
Serve with steamed or stir-fried asian greens.

tips Pork can be poached and weighted a day in advance; keep covered in the fridge. If skin is not crisp, place under hot grill (broiler) for a few seconds.

not suitable to freeze

SLOW-ROASTED TURKEY WITH WILD RICE SEASONING

prep + cook time 5 hours 10 minutes (+ standing) **serves** 10

4kg (8-pound) whole turkey

90g (3 ounces) butter, melted

1 litre (4 cups) water

45g (1½ ounces) butter, extra

¼ cup (35g) plain (all-purpose) flour

⅓ cup (80ml) port

2 cups (500ml) chicken stock

WILD RICE SEASONING

45g (1½ ounces) butter

1 large brown onion (200g), chopped coarsely

2 cloves garlic, crushed

⅓ cup (60g) wild rice

½ cup (125ml) dry white wine

1 cup (250ml) water

⅔ cup (130g) basmati rice

2 cups (500ml) chicken stock

2 medium zucchini (240g), grated coarsely

2 teaspoons finely grated lemon rind

2 teaspoons lemon thyme leaves

1 cup (70g) stale breadcrumbs

1 Make wild rice seasoning.

2 Preheat oven to 150°C/300°F.

3 Discard neck from turkey. Rinse turkey under cold water, pat dry inside and out. Fill neck cavity with seasoning; secure skin over opening with toothpicks. Fill large cavity with seasoning; tie legs together with kitchen string, tuck wing tips under turkey. Place on an oiled wire rack in a flameproof baking dish.

4 Dip 50cm (20-inch) piece of muslin into the melted butter; place over turkey. Add the water to dish, cover with foil. Roast 4 hours.

5 Remove foil and muslin from turkey, brush with pan juices. Increase oven to 200°C/400°F; roast 30 minutes or until turkey is cooked. Remove from oven; cover, stand 20 minutes. Drain pan juices into a large jug; skim fat from top of juices, discard. You will need about 2 cups of pan juices.

6 Place same dish over medium heat on stove top; melt extra butter, add flour. Cook, stirring, until well browned. Gradually stir in port, reserved juices and stock; cook, stirring, until mixture boils and thickens. Strain into a large jug.

7 Serve turkey and seasoning with gravy.

WILD RICE SEASONING Heat butter in a large frying pan; cook onion and garlic, stirring, until onion is soft. Add wild rice; cook, stirring, 1 minute. Add wine; simmer, covered, 10 minutes or until almost all the liquid is absorbed. Add the water; simmer, covered, 10 minutes or until liquid is absorbed. Add basmati rice; cook, stirring, 1 minute. Add stock; simmer, covered, 10 minutes or until liquid is absorbed and rice is tender. Stir in zucchini, rind and thyme; cool. Add breadcrumbs; mix well.

not suitable to freeze

nutritional count per serving
44.4g total fat
19.6g saturated fat
2947kJ (705 cal)
25.2g carbohydrate
47.4g protein
1.7g fibre

serving suggestion
Serve with steamed green beans and baby carrots.

SLOW-COOKED DUCK WITH CABBAGE AND FENNEL

prep + cook time 2 hours 40 minutes **serves** 4

½ small red cabbage (600g), cut into four wedges

1 large leek (500g), chopped coarsely

4 baby fennel bulbs (520g), trimmed, halved lengthways

1 tablespoon fresh rosemary leaves

2 cloves garlic, sliced thinly

1 cup (250ml) chicken stock

⅓ cup (80ml) cider vinegar

2 tablespoons redcurrant jelly

4 duck marylands (1.2kg), trimmed

1 tablespoon coarse cooking salt (kosher salt)

1. Preheat oven to 160°C/325°F.
2. Combine cabbage, leek, fennel, rosemary, garlic, stock, vinegar and jelly in a medium deep baking dish. Rub duck skin with salt; place duck, skin-side up, on cabbage mixture.
3. Roast, uncovered, 2¼ hours or until duck meat is tender and skin is crisp.
4. Strain pan juices through a muslin-lined sieve into a medium saucepan; cover duck and cabbage mixture to keep warm. Skim fat from surface of pan juices; bring to the boil. Boil, uncovered, 5 minutes or until sauce thickens slightly.
5. Serve duck with cabbage mixture, drizzled with sauce.

nutritional count per serving
60.5g total fat
5.4g saturated fat
2096kJ (501 cal)
18.4g carbohydrates
60.6g protein
9.8g fibre

serving suggestion
Serve with roast potatoes (see page 172).

to freeze Complete the recipe to the end of step 3. Pack into freezer-proof containers, leaving a 2.5cm (1 inch) space to allow for expansion. Seal, label and freeze for up to 3 months. Thaw overnight in the fridge. Reheat in oven or microwave on medium power (50%) until heated through, then continue from step 4.

ROASTED CHICKEN WITH GREMOLATA

prep + cook time 1 hour 30 minutes **serves** 4

2kg (4-pound) whole chicken

¼ cup loosely packed fresh oregano leaves

1 tablespoon olive oil

6 medium roma (egg) tomatoes (450g), halved

GREMOLATA

1 clove garlic, crushed

1 tablespoon finely shredded lemon rind

½ cup coarsely chopped fresh flat-leaf parsley

1 Preheat oven to 220°C/425°F.

2 Wash chicken under cold water; pat dry inside and out with absorbent paper. Using kitchen scissors, cut along both sides of backbone; discard backbone. Place chicken on bench, breast-side up; press down on breastbone with heel of hand to flatten.

3 Place chicken in a large baking dish; rub chicken all over with combined oregano and oil, season. Roast, uncovered, 1 hour, or until chicken is cooked. Remove from dish, cover; stand while tomatoes cook.

4 Add tomatoes to dish, season; roast, uncovered, 15 minutes.

5 Meanwhile, make gremolata.

6 Top tomatoes with gremolata; serve with chicken.

GREMOLATA Combine ingredients in a small bowl.

nutritional count per serving
50.1g total fat
15.1g saturated fat
22904kJ (694 cal)
1.5g carbohydrate
59.3g protein
1.4g fibre

serving suggestion
Serve with a green salad.

tips Ask the butcher to butterfly the chicken for you. Use a zester to shred the lemon rind finely.

not suitable to freeze

SLOW-ROASTED DUCK WITH BALSAMIC GLAZED VEGETABLES

prep + cook time 1 hour 50 minutes **serves** 4

4 duck marylands (1.2kg), trimmed

2 teaspoons sea salt

2 medium potatoes (400g), chopped coarsely

2 medium carrots (240g), chopped coarsely

2 medium parsnips (460g), chopped coarsely

¼ cup (60ml) balsamic vinegar

20g (¾ ounce) butter, melted

½ cup firmly packed fresh flat-leaf parsley leaves

⅓ cup (55g) almond kernels

1 Preheat oven to 180°C/350°F.

2 Rub duck skin with sea salt.

3 Combine vegetables, vinegar and butter in a large shallow baking dish; arrange vegetables in a single layer. Place duck, skin-side up, on top of vegetables. Roast 1¼ hours.

4 Increase oven to 220°C/425°F; roast a further 15 minutes or until duck skin is crisp and vegetables are glazed. Remove duck from dish.

5 Add parsley and nuts to vegetables in baking dish; toss to combine. Serve vegetable mixture topped with duck.

nutritional count per serving   **not suitable to freeze**
66.3g total fat
19.5g saturated fat
3334kJ (797 cal)
24.5g carbohydrate
26.3g protein
7.2g fibre

CHICKEN STUFFED WITH RICOTTA, BASIL AND PROSCIUTTO

prep + cook time 2 hours 30 minutes **serves** 4

8 chicken thigh cutlets (1.3kg)

⅔ cup (130g) ricotta cheese

4 slices prosciutto (60g), halved lengthways

8 large fresh basil leaves

1 tablespoon olive oil

1 medium brown onion (150g), chopped finely

2 cloves garlic, chopped finely

1 medium carrot (120g), chopped finely

1 stick celery (150g), trimmed, chopped finely

2 tablespoons tomato paste

½ cup (125ml) dry white wine

8 small tomatoes (720g), peeled, chopped coarsely

425g (13½ ounces) canned diced tomatoes

½ cup (125ml) water

1 Preheat oven to 160°C/325°F.

2 Using a small sharp knife, cut a pocket through the thickest part of each cutlet over the bone. Push 1 tablespoon of the cheese, one slice of prosciutto and one basil leaf into each pocket; secure pocket closed with toothpick.

3 Heat oil in a large deep flameproof baking dish; cook chicken, in batches, until browned all over. Remove from dish.

4 Cook onion, garlic, carrot and celery in same dish, stirring, 5 minutes or until onion softens. Add paste; cook, stirring, 2 minutes. Add wine; bring to the boil. Reduce heat; simmer, uncovered, 1 minute. Add fresh and canned tomatoes, and the water; bring to the boil. Reduce heat; simmer, uncovered, 10 minutes.

5 Return chicken to dish; bake, covered, 1 hour. Remove lid; bake a further 20 minutes or until chicken is cooked through. Season to taste. Remove toothpicks before serving; top with extra basil leaves, if you like.

nutritional count per serving
46.8g total fat
15.5g saturated fat
2922kJ (699 cal)
11.2g carbohydrate
53.3g protein
5.5g fibre

to freeze Pack into freezer-proof containers, leaving a 2.5cm (1 inch) space to allow for expansion. Seal, label and freeze for up to 3 months. Thaw overnight in the fridge. Reheat in oven or microwave on medium power (50%) until heated through.

MOROCCAN CHICKEN WITH COUSCOUS STUFFING

prep + cook time 2 hours 30 minutes (+ standing) **serves** 4

1.6kg (3¼-pound) whole chicken

20g (¾ ounces) butter, melted

20 vine-ripened truss cherry tomatoes (400g)

1 tablespoon olive oil

COUSCOUS STUFFING

1 teaspoon olive oil

1 medium brown onion (150g), chopped finely

1½ cups (375ml) chicken stock

¼ cup (60ml) olive oil

1 tablespoon finely grated lemon rind

¼ cup (60ml) lemon juice

1 cup (200g) couscous

½ cup (70g) roasted slivered almonds

1 cup (140g) pitted dried dates, chopped finely

1 teaspoon ground cinnamon

1 teaspoon smoked paprika

1 egg, beaten lightly

1 Make couscous stuffing.

2 Preheat oven to 200°C/400°F.

3 Wash chicken under cold water; pat dry inside and out with absorbent paper. Fill large cavity loosely with couscous stuffing; tie legs together with kitchen string. Place chicken on an oiled wire rack over a large baking dish; half fill with water. Brush butter all over chicken; roast, uncovered, 15 minutes.

4 Reduce oven to 180°C/350°F; roast, uncovered, further 1½ hours or until cooked through. Remove chicken from rack; cover, stand 20 minutes.

5 Meanwhile, place tomatoes on oven tray; drizzle with oil. Roast, uncovered, 20 minutes or until softened and browned.

6 Serve chicken with tomatoes.

COUSCOUS STUFFING Heat oil in a small frying pan; cook onion, stirring, until soft. Combine stock, oil, rind and juice in a medium saucepan; bring to the boil. Remove from heat. Add couscous, cover; stand 5 minutes or until stock is absorbed, fluffing with fork occasionally. Stir in onion, nuts, dates, spices and egg.

nutritional count per serving   **not suitable to freeze**

67.5g total fat

16.7g saturated fat

4631kJ (1108 cal)

67.8g carbohydrate

54.9g protein

7.2g fibre

CONFIT OF SALMON WITH HERB SALAD

prep + cook time 4 hours **serves** 4

1 large red capsicum (bell pepper) (350g)

2 baby fennel bulbs (260g), trimmed, halved, cored

2 small leeks (400g), white part only, halved lengthways

2 cloves garlic, bruised

1 fresh bay leaf

2 cups (500ml) light olive oil

1 cup (250ml) extra virgin olive oil

4 x 180g (5½-ounce) salmon fillets, skin on

¼ cup firmly packed fresh dill sprigs

¼ cup firmly packed fresh flat-leaf parsley leaves

¼ cup firmly packed fresh coriander (cilantro) leaves

¼ cup firmly packed fresh basil leaves

1 tablespoon lemon juice

1 tablespoon extra virgin olive oil, extra

DILL MAYONNAISE

2 egg yolks

2 tablespoons lemon juice

1 teaspoon dijon mustard

¾ cup (180ml) light olive oil

2 tablespoons finely chopped fresh dill

1 Preheat oven to 200°C/400°F.

2 Roast capsicum, uncovered, 30 minutes or until skin blisters and blackens. Cover with paper or plastic; stand 5 minutes, peel away skin. Discard seeds and membrane; slice capsicum thinly.

3 Reduce oven to 125°C/250°F.

4 Place fennel and leek, cut-side down, in a single layer, in a large baking dish. Add garlic, bay leaf and combined oils. Cover with baking paper; bake 1 hour or until vegetables are tender. Remove vegetables from dish; drain on absorbent paper.

5 Reduce oven to 50°C/100°F.

6 Place salmon, skin-side down, in oil in dish; cover with baking paper. Bake 2½ hours or until salmon is heated through, but still looks glassy. Remove salmon; drain on absorbent paper.

7 Meanwhile, make dill mayonnaise.

8 Combine herbs, juice and extra oil in a medium bowl; season to taste.

9 Serve salmon topped with dill mayonnaise and herb salad, and with vegetables.

DILL MAYONNAISE Blend or process egg yolks, juice and mustard until smooth. With motor operating, gradually add oil in a thin, steady stream until thick. Stir in dill; season to taste. Add a little boiling water if mayonnaise is too thick.

nutritional count per serving
70.1g total fat
11.6g saturated fat
3465kJ (829 cal)
7.2g carbohydrate
40g protein
4.8g fibre

serving suggestion
Serve with steamed baby potatoes.

tips Confit is a cooking term for foods that are preserved either by being salted and cooked slowly in their fat, or are cooked and preserved in oil in a similar method.

You can use ocean trout instead of the salmon. Mayonnaise can be made a day ahead; cover, refrigerate.

not suitable to freeze

RICOTTA AND CAPSICUM BAKE

prep + cook time 2 hours (+ standing) **serves** 6

1kg (2 pounds) firm ricotta cheese

2 cups (160g) finely grated parmesan cheese

2 eggs

2 egg yolks

1 clove garlic, crushed

200g (6½ ounces) drained roasted red capsicum
  (bell pepper), sliced thickly

40g (1½ ounces) baby spinach leaves

¾ cup loosely packed fresh basil leaves

1 tablespoon olive oil

¼ cup (65g) basil pesto

2 tablespoons water

1 Preheat oven to 160°C/325°F. Oil a 22cm (9-inch) round springform pan; line base and side with baking paper.

2 Combine cheeses, eggs, egg yolks and garlic in a medium bowl; season. Spread half the cheese mixture over base of pan; top with capsicum, spinach and ½ cup of the basil leaves. Spread the remaining cheese mixture over basil; drizzle with oil.

3 Bake, uncovered, 1½ hours or until browned lightly. Stand 30 minutes.

4 Meanwhile, combine pesto and the water in a small bowl.

5 Serve ricotta bake drizzled with pesto and topped with remaining basil leaves.

nutritional count per serving
38.1g total fat
19.9g saturated fat
2040kJ (488 cal)
3.8g carbohydrate
32.7g protein
1.1g fibre

serving suggestion
Serve with a green salad.

tip This is delicious served warm or cold, making it perfect for picnics or to take to work the next day.

not suitable to freeze

ROASTED SALMON WITH MANGO AND LIME MAYONNAISE

prep + cook time 1 hour 40 minutes **serves** 8

3kg (6-pound) whole salmon

1 medium lime, sliced thinly

3 sprigs fresh dill

cooking-oil spray

¼ cup (60ml) olive oil

2 tablespoons drained capers

MANGO AND LIME MAYONNAISE

2 egg yolks

½ teaspoon dry mustard

½ cup (125ml) light olive oil

¼ cup (60ml) olive oil

2 tablespoons lime juice

1 teaspoon finely grated lime rind

1 medium mango (430g), peeled, quartered

1 Preheat oven to 180°C/350°F.

2 Wash fish, pat dry inside and out with absorbent paper; place lime and dill inside cavity. Place two large pieces of foil, overlapping slightly, on an oven tray; coat with cooking oil-spray. Place fish on foil, fold foil over to completely enclose fish. Roast 1 hour or until cooked as desired.

3 Meanwhile, heat oil in a small frying pan; cook capers, stirring, until crisp. Drain on absorbent paper.

4 Make mango and lime mayonnaise.

5 Starting behind the gills of the salmon, peel away then discard skin; scrape away any dark flesh. Flake salmon coarsely; sprinkle with capers.

6 Serve salmon warm or cold with mayonnaise.

MANGO AND LIME MAYONNAISE Blend or process egg yolks and mustard until smooth. With motor operating, gradually add combined oils in a thin stream until mixture is thick. Add remaining ingredients; blend until smooth.

nutritional count per serving
43.7g total fat
7.6g saturated fat
2391kJ (572 cal)
5.3g carbohydrate
40g protein
0.8g fibre

tip Salmon is best served rare in the centre so it remains moist.

not suitable to freeze

CREAM OF ROASTED FENNEL SOUP WITH CAPSICUM AÏOLI

prep + cook time 1 hour 20 minutes (+ cooling) **serves** 4

2 medium fennel bulbs (600g)

1 large brown onion (200g), chopped coarsely

4 cloves garlic, unpeeled, bruised

2 teaspoons dried fennel seeds

1 tablespoon olive oil

2 cups (500ml) vegetable stock

1 cup (250ml) milk

1 cup (250ml) water

2 teaspoons lemon juice

CAPSICUM AÏOLI

1 medium red capsicum (bell pepper) (200g)

2 cloves garlic

1 egg yolk

1 tablespoon lemon juice

½ teaspoon dijon mustard

⅓ cup (80ml) olive oil

1 Preheat oven to 200°C/400°F.

2 Trim fennel; reserve four frond tips. Chop fennel coarsely; combine with onion, garlic, seeds and oil in a shallow medium baking dish. Roast, uncovered, 30 minutes; cover, roast 20 minutes or until tender.

3 When cool enough to handle, squeeze garlic into a large saucepan; discard skins. Add roasted fennel mixture to pan with stock, milk and the water; bring to the boil. Reduce heat; simmer, uncovered, 10 minutes. Cool 15 minutes.

4 Meanwhile, make capsicum aïoli.

5 Blend or process soup, in batches, until smooth. Return soup to same cleaned pan, add juice; stir over medium heat until hot.

6 Serve bowls of soup with aïoli and reserved fronds.

CAPSICUM AÏOLI Quarter capsicum; discard seeds and membrane. Roast under grill (broiler) or in hot oven, skin-side up, until skin blisters and blackens. Cover capsicum in plastic or paper for 5 minutes; peel away skin then chop capsicum coarsely. Blend or process garlic, yolk, juice and mustard until mixture is smooth. With motor operating, add oil in a thin, steady stream; process until aïoli thickens. Add capsicum; process until smooth.

nutritional count per serving
27g total fat
5.3g saturated fat
1367kJ (327 cal)
13g carbohydrate
5.6g protein
6g fibre

tips Making your own vegetable stock will enhance the flavour of this dish – see page 471 for the recipe. Capsicum aïoli can be made a day ahead; cover, refrigerate until required.

not suitable to freeze

QUINCE SPONGE PUDDING

prep + cook time 2 hours 30 minutes **serves** 8

4 medium quinces (1.25kg)

1½ cups (330g) caster (superfine) sugar

3 cups (750ml) water

4 whole cloves

1 cinnamon stick

2 whole star anise

2 tablespoons icing (confectioners') sugar

¼ teaspoon ground cinnamon

SPONGE TOPPING

3 eggs

½ cup (110g) caster (superfine) sugar

¼ cup (35g) plain (all-purpose) flour

¼ cup (35g) self-raising flour

¼ cup (35g) cornflour (cornstarch)

1 Preheat oven to 200°C/400°F.

2 Peel, core and slice quinces; place in a shallow 2.5-litre (10-cup) ovenproof dish.

3 Stir sugar, the water, cloves, cinnamon and star anise in a medium saucepan over heat, without boiling, until sugar is dissolved. Reduce heat; simmer, uncovered, without stirring, 2 minutes. Pour syrup over quince.

4 Bake quince, covered, 2 hours or until quince is tender and pink. Carefully drain away 2 cups of the hot liquid from quince.

5 Make sponge topping; spread over hot quince.

6 Bake pudding 30 minutes or until browned. Serve dusted with sifted icing sugar and cinnamon.

SPONGE TOPPING Beat eggs in a small bowl with an electric mixer until thick and creamy. Gradually add sugar, beating until dissolved after each addition. Fold in sifted flours.

nutritional count per serving
2.3g total fat
0.6g saturated fat
1514kJ (362 cal)
79.6g carbohydrate
4g protein
8.5g fibre

serving suggestion
Serve with vanilla ice-cream or cream.

not suitable to freeze

CHOCOLATE CINNAMON CAKE WITH CHERRY AND RED WINE SYRUP

prep + cook time 1 hour 30 minutes **serves** 8

125g (4 ounces) butter, softened

1 cup (220g) firmly packed light brown sugar

3 eggs

100g (3 ounces) dark (semi-sweet) chocolate, chopped coarsely

½ cup (75g) plain (all-purpose) flour

¼ cup (35g) self-raising flour

¼ cup (25g) cocoa powder

1½ teaspoons ground cinnamon

½ cup (60g) ground almonds

⅓ cup (80g) sour cream

CHERRY AND RED WINE SYRUP

415g (13 ounces) canned seedless black cherries in syrup

½ cup (125ml) dry red wine

¼ cup (55g) caster (superfine) sugar

1 cinnamon stick

1 Preheat oven to 180°C/350°F. Grease a 21cm (8-inch) baba pan with some butter.

2 Beat butter and sugar in a small bowl with an electric mixer until light and fluffy. Beat in eggs, one at a time. Transfer mixture to a large bowl.

3 Melt chocolate in a small heatproof bowl over a small saucepan of simmering water; cool slightly.

4 Stir sifted flours, cocoa and cinnamon, ground almonds, sour cream and chocolate into egg mixture. Spoon mixture into pan.

5 Bake cake 50 minutes. Stand in pan 5 minutes before turning onto a wire rack over a tray.

6 Meanwhile, make cherry and red wine syrup.

7 Pour hot syrup over hot cake. Serve cake warm or cold with cream or ice-cream.

CHERRY AND RED WINE SYRUP Strain syrup from cherries into a small saucepan; reserve cherries. Add wine, sugar and cinnamon to pan; stir over high heat, without boiling, until sugar dissolves. Bring to the boil; reduce heat, simmer, uncovered, without stirring, 10 minutes or until syrup has thickened slightly. Remove cinnamon stick; stir in reserved cherries.

nutritional count per serving
27.4g total fat;
14.4g saturated fat
2125kJ (507 cal);
56.7g carbohydrate;
7.8g protein;
2.2g fibre

tip This cake will keep in an airtight container at room temperature for 2 days, in the fridge for 1 week, or in the freezer for 2 months.

ACCOMPANIMENTS

vegetables

STEAMED GAI LAN IN OYSTER SAUCE

prep + cook time 25 minutes **serves** 6

Boil, steam or microwave 1kg (2 pounds) gai lan until just tender; drain. Heat 1 tablespoon peanut oil in a wok; stir-fry gai lan, 1 tablespoon japanese soy sauce and 2 tablespoons oyster sauce, 2 minutes or until gai lan is tender. Season to taste.

nutritional count per serving 3.4g total fat (0.6g saturated fat); 226kJ (54 cal); 2.6g carbohydrate; 2.1g protein; 2.2g fibre

GARLICKY BEANS WITH PINE NUTS

prep + cook time 45 minutes **serves** 4

Boil, steam or microwave 400g (12½ ounces) trimmed baby beans until just tender; drain. Add beans to a large bowl of iced water; drain well. Place in a large bowl. Heat ¼ cup olive oil and 1 clove thinly sliced garlic in a small frying pan over low heat until garlic just changes colour. Add 2 tablespoons roasted chopped pine nuts; stir until heated through. Drizzle garlic mixture over beans. Season to taste.

nutritional count per serving 18.9g total fat (2.2g saturated fat); 828kJ (198 cal); 2.8g carbohydrate; 3.2g protein; 3.2g fibre

CREAMED SPINACH

prep + cook time 15 minutes serves 4

Melt 20g (¾ ounce) butter in a large frying pan; cook 600g (1¼ pounds) spinach, stirring, until wilted. Add ½ cup pouring cream; bring to the boil. Reduce heat; simmer, uncovered, until liquid reduces by half. Blend or process mixture until smooth; season to taste.

nutritional count per serving 38.7g total fat (25.4g saturated fat); 1555kJ (372 cal); 2.8g carbohydrate; 3.5g protein; 2.1g fibre

TOMATO BRAISED BEANS

prep + cook time 35 minutes serves 6

Heat 1 tablespoon olive oil in a large saucepan; cook 1 coarsely chopped medium brown onion and 2 crushed garlic cloves, stirring, until onion softens. Add 1kg (2 pounds) trimmed green beans and 4 coarsely chopped medium tomatoes; cook, covered, stirring occasionally, 20 minutes or until vegetables soften slightly. Season to taste.

nutritional count per serving 3.5g total fat (0.4g saturated fat); 397kJ (95 cal); 7.4g carbohydrate; 5.1g protein; 6.2g fibre

ORANGE AND MAPLE GLAZED BABY CARROTS

prep + cook time 25 minutes **serves** 4

Melt 30g (1 ounce) butter in a large frying pan; cook 800g (1½ pounds) trimmed peeled baby carrots, turning occasionally, until almost tender. Add 2 teaspoons orange rind, ¼ cup orange juice and 2 tablespoons dry white wine and 2 tablespoons maple syrup; bring to the boil. Reduce heat; simmer, uncovered, until liquid has almost evaporated and carrots are tender and caramelised. Serve carrots toppd with ½ cup coarsely chopped roasted hazelnuts.

nutritional count per serving 17.2g total fat (4.5g saturated fat); 1145kJ (274 cal); 20.8g carbohydrate; 4.1g protein; 7.7g fibre

ROASTED CARAMELISED PARSNIPS

prep + cook time 1 hour 10 minutes **serves** 4

Preheat oven to 220°C/425°F. Halve 1kg (2 pounds) parsnips lengthways. Combine parsnips in a large baking dish with 2 tablespoons olive oil, ¼ cup firmly packed light brown sugar and 1 teaspoon ground nutmeg; season. Roast 1 hour or until parsnips are browned and tender. Serve parsnips topped with 1 tablespoon finely chopped fresh flat-leaf parsley.

nutritional count per serving 9.6g total fat (1.3g saturated fat); 1074kJ (257 cal); 35.8g carbohydrate; 4.1g protein; 5.7g fibre

BROCCOLINI AND BEANS WITH GARLIC AND ANCHOVIES

prep + cook time 20 minutes **serves** 8

Boil, steam or microwave 350g (11 ounces) trimmed broccolini and 350g (11 ounces) trimmed baby green beans, separately, until just tender; drain. Heat 2 tablespoons olive oil in a large frying pan; cook 2 cloves finely chopped garlic and 6 finely chopped drained anchovies until garlic softens. Add beans and broccolini; toss gently to combine.

nutritional count per serving 4.9g total fat (0.7g saturated fat); 280kJ (67 cal); 1.3g carbohydrate; 3.2g protein; 2.5g fibre

FRESH PEAS WITH CARAWAY AND PARMESAN

prep + cook time 40 minutes **serves** 6

Melt 60g (2 ounces) butter in a large frying pan; cook 1 teaspoon caraway seeds, 2 teaspoons finely grated lemon rind and 1 thinly sliced small red onion, stirring, until onion softens. Add 4 cups shelled fresh peas; cook, stirring, until peas are just tender. Stir in ⅓ cup coarsely chopped fresh flat-leaf parsley; top with ½ cup finely grated parmesan cheese.

nutritional count per serving 8.1g total fat (5.1g saturated fat); 598kJ (143 cal); 8.5g carbohydrate; 6.8g protein; 4.8g fibre
tip You need about 1.3kg (2¾ pounds) fresh peas to get the amount of podded peas required for this recipe.

STOCKS

BEEF

prep + cooking time 5 hours 10 minutes
(+ cooling & refrigeration) makes 3.5 litres (14 cups)

2kg (4 pounds) meaty beef bones

2 medium brown onions (300g), chopped coarsely

2 medium carrots (240g), chopped coarsely

2 stalks celery (300g), trimmed, chopped coarsely

5.5 litres (22 cups) water

3 bay leaves

2 teaspoons black peppercorns

3 litres (12 cups) water, extra

1 Preheat oven to 200°C/400°F.

2 Roast bones on an oven tray, uncovered, 1 hour
   or until browned.

3 Place bones in a large saucepan or boiler with
   onion, carrot, celery, the water, bay leaves and
   peppercorns; bring to the boil. Reduce heat; simmer,
   uncovered, 3 hours, skimming surface occasionally.
   Add the extra water; simmer, uncovered, 1 hour.

4 Strain stock through a muslin-lined sieve or
   colander into a large heatproof bowl; discard
   solids. Allow stock to cool. Cover; refrigerate until
   cold. Skim and discard surface fat before using.

nutritional count per 1 cup (250ml) 2g total fat
(0.9g saturated fat); 259kJ (62 cal); 2.3g carbohydrate;
8g protein; 1.1g fibre

CHICKEN

prep + cook time 2 hours 10 minutes
(+ cooling & refrigeration) makes 3.5 litres (14 cups)

2kg (4 pounds) chicken bones

2 medium onions (300g), chopped coarsely

2 medium carrots (240g), chopped coarsely

2 stalks celery (300g), trimmed, chopped coarsely

5 litres (20 cups) water

3 bay leaves

2 teaspoons black peppercorns

1 Place ingredients in a large saucepan or boiler;
   simmer, uncovered, 2 hours, skimming surface
   occasionally.

2 Strain stock through a muslin-lined sieve or
   colander into a large heatproof bowl; discard
   solids. Allow stock to cool. Cover; refrigerate until
   cold. Skim and discard surface fat before using.

nutritional count per 1 cup (250ml) 0.6g total fat
(0.2g saturated fat); 105kJ (25 cal); 2.3g carbohydrate;
1.9g protein; 1.1g fibre

VEGETABLE

prep + cooking time 1 hour 40 minutes
(+ cooling & refrigeration) makes 3.5 litres (14 cups)

4 medium onions (600g), chopped coarsely

2 large carrots (360g), chopped coarsely

10 stalks celery (1.5kg), trimmed, chopped coarsely

2 large parsnips (700g), chopped coarsely

6 litres (24 cups) water

4 bay leaves

2 teaspoons black peppercorns

1 Place ingredients in a large saucepan; simmer, uncovered, 1½ hours.

2 Strain stock through a muslin-lined sieve or colander into a large heatproof bowl; discard solids. Allow stock to cool. Cover; refrigerate until cold. Skim and discard surface fat before using.

nutritional count per 1 cup (250ml) 0.2g total fat (0g saturated fat); 151kJ (36 cal); 5.7g carbohydrate; 1.4g protein; 2.9g fibre

FISH

prep + cook time 25 minutes (+ cooling & refrigeration)
makes 2.5 litres (10 cups)

1.5kg (3 pounds) fish bones

3 litres (12 cups) water

1 medium onion (150g), chopped coarsely

2 stalks celery (300g), trimmed, chopped coarsely

2 bay leaves

1 teaspoon black peppercorns

1 Place ingredients in a large saucepan; simmer, uncovered, 20 minutes.

2 Strain stock through a muslin-lined sieve or colander into a large heatproof bowl; discard solids. Allow stock to cool. Cover; refrigerate until cold. Skim and discard surface fat before using.

nutritional count per 1 cup (250ml) 0.2g total fat (0.1g saturated fat); 63kJ (15 cal); 1.1g carbohydrate; 1.9g protein; 0.6g fibre

GLOSSARY

ALLSPICE also known as pimento or jamaican pepper; so-named because it tastes like a combination of nutmeg, cumin, clove and cinnamon. Available whole (a dark-brown berry the size of a pea) or ground.

ALMONDS flat, pointy-tipped nuts with a pitted brown shell enclosing a creamy white kernel which is covered by a brown skin.
blanched brown skins removed.
flaked paper-thin slices.
ground also called almond meal; nuts are powdered to a coarse flour-like texture.
silvered small pieces cut lengthways.

ARTICHOKES
globe large flower-bud member of the thistle family; it has tough petal-like leaves, and is edible in part when cooked.
hearts tender centre of the globe artichoke; can be harvested from the plant after the prickly choke is removed. Cooked hearts can be bought from delicatessens or canned in brine.
jerusalem neither from Jerusalem nor an artichoke, this crunchy brown-skinned tuber tastes a bit like a water chestnut and belongs to the sunflower family. Eat raw in salads or cooked like potatoes.

BACON also known as bacon slices.

BAKE BLIND a cooking term to describe baking a pie shell or pastry case before the filling is added. If a filling does not need to be baked or is very wet, you may need to "blind-bake" the unfilled shell. To bake blind, ease the pastry into a pan or dish, place on an oven tray; line the pastry with baking paper then fill with dried beans, uncooked rice or "baking beans" (also called pie weights). Bake according to the recipe's directions then cool before adding the suggested filling.

BAKING PAPER also called parchment paper or baking parchment – is a silicone-coated paper that is primarily used for lining baking pans and oven trays so cakes and biscuits won't stick, making removal easy.

BAKING POWDER a raising agent consisting mainly of two parts cream of tartar to one part bicarbonate of soda (baking soda).

BARLEY a nutritious grain used in soups and stews. Hulled barley, the least processed, is high in fibre. Pearl barley has had the husk removed then been steamed and polished so that only the "pearl" of the original grain remains, much the same as white rice.

BASIL
holy also called kra pao or hot basil; different from thai and sweet basil, having an almost hot, spicy flavour similar to clove. Used in many Thai dishes, especially curries; distinguished from thai basil by tiny "hairs" on its leaves and stems.
sweet the most common type of basil; used extensively in Italian dishes and one of the main ingredients in pesto.
thai also called horapa; different from holy basil and sweet basil in both look and taste, having smaller leaves and purplish stems. It has a slight aniseed taste and is one of the identifying flavours of Thai food.

BAY LEAVES aromatic leaves from the bay tree available fresh or dried; adds a strong, slightly peppery flavour.

BEANS
black-eyed also called black-eyed peas or cow peas. Mild-flavoured and thin-skinned, so they cook faster than most other beans. Often served in the American south with pork and cornbread.
black turtle also known as black or black kidney beans; an earthy-flavoured dried bean completely different from the better-known chinese black beans (which are fermented soya beans).
borlotti also called roman beans or pink beans, can be eaten fresh or dried. Interchangeable with pinto beans due to their similarity in appearance – pale pink or beige with dark red streaks.
broad (fava) also called windsor and horse beans; available dried, fresh,

canned and frozen. Fresh should be peeled twice (discarding both the outer long green pod and the beige-green tough inner shell); the frozen beans have had their pods removed but the beige shell still needs removal.
butter cans labelled butter beans are, in fact, cannellini beans. Confusingly butter is also another name for lima beans, sold both dried and canned; a large beige bean having a mealy texture and mild taste.
cannellini small white bean similar in appearance and flavour to haricot, great northern and navy beans, all of which can be substituted for the other.
green also known as french or string beans (although the tough string they once had has generally been bred out of them), this long thin fresh bean is consumed in its entirety once cooked.
haricot the haricot bean family includes navy beans and cannellini. All are mild-flavoured white beans which can be interchangeable.
kidney medium-sized red bean, slightly floury in texture, yet sweet in flavour.
lima large, flat kidney-shaped, beige dried and canned beans. Also known as butter beans.
snake long (about 40cm/16 inches), thin, round, fresh green bean; Asian in origin with a taste similar to green beans. Are also known as yard-long beans because of their (pre-metric) length.
soy the most nutritious of all legumes; high in protein and low in carbohydrate and the source of products such as tofu, soy milk, soy sauce, tamari and miso. Also available dried and canned.
white a generic term we use for canned or dried cannellini, haricot, navy or great northern beans belonging to the same family, *phaseolus vulgaris*.

BEEF
blade from the shoulder; isn't as tender as other cuts, so it needs slow-roasting.
brisket a cheaper cut from the belly; available with or without bones as a joint for slow-roasting, or for stewing and casseroling as cubes or mince.

cheeks the cheek muscle. A very tough and lean cut of meat; often used for braising or slow cooking to produce a tender result.

chuck from the neck and shoulder of the beef; tends to be chewy but flavourful and inexpensive. A good cut for stewing or braising.

corned silverside also known as topside roast; sold vacuum-sealed in brine.

gravy beef also known as beef shin or shank, cut from the lower shin.

osso buco literally meaning 'bone with a hole', osso buco is cut from the shin of the hind leg. It is also known as knuckle.

oxtail a flavourful cut originally from the ox but today more likely to be from any beef cattle; requires long, slow cooking so it is perfect for curries and stews.

sausages seasoned and spiced minced (ground) beef mixed with cereal and packed into casings. Also known as snags or bangers.

shank see gravy beef, above.

short ribs cut from the rib section; usually larger, more tender and meatier than pork spare ribs.

BEETROOT (BEETS) also known as red beets; firm, round root vegetable.

BICARBONATE OF SODA (BAKING SODA) a raising agent.

BRANDY a general term for a liqueur distilled from wine grapes (usually white), it is used as the basis for many sweet-to-dry spirits made with fruits. Cognac and Armagnac are two of the finest aged brandies available.

BREAD
brioche French in origin; a rich, yeast-leavened, cake-like bread made with butter and eggs. Available from cake or specialty bread shops.

ciabatta in Italian, the word means slipper, the traditional shape of this popular crisp-crusted, open-textured white sourdough bread.

french stick a long, narrow cylindrical loaf with a crisp brown crust and a light chewy interior. Also called french loaf.

naan the rather thick, leavened bread associated with the tandoori dishes of northern India, where it is baked pressed against the inside wall of a heated tandoor (clay oven). Sold in most supermarkets.

pitta also known as lebanese bread. This wheat-flour pocket bread is sold in large, flat pieces that separate into two thin rounds. Also available in small thick pieces called pocket pitta.

sourdough so-named, not because it's sour in taste, but because it's made by using a small amount of 'starter dough', which contains a yeast culture, mixed into flour and water. Part of the resulting dough is then saved to use as the starter dough next time.

tortilla thin, round unleavened bread; can be made at home or purchased frozen, fresh or vacuum-packed. Two kinds are available, one made from wheat flour and the other from corn.

turkish also called pide. Sold in long (about 45cm/18 inches) flat loaves and individual rounds; made from wheat flour and sprinkled with black onion seeds.

BREADCRUMBS
fresh bread, usually white, processed into crumbs.

packaged prepared fine-textured but crunchy white breadcrumbs; good for coating foods that are to be fried.

panko (japanese breadcrumbs) are available in two kinds: larger pieces and fine crumbs; have a lighter texture than Western-style ones. Available from Asian food stores and most supermarkets.

stale crumbs made by grating, blending or processing 1- or 2-day-old bread.

BROCCOLINI a cross between broccoli and chinese kale; long asparagus-like stems with a long loose floret, both completely edible. Resembles broccoli but is milder and sweeter in taste.

BRUISE a cooking term to describe the slight crushing given to aromatic ingredients, such as lemon grass and cardamom pods, with the flat side of a heavy knife to release flavour and aroma.

BUK CHOY also called bok choy, pak choi, chinese white cabbage or chinese chard; has a fresh, mild mustard taste.

BURGHUL also called bulgar wheat; hulled steamed wheat kernels that, once dried, are crushed into various sized grains. Used in Middle Eastern dishes such as felafel, kibbeh and tabbouleh. Is not the same as cracked wheat.

BUTTER we use salted butter unless stated otherwise; 125g is equal to 1 stick (4 ounces). Unsalted or "sweet" butter has no salt added and is perhaps the most popular butter among pastry-chefs.

BUTTERMILK originally the term given to the slightly sour liquid left after butter was churned from cream, today it is made from no-fat or low-fat milk to which specific bacterial cultures have neen added. Despite its name, it is actually low in fat.

CAPERBERRIES olive-sized fruit formed after the buds of the caper bush have flowered; are usually sold pickled in a vinegar brine with stalks intact.

CAPERS grey-green buds of a warm climate (usually Mediterranean) shrub, sold either dried and salted or pickled in a vinegar brine. Capers must be rinsed well before using.

CAPSICUM (BELL PEPPER) also called pepper. Comes in many colours: red, green, yellow, orange and purplish-black. Be sure to discard seeds and membranes before use.

CARAWAY SEEDS the small, half-moon-shaped dried seed from a member of the parsley family; adds a sharp anise flavour when used in both sweet and savoury dishes. Used widely, in foods such as rye bread, harissa and the classic Hungarian fresh cheese, liptauer.

CARDAMOM a spice native to India and used extensively in its cuisine; can be purchased in pod, seed or ground form. Has a distinctive aromatic, sweetly rich flavour.

CASHEWS plump, kidney-shaped, golden-brown nuts having a distinctive sweet, buttery flavour and containing about 48% fat. Because of this high fat content, they should be kept, sealed tightly, in the fridge to avoid becoming rancid. We use roasted unsalted cashews unless stated otherwise; they are available from health-food stores and most major supermarkets. Roasting cashews brings out their intense nutty flavour. See roasting/toasting.

CAVOLO NERO, or tuscan cabbage, is a staple in Tuscan country cooking. It has long, narrow, wrinkled leaves and a rich and astringent, mild cabbage flavour. It doesn't lose its volume like silver beet or spinach when cooked, but it does need longer cooking.

CELERIAC (CELERY ROOT) tuberous root with knobbly brown skin, white flesh and a celery-like flavour. Keep peeled celeriac in acidulated water to stop it discolouring. It can be grated and eaten raw in salads; used in soups and stews; boiled and mashed like potatoes; or sliced thinly and deep-fried as chips.

CHAR SIU SAUCE a Chinese barbecue sauce made from sugar, water, salt, fermented soya bean paste, honey, soy sauce, malt syrup and spices. Found at most supermarkets.

CHEESE
bocconcini from the diminutive of "boccone", meaning mouthful in Italian; walnut-sized, baby mozzarella, a delicate, semi-soft, white cheese traditionally made from buffalo milk. Sold fresh, it spoils rapidly so will only keep, refrigerated in brine, for 1 or 2 days at the most.
cheddar the most common cow's milk 'tasty' cheese; should be aged, hard and have a pronounced bite.
cottage fresh, white, unripened curd cheese with a grainy consistency and a fat content of 15% to 55%.
cream commonly called philadelphia or philly; a soft cow-milk cheese, its fat content ranges from 14% to 33%.

fetta Greek in origin; a crumbly textured goat- or sheep-milk cheese having a sharp, salty taste. Ripened and stored in salted whey; particularly good cubed and tossed into salads.
goat's made from goat's milk, has an earthy, strong taste. Available in soft, crumbly and firm textures, in various shapes and sizes, and sometimes rolled in ash or herbs.
gruyère a hard-rind Swiss cheese with small holes and a nutty, slightly salty flavour. A popular cheese for soufflés.
haloumi a Greek Cypriot cheese with a semi-firm, spongy texture and very salty sweet flavour. Ripened and stored in salted whey; best grilled or fried, it holds its shape well on being heated. Eat while still warm as it becomes tough and rubbery on cooling.
kefalotyri is a hard, salty cheese made from sheep and/or goat's milk. Its colour varies from white to yellow depending on the mixture of milk used in the process and its age. It is a great cheese for grating over pasta or salads, it can replace parmesan.
mascarpone an Italian fresh cultured-cream product made in much the same way as yoghurt. Whiteish to creamy yellow in colour, with a buttery-rich, luscious texture. Soft, creamy and spreadable, it is used in Italian desserts and as an accompaniment to fresh fruit.
mozzarella soft, spun-curd cheese; originating in southern Italy where it was traditionally made from water-buffalo milk. Now generally made from cow's milk, it is the most popular pizza cheese because of its low melting point and elasticity when heated.
parmesan also called parmigiano; is a hard, grainy cow-milk cheese originating in Italy. Reggiano is the best variety.
pecorino the Italian generic name for cheeses made from sheep's milk. This family of hard, white to pale-yellow cheeses, traditionally made in the Italian winter and spring when sheep graze on natural pastures, have been matured for 8 to 12 months. They are classified according to the area in which they were

produced – romano from Rome, sardo from Sardinia, siciliano from Sicily and toscano from Tuscany. If you can't find it, use parmesan.
ricotta a soft, sweet, moist, white cow-milk cheese with a low fat content and a slightly grainy texture. The name roughly translates as "cooked again" and refers to ricotta's manufacture from a whey that is itself a by-product of other cheese making.

CHERVIL also called cicily; mildly fennel-flavoured member of the parsley family with curly dark-green leaves. Available fresh and dried but, like all herbs, is best used fresh; like coriander and parsley, its delicate flavour diminishes the longer it's cooked.

CHICKEN
breast fillet breast halved, skinned and boned.
drumsticks leg with skin and bone intact.
maryland leg and thigh still connected in a single piece; bones and skin intact.
small chicken also known as spatchcock or poussin; no more than 6 weeks old, weighing a maximum of 500g (1 pound). Also a cooking term to describe splitting a small chicken open, flattening out then grilling.
thigh skin and bone intact.
thigh cutlets thigh with skin and centre bone intact; sometimes found skinned with bone intact.
thigh fillets the skin and bone removed.

CHILLI available in many types and sizes. Use rubber gloves when seeding and chopping fresh chillies as they can burn your skin. Removing membranes and seeds lessens the heat level.
ancho mild, dried chillies commonly used in Mexican cooking.
cayenne pepper dried, long, thin-fleshed, extremely hot, ground red chilli.
chipotle pronounced cheh-pote-lay. The name used for jalapeño chillies once they've been dried and smoked. With a deep, intensely smoky flavour, rather than a searing heat, chipotles are dark brown, almost black, and wrinkled in appearance.

flakes dried, deep-red, dehydrated chilli slices and whole seeds.

green any unripened chilli; also some particular varieties that are ripe when green, such as jalapeño, habanero, poblano or serrano.

jalapeño pronounced hah-lah-pain-yo. Fairly hot, medium-sized, plump, dark green chilli; available pickled, sold canned or bottled, and fresh, from greengrocers.

long red available both fresh and dried; a generic term used for any moderately hot, thin, long (6-8cm/2¼-3¼ inch) chilli.

powder can be used as a substitute for fresh chillies (½ teaspoon ground chilli powder to 1 chopped medium fresh chilli).

thai (serrano) also known as "scuds"; tiny, very hot and bright red in colour.

CHINESE COOKING WINE (SHAO HSING)
also called chinese rice wine; made from fermented rice, wheat, sugar and salt. Found in Asian food shops; if you can't find it, use mirin or sherry.

CHIVES
related to the onion and leek; has a subtle onion flavour. Used more for flavour than as an ingredient; chopped finely, they're good in sauces, dressings, omelettes or as a garnish.

garlic chives also known as chinese chives; are strongly flavoured, have flat leaves and are eaten as a vegetable, usually in stir-fries.

CHOCOLATE
choc bits also called chocolate chips or chocolate morsels; available in milk, white and dark chocolate. Made of cocoa liquor, cocoa butter, sugar and an emulsifier, these hold their shape in baking and are ideal for decorating.

couverture a term used to describe a fine quality, very rich chocolate high in both cocoa butter and cocoa liquor. This type of chocolate requires tempering when used to coat but not if used in baking, mousses or fillings.

dark (semi-sweet) also called luxury chocolate; made of a high percentage of cocoa liquor and cocoa butter, and little added sugar. Unless stated otherwise, we use dark chocolate in this book as it's ideal for use in desserts and cakes.

melts small discs of compounded milk, white or dark chocolate ideal for melting and moulding.

milk most popular eating chocolate, mild and very sweet; similar in make-up to dark with the difference being the addition of milk solids.

white contains no cocoa solids but derives its sweet flavour from cocoa butter. Very sensitive to heat.

CHORIZO SAUSAGES
a sausage of Spanish origin, made from coarsely minced (ground) smoked pork and highly seasoned with garlic, chilli powder and other spices.

CHOY SUM
also known as pakaukeo or flowering cabbage, a member of the buk choy family; easy to identify with its long stems, light green leaves and yellow flowers. Stems and leaves are both edible, steamed or stir-fried.

CINNAMON
available in pieces (called sticks or quills) and ground into powder; one of the world's most common spices, used as a sweet, fragrant flavouring for both sweet and savoury foods.

CLOVES
dried flower buds of a tropical tree; can be used whole or in ground form. They have a strong scent and taste so should be used sparingly.

COCOA POWDER
also unsweetened cocoa; cocoa beans (cacao seeds) that have been fermented, roasted, shelled, ground into powder then cleared of most of the fat content. Unsweetened cocoa is used in hot chocolate drink mixtures; milk powder and sugar are added to the ground product.

COCONUT
cream obtained commercially from the first pressing of the coconut flesh alone, without the addition of water; the second pressing (less rich) is sold as coconut milk. Available in cans and cartons at most supermarkets.

desiccated concentrated, dried, unsweetened and finely shredded coconut flesh.

flaked dried flaked coconut flesh.

milk not the liquid found inside the fruit (coconut water), but the diluted liquid from the second pressing of the white flesh of a mature coconut (the first pressing produces coconut cream). Available in cans and cartons at most supermarkets.

shredded unsweetened thin strips of dried coconut flesh.

CORIANDER (CILANTRO)
also called pak chee or chinese parsley; bright-green-leafed herb with a pungent flavour. The leaves, stems and roots of coriander are also used. Wash under cold water, removing any dirt clinging to the roots; scrape the roots with a small flat knife to remove some of the outer fibrous skin. Chop roots and stems together to obtain the amount specified. Also available ground or as seeds; these should not be substituted for fresh coriander as the tastes are completely different.

CORNFLOUR (CORNSTARCH)
available made from corn or wheat (wheaten cornflour, gluten-free, gives a lighter texture in cakes); used as a thickening agent in cooking.

COUSCOUS
a fine, dehydrated, grain-like cereal product made from semolina; it swells to three or four times its original size when liquid is added. It is eaten like rice with a tagine, as a side dish or salad ingredient.

CRANBERRIES
available dried and frozen; have a rich, astringent flavour and can be used in cooking sweet and savoury dishes. The dried version can usually be substituted for or with other dried fruit.

CREAM
pouring also known as pure or fresh cream. It has no additives and contains a minimum fat content of 35%.

sour a thick, commercially-cultured sour cream with a minimum fat content of 35%.

thick (double) a dolloping cream with a minimum fat content of 45%.

thickened (heavy) a whipping cream that contains a thickener. It has a minimum fat content of 35%.

CREAM OF TARTAR the acid ingredient in baking powder; added to confectionery mixtures to help prevent sugar from crystallising. Keeps frostings creamy and improves volume when beating egg whites.

CREME FRAICHE a mature, naturally fermented cream (minimum fat content 35%) having a velvety texture and slightly tangy, nutty flavour. Crème fraîche, a French variation of sour cream, can boil without curdling and be used in sweet and savoury dishes.

CUCUMBER, LEBANESE short, slender and thin-skinned cucumber. Probably the most popular variety because of its tender, edible skin, tiny, yielding seeds, and sweet, fresh and flavoursome taste.

CUMIN also known as zeera or comino; resembling caraway in size, cumin is the dried seed of a plant related to the parsley family. Its spicy, almost curry-like flavour is essential to the traditional foods of Mexico, India, North Africa and the Middle East. Available dried as seeds or ground.

CURRY LEAVES available fresh or dried and have a mild curry flavour; use like bay leaves.

CURRY PASTES some recipes in this book call for commercially prepared pastes of varying strengths and flavours. Use whichever one you feel best suits your spice-level tolerance.

green hottest of the traditional thai pastes; particularly good in chicken and vegetable curries, and a great addition to stir-fry and noodle dishes.

korma a mix of mostly heat-free spices; forms the base of a mild, slightly nutty-tasting, slow-cooked curry.

massaman rich, spicy flavour reminiscent of Middle Eastern cooking; favoured by southern Thai cooks for use in hot and sour stew-like curries and satay sauces.

panang based on the curries of Penang, an island off the north-west coast of Malaysia, close to the Thai border. A complex, sweet and milder variation of red curry paste; good with seafood and for adding to soups and salad dressings.

red a popular curry paste; a hot blend of red chilli, garlic, shallot, lemon grass, salt, galangal, shrimp paste, kaffir lime peel, coriander, cumin and paprika. It is milder than the hotter thai green curry paste.

rogan josh a medium-hot blend that is a specialty of Kashmir in northern India. It contains tomatoes, fenugreek, coriander, paprika and cumin.

tikka in Indian cooking, the word "masala" loosely translates as paste and the word "tikka" means a bite-sized piece of meat, poultry or fish, or sometimes a cutlet. Tikka paste is any maker's choice of spices and oils, mixed into a mild paste, frequently coloured red. Used for marinating or for brushing over meat, seafood or poultry, before or during cooking instead of as an ingredient.

vindaloo a Goan combination of vinegar, tomatoes, pepper and other spices that exemplifies the Portuguese influence on this part of India's coast.

yellow one of the mildest thai pastes; it is similar in appearance to Indian curries as they both include yellow chilli and fresh turmeric. Good blended with coconut in vegetable, rice and noodle dishes.

CURRY POWDER a blend of ground spices used for making Indian and some South-East Asian dishes. Consists of some of the following spices: dried chilli, cumin, cinnamon, coriander, fennel, mace, fenugreek, cardamom and turmeric. Available mild or hot.

CUSTARD POWDER instant mixture used to make pouring custard; similar to North American instant pudding mixes.

DATES fruit of the date palm tree, eaten fresh or dried. About 4-6cm (1½-2¼ inches) in length, oval and plump, thin-skinned, with a honey-sweet flavour and sticky texture.

DEGLAZE a cooking term to describe making the base for a sauce by heating a small amount of wine, stock or water in a pan in which meat or poultry has been cooked (with most of the excess fat removed) then stirring to loosen the browned bits of food adhering to the bottom. After "deglazing" a pan, it is used as part of the sauce accompanying the food cooked earlier in the pan.

DILL also called dill weed; used fresh or dried, in seed form or ground. Its anise/celery sweetness flavours the food of the Scandinavian countries, and Germany and Greece. Its feathery, frond-like fresh leaves are grassier and more subtle than the dried version or the seeds (which slightly resemble caraway in flavour). Use dill leaves with smoked salmon and sour cream, poached fish or roast chicken; use the seeds with simply cooked vegetables, or home-baked dark breads.

DRIED CURRANTS dried tiny, almost black raisins so named from the grape type native to Corinth, Greece; most often used in jams, jellies and sauces (the best-known of which is the English cumberland sauce). These are not the same as fresh currants, which are the fruit of a plant in the gooseberry family.

DUCK we use whole ducks in some recipes; available from specialty chicken shops, markets and some supermarkets.

breast fillets boneless whole breasts, with the skin on.

chinese barbecued traditionally, in China, cooked in special ovens; dipped into and brushed during roasting with a sticky sweet coating made from soy sauce, sherry, ginger, five-spice, star anise and hoisin sauce. Available from Asian food shops as well as dedicated Chinese barbecued meat shops.

maryland thigh and drumstick still connected, skin on.

DUKKAH an Egyptian specialty spice mixture made up of roasted nuts, seeds and an array of aromatic spices.

EGGPLANT also known as aubergine. Ranging in size from tiny to very large and in colour from pale green to deep purple. Can also be purchased char-grilled, packed in oil, in jars.
baby also known as finger or japanese eggplant; very small and slender.
thai also known as makeua prao, golf-ball sized eggplants available in different colours but most commonly green traced in off-white; crisper than the common purple variety, they have bitter seeds that must be removed before using.

EGGS we use large chicken eggs weighing an average of 60g (2 ounces). If a recipe calls for raw or barely cooked eggs, exercise caution if there is a salmonella problem in your area, particularly in food eaten by children and pregnant women.

EGGWASH beaten egg (white, yolk or both) and milk or water; often brushed over pastry or bread to impart colour or gloss.

FENNEL also called finocchio or anise; a crunchy green vegetable slightly resembling celery that's eaten raw in salads; fried as an accompaniment; or used as an ingredient in soups and sauces. Also the name given to the dried seeds of the plant which have a stronger licorice flavour.

FENUGREEK a member of the pea family, the seeds have a bitter taste; the ground seeds are used in Indian curries, powders and pastes.

FIGS are best eaten in peak season, at the height of summer. Vary in skin and flesh colour according to type not ripeness. When ripe, figs should be unblemished and bursting with flesh; nectar beads at the base indicate when a fig is at its best. Figs are also glacéd, dried or canned in sugar syrup; these

are usually sold at health-food stores, Middle Eastern food shops or specialty cheese counters.

FISH SAUCE called naam pla if Thai-made, nuoc naam if Vietnamese; the two are almost identical. Made from pulverised salted fermented fish (most often anchovies); has a pungent smell and strong taste. Available in varying degrees of intensity, so use according to your taste.

FIVE-SPICE POWDER (chinese five-spice) a fragrant mixture of ground cinnamon, cloves, star anise, sichuan pepper and fennel seeds.

FLOUR
plain (all-purpose) unbleached wheat flour, is the best for baking: the gluten content ensures a strong dough, for a light result.
rice very fine, almost powdery, gluten-free flour; made from ground white rice. Used in baking, as a thickener, and in some Asian noodles and desserts. Another variety, made from glutinous sweet rice, is used for chinese dumplings and rice paper.
self-raising all-purpose plain or wholemeal flour with baking powder and salt added; make at home in the proportion of 1 cup plain or wholemeal flour to 2 teaspoons baking powder.
wholemeal also known as wholewheat flour; milled with the wheat germ so is higher in fibre and more nutritional than plain flour.

GAI LAN also known as chinese broccoli, gai larn, kanah, gai lum and chinese kale; appreciated more for its stems than its coarse leaves.

GALANGAL a rhizome with a hot ginger-citrusy flavour; used similarly to ginger and garlic. Use fresh ginger if unavailable.

GARAM MASALA a blend of spices that includes cardamom, cinnamon, coriander, cloves, fennel and cumin. Black pepper and chilli can be added for heat.

GHEE also known as clarified butter; with the milk solids removed, this fat has a high smoking point so can be heated to a high temperature without burning. Used as a cooking medium in most Indian recipes.

GINGER
fresh also called green or root ginger; the thick gnarled root of a tropical plant.
ground also called powdered ginger; used as a flavouring in baking but cannot be substituted for fresh ginger.

GNOCCHI see pasta.

GREASING/OILING PANS use butter or margarine (for sweet baking), oil or cooking-oil spray (for savoury baking) to grease baking pans; overgreasing pans can cause food to overbrown. Use absorbent paper or a pastry brush to spread the oil or butter over the pan. Try covering your hand with a small plastic bag then swiping if into the butter or margarine.

HARISSA a Moroccan paste made from dried chillies, cumin, garlic, oil and caraway seeds. Available from Middle-Eastern food shops and some supermarkets.

HAZELNUTS also known as filberts; plump, grape-sized, rich, sweet nut having a brown skin that is removed by rubbing heated nuts together vigorously in a tea-towel.
ground is made by grounding the hazelnuts to a coarse flour texture for use in baking or as a thickening agent.

HOISIN SAUCE barbecue sauce made from salted fermented soybeans, onions and garlic; used as a marinade or baste, or to accent stir-fries and barbecued or roasted foods. Available from Asian food shops and supermarkets.

HONEY the variety sold in a squeezable container is not suitable for the recipes in this book.

HORSERADISH a vegetable with edible green leaves but mainly grown for its long, pungent white root. Occasionally found fresh in specialty greengrocers and some Asian food shops, but commonly purchased in bottles at the supermarket as horseradish cream and prepared horseradish. These cannot be substituted one for the other in cooking but both can be used as table condiments.
cream a paste of grated horseradish, mustard seeds, oil and sugar.
prepared preserved grated horseradish.

HUMMUS a Middle Eastern salad or dip made from softened dried chickpeas, garlic, lemon juice and tahini; can be purchased ready-made from most delicatessens and supermarkets. Also the Arabic word for chickpeas.

KAFFIR LIME also known as magrood, leech lime or jeruk purut. The wrinkled, bumpy-skinned green fruit of a small citrus tree originally grown in South Africa and South-East Asia. As a rule, only the rind and leaves are used.

KAFFIR LIME LEAVES also known as bai magrood, sold fresh, dried or frozen; looks like two glossy dark green leaves joined end to end, forming a rounded hourglass shape. A strip of fresh lime peel may be substituted for each kaffir lime leaf.

KITCHEN STRING made of a natural product such as cotton or hemp so that it neither affects the flavour of the food it's tied around nor melts when heated.

KUMARA Polynesian name of an orange-fleshed sweet potato often confused with yam.

LAMB
chump cut from just above the hind legs to the mid-loin section; can be used as a piece for roasting or cut into chops.
cutlet small, tender rib chop; sometimes sold french-trimmed, with all the fat and gristle at the narrow end of the bone removed.

forequarter chops are cut from the shoulder end.
leg cut from the hindquarter; can be boned, butterflied, rolled and tied, or cut into dice.
rolled shoulder boneless section of the forequarter, rolled and secured with string or netting.
shank forequarter leg; sometimes sold as drumsticks or frenched shanks if the gristle and narrow end of the bone are discarded and the remaining meat trimmed.
shoulder large, tasty piece having much connective tissue so is best pot-roasted or braised. Makes the best mince.

LEEKS a member of the onion family, the leek resembles a green onion but is much larger and more subtle in flavour. Tender baby or pencil leeks can be eaten whole with minimal cooking but adult leeks are usually trimmed of most of the green tops then chopped or sliced and cooked as an ingredient in stews, casseroles and soups.

LEMON GRASS also known as takrai, serai or serah. A tall, clumping, lemon-smelling and tasting, sharp-edged aromatic tropical grass; the white lower part of the stem is used, finely chopped, in many South-East Asian dishes. Can be found fresh, dried, powdered and frozen, in supermarkets, greengrocers and Asian food shops.

LENTILS (red, brown, yellow) dried pulses often identified by and named after their colour. Eaten by cultures all over the world, most famously perhaps in the dhals of India, lentils have high food value.
french-style are a local cousin to the famous (and very expensive) French lentils du puy; green-blue, tiny lentils with a nutty, earthy flavour and a hardy nature that allows them to be rapidly cooked without disintegrating.

LIQUEUR, ORANGE-FLAVOURED such as curaçao, Grand Marnier or Cointreau.

MACADAMIAS native to Australia; fairly large, slightly soft, buttery rich nut. Should always be stored in the fridge to prevent their high oil content turning them rancid.

MANGO tropical fruit originally from India and South-East Asia. With skin colour ranging from green to yellow and deep red; fragrant, deep yellow flesh surrounds a large flat seed. Slicing off the cheeks, cross-hatching them with a knife then turning them inside out shows the sweet, juicy flesh at its best. Mangoes can also be used in curries and salsas, or pureed for ice-cream, smoothies or mousse.

MAPLE-FLAVOURED SYRUP is made from sugar cane and is also called golden or pancake syrup. It is not a substitute for pure maple syrup.

MAPLE SYRUP also called pure maple syrup; distilled from the sap of sugar maple trees found only in Canada and the USA. Maple-flavoured syrup or pancake syrup is not an adequate substitute for the real thing.

MARJORAM closely related to and similar in flavour to oregano, but milder and sweeter. Delicious in herb mixtures for omelettes, stuffings, herb scones and herb and cream cheese sandwiches. As with oregano, many chefs prefer dried marjoram to fresh.

MARSALA a fortified Italian wine produced in the region surrounding the Sicilian city of Marsala; recognisable by its intense amber colour and complex aroma. Often used in cooking, especially in sauces, risottos and desserts.

MAYONNAISE, WHOLE-EGG commercial mayonnaise of high quality made with whole eggs and labelled as such; some prepared mayonnaises substitute emulsifiers such as food starch, cellulose gel or other thickeners to achieve the same thick and creamy consistency but never achieve the same rich flavour. Must be refrigerated once opened.

MERGUEZ SAUSAGES small, spicy sausage believed to have originated in Tunisia but eaten in North Africa, France and Spain; is traditionally made with lamb meat and is easily recognised because of its chilli-red colour. Can be fried, grilled or roasted; available from many butchers, delis and specialty sausage stores.

MINT the most commonly used variety of mint is spearmint; it has pointed, bright-green leaves and a fresh flavour.

MIRIN a Japanese champagne-coloured cooking wine, made of glutinous rice and alcohol. It is used just for cooking and should not be confused with sake. A seasoned sweet mirin, manjo mirin, made of water, rice, corn syrup and alcohol, is used in dipping sauces.

MIXED SALAD LEAVES also called mesclun; a salad mix of young lettuce and other green leaves, including baby spinach leaves, mizuna and curly endive.

MIXED SPICE a classic spice mixture generally containing caraway, allspice, coriander, cumin, nutmeg and ginger, although cinnamon and other spices can be added. It is used with fruit and in cakes.

MOLASSES a thick, dark brown syrup, the residue from the refining of sugar; available in light, dark and blackstrap varieties. Its slightly bitter taste is an essential ingredient in American cooking, found in foods such as gingerbread, shoofly pie and boston baked beans.

MOROCCAN SEASONING available from most Middle-Eastern food stores, spice shops and major supermarkets. A blend of turmeric, cinnamon and cumin adds a Moroccan flavour to cooking.

MORTAR AND PESTLE a cooking tool whose design has remained the same over the centuries: the mortar is a bowl-shaped container and the pestle a rounded, bat-shaped tool. Together, they grind and pulverise spices, herbs and other foods. The pestle is pressed against the mortar and rotated, grinding the ingredient between the two surfaces. Essential for curry pastes and crushing spices.

MOULI also known as a food mill; an essential kitchen tool in terms of versatility, ease of use and multi-task function. It's a rotary grater large enough to fit over a saucepan or bowl which comes with variety of interchangeable plates for processing different textures; it strains, pulps, rices, mashes, purees and even dices. Unlike a blender or processor, it separates the peel, seeds, cores etc, from the puree and allows the cook a degree of control over the final texture.

MUSHROOMS
button small, cultivated white mushrooms with a mild flavour.
dried porcini also known as cèpes; the richest-flavoured mushrooms. Expensive, but because they're so strongly flavoured, only a small amount is required.
enoki cultivated mushrooms also called enokitake; are tiny long-stemmed, pale mushrooms that grow and are sold in clusters, and can be used that way or separated by slicing off the base. They have a mild fruity flavour and are slightly crisp in texture.
flat large, flat mushrooms with a rich earthy flavour, ideal for filling and barbecuing. They are sometimes misnamed field mushrooms which are wild mushrooms.
oyster also called abalone; grey-white mushrooms shaped like a fan. Prized for their smooth texture and subtle, oyster-like flavour. Also available pink.
portobello are mature, fully opened swiss browns; they are larger and bigger in flavour.
shiitake when fresh are also known as chinese black, forest or golden oak mushrooms. Are large and meaty and, although cultivated, have the earthiness and taste of wild mushrooms.

swiss brown also known as roman or cremini. Light to dark brown mushrooms with full-bodied flavour; suited for use in casseroles or being stuffed and baked.

MUSLIN inexpensive, undyed, finely woven cotton fabric called for in cooking to strain stocks and sauces; if unavailable, use disposable coffee filter papers.

MUSSELS see seafood.

MUSTARD
dijon pale brown, distinctively flavoured, fairly mild-tasting french mustard.
seeds, black also called brown mustard seeds; more pungent than the yellow (or white) seeds used in prepared mustards.
wholegrain also known as seeded. A french-style coarse-grain mustard made from crushed mustard seeds and dijon-style french mustard.

NOODLES
dried rice also called rice stick noodles. Made from rice flour and water, available flat and wide or very thin (vermicelli). Must be soaked in boiling water to soften.
fresh rice also called ho fun, khao pun, sen yau, pho or kway tiau, depending on the country of manufacture; the most common form of noodle used in Thailand. Can be purchased in strands of various widths or large sheets of about 500g (1 pound) which are to be cut into the desired size. Chewy and pure white, they do not need pre-cooking before use.
rice stick also called sen lek, ho fun or kway teow; especially popular South-East Asian dried rice noodles. They come in different widths (thin used in soups, wide in stir-fries), but all should be soaked in hot water to soften. The traditional noodle used in pad thai which, before soaking, measures about 5mm in width.
rice vermicelli also called sen mee, mei fun or bee hoon. Used throughout Asia in spring rolls and cold salads; similar to bean threads, only longer and made with rice flour instead of mung bean starch. Before using, soak the dried noodles in hot water until softened, boil them briefly then rinse with hot water.

NUTMEG a strong and pungent spice ground from the dried nut of an evergreen tree native to Indonesia. Usually found ground but the flavour is more intense from a whole nut, available from spice shops, so it's best to grate your own.

OCTOPUS see seafood.

OIL
cooking spray we use a cholesterol-free cooking spray made from canola oil.
olive made from ripened olives. Extra virgin and virgin are the first and second press, respectively, of the olives and are therefore considered the best; "light" refers to taste not fat levels.
peanut pressed from ground peanuts; most commonly used oil in Asian cooking because of its high smoke point (capacity to handle high heat without burning).
sesame roasted, crushed, white sesame seeds; a flavouring rather than a cooking medium.
vegetable oils sourced from plant rather than animal fats.

OKRA also called bamia or lady fingers. A green, ridged, oblong pod with a furry skin. Native to Africa, this vegetable is used in Indian, Middle Eastern and South American cooking. Can be eaten on its own; as part of a casserole, curry or gumbo; used to thicken stews or gravies.

ONIONS
baby also called pickling and cocktail onions; are baby brown onions, though are larger than shallots. To peel, cover with boiling water and stand for 2 minutes, then drain. The skins will slip off easily.
brown and white are interchangeable; white onions have a more pungent flesh.
green (scallions) also called, incorrectly, shallot; an immature onion picked before the bulb has formed, has a long, bright-green stalk.
red also known as spanish, red spanish or bermuda onion; a sweet-flavoured, large, purple-red onion.
shallots also called french or golden shallots or eschalots; small and brown-skinned.

spring an onion with a small white bulb and long, narrow green-leafed tops.

ORANGE FLOWER WATER concentrated flavouring made from orange blossoms.

OREGANO a herb, also known as wild marjoram; has a woody stalk and clumps of tiny, dark-green leaves. Has a pungent, peppery flavour.

OYSTER SAUCE Asian in origin, this thick, richly flavoured brown sauce is made from oysters and their brine, cooked with salt and soy sauce, and thickened with starches. Use as a condiment.
vegetarian mushrom a "vegetarian" oyster sauce made from blended mushrooms and soy sauce.

PANCETTA see pork.

PANKO see breadcrumbs.

PAPRIKA ground, dried, sweet red capsicum (bell pepper); there are many grades and types available, including sweet, hot, mild and smoked.

PARSLEY a versatile herb with a fresh, earthy flavour. There are about 30 varieties of curly parsley; the flat-leaf variety (also called continental or italian parsley) is stronger in flavour and darker in colour.

PARSNIP their nutty sweetness is especially good when steamed and dressed with a garlic and cream sauce or in a curried parsnip soup, or simply baked. Can be substituted for potatoes. Available all year but the cold develops their sweet/savoury flavour in winter.

PASTA
fettuccine fresh or dried ribbon pasta made from durum wheat, semolina and egg. Also available plain or flavoured.
fresh lasagne sheets thinly rolled wide sheets of plain or flavoured pasta; they do not need par-boiling before being used in cooking.

gnocchi Italian 'dumplings' made of potatoes, semolina or flour; can be cooked in boiling water or baked with sauce.
macaroni tube-shaped pasta available in various sizes; made from semolina and water; does not contain eggs.
pappardelle from the Italian verb pappare, meaning "to gobble up", pappardelle are broad, flat or frilly, ribbons of pasta. Go well with red meat sauces (rabbit is a Tuscan favourite), chunky tomato and mushroom sauces as in pappardelle boscaiola, or with cream.
penne Italian for "pen", this dried pasta resembles a quill, and has angled ends and ridges to hold chunky sauces. Penne are also available in a smooth variety to complement finer sauces.
risoni small rice-shape pasta; very similar to orzo, another small pasta.
spaghetti long, thin solid strands of pasta.
tagliatelle long, flat strips of wheat pasta, slightly narrower and thinner than fettuccine.

PASTRY SHEETS ready-rolled packaged sheets of frozen puff and shortcrust pastry, available from supermarkets.

PATTY-PAN SQUASH also known as crookneck or custard marrow pumpkins; a round, slightly flat summer squash being yellow to pale-green in colour and having a scalloped edge. It has a firm white flesh and a distinct flavour.

PEANUTS also called groundnut, not in fact a nut but the pod of a legume. We mainly use raw (unroasted) or unsalted roasted peanuts.

PEARL BARLEY see barley.

PEAS
green also known as garden peas, must be shelled and their pods never eaten. Peas in the pod will yield just under half their weight of shelled peas; 1kg (2 pounds) will serve 4. Peas in the pod are available fresh and shelled peas are available frozen.

snow also called mangetout; a variety of garden pea, eaten pod and all (although you may need to string them). Used in stir-fries or eaten raw in salads. Snow pea sprouts are available from supermarkets or greengrocers and are usually eaten raw in salads or sandwiches.
sugar snap also called honey snap peas; fresh small pea which can be eaten, whole, pod and all, similarly to snow peas.

PECANS native to the US and now grown locally; pecans are golden brown, buttery and rich. Good in savoury as well as sweet dishes; walnuts are a good substitute.

PEPITAS (PUMPKIN SEEDS) are the pale green kernels of dried pumpkin seeds; they can be bought plain or salted.

PINE NUTS also called pignoli; not a nut but a small, cream-coloured kernel from pine cones. They are best roasted before use to bring out the flavour.

PISTACHIOS green, delicately flavoured nuts inside hard off-white shells. Available salted or unsalted in their shells; you can also get them shelled.

POACH a cooking term to describe gentle simmering of food in liquid (generally water or stock); spices or herbs can be added to impart their flavour.

POLENTA also known as cornmeal; a ground, flour-like cereal made of dried corn (maize). Also the name of the dish made from it.

POMEGRANATE dark-red, leathery-skinned fresh fruit about the size of an orange filled with hundreds of seeds, each wrapped in an edible lucent-crimson pulp having a unique tangy sweet-sour flavour.

POPPY SEEDS small, dried, bluish-grey seeds of the poppy plant, with a crunchy texture and a nutty flavour. Can be purchased whole or ground from most supermarkets and delicatessens.

PORK
belly fatty cut sold in rashers or in a piece, with or without rind or bone.
cutlets cut from ribs.
ham hock the lower portion of the leg; includes the meat, fat and bone. Most have been cured, smoked or both.
loin chops or roasting cut from the loin.
neck sometimes called pork scotch; a boneless cut from the foreloin.
pancetta an Italian unsmoked bacon; pork belly cured in salt and spices then rolled into a sausage shape and dried for several weeks. Used, sliced or chopped, as an ingredient rather than eaten on its own.
prosciutto a kind of unsmoked Italian ham; salted, air-cured and aged, it is usually eaten uncooked.
sausage, italian pork available as both sweet, which is flavoured with garlic and fennel seed, and hot, which has chilli.
shoulder joint sold with the bone in or out.
spare ribs (american-style spareribs); well-trimmed mid-loin ribs.

POTATOES
baby also called chats; not a separate variety but an early harvest with very thin skin.
coliban round, smooth white skin and flesh; good for baking and mashing.
desiree oval, smooth and pink-skinned, waxy yellow flesh; good in salads, boiled and roasted.
idaho also known as russet burbank; russet in colour, fabulous baked.
king edward slightly plump and rosy; great mashed.
lasoda round, red skin with deep eyes, white flesh; good for mashing or roasting.
pink-eye small, off-white skin, deep purple eyes; good steamed and boiled, great baked.
pontiac large, red skin, deep eyes, white flesh; good grated, boiled and baked.
sebago white skin, oval; good fried, mashed and baked.
spunta large, long, yellow flesh, floury; great mashed and fried.

PRAWNS (SHRIMP) see seafood.

PRESERVED LEMON RIND a North African specialty; lemons are quartered and preserved in salt and lemon juice or water. To use, remove and discard pulp. Squeeze juice from rind, then rinse well and slice thinly. Sold in delicatessens and major supermarkets.

PROSCIUTTO see pork.

QUINCE yellow-skinned fruit with hard texture and astringent, tart taste; eaten cooked or as a preserve. Long, slow cooking makes the flesh a deep rose pink.

QUINCE PASTE a thick quince preserve which is sliceable; served on a cheese platter, it goes well with cheeses such as brie and camembert. Available from most supermarkets and delicatessens.

RADICCHIO a red-leafed Italian chicory with a refreshing bitter taste that's eaten raw and grilled. Comes in varieties named after their places of origin, such as round-headed Verona or long-headed Treviso.

RAISINS dried sweet grapes (traditionally muscatel grapes).

RAITA a minted yoghurt and cucumber dish. It is a cooling accompaniment to fiery curries.

RAS EL HANOUT a classic spice blend used in Moroccan cooking. The name means 'top of the shop' and is the very best spice blend a spice merchant has to offer. Most versions contain over a dozen spices, including cardamom, nutmeg, mace, cinnamon and ground chilli.

RHUBARB a plant with long, green-red stalks; becomes sweet and edible when cooked.

RICE
arborio small, round grain rice well-suited to absorb a large amount of liquid; the high level of starch makes it especially suitable for risottos for its classic creaminess.

basmati a white, fragrant long-grained rice; the grains fluff up when cooked. Wash several times before cooking.
brown retains the high-fibre, nutritious bran coating that's removed from white rice when hulled. It takes longer to cook than white rice and has a chewier texture. Once cooked, the long grains stay separate, while the short grains are soft and stickier.
jasmine is a long-grain white rice recognised around the world as having a perfumed aromatic quality; moist in texture, it clings together after cooking. Sometimes substituted for basmati rice.
wild not a member of the rice family but the seed of an aquatic grass native to the cold regions of North America. Wild rice has a strong nutty taste and can be expensive, so is best combined with brown and white rices in pulaos, stuffings and salads.
wild rice blend a packaged blend of white long-grain rice and wild rice. With its dark brown, almost black grains, crunchy, resilient texture and smokey-like flavour, wild rice contrasts nicely with mild-tasting white rice. Perfect with fish, lentils, in pulaos or added to soups.

RISONI see pasta.

ROASTING/TOASTING nuts and dried coconut can be roasted in the oven to restore their fresh flavour and release their aromatic essential oils. Spread them evenly onto an oven tray then roast in a moderate oven for about 5 minutes. Desiccated coconut, pine nuts and sesame seeds roast more evenly if stirred over low heat in a heavy-based frying pan; their natural oils will help turn them golden brown.

ROCKET (ARUGULA) also called rugula and rucola; peppery green leaf eaten raw in salads or used in cooking. Baby rocket leaves are smaller and less peppery.

ROSEMARY pungent herb with long, thin pointy leaves; use large and small sprigs, and finely chop leaves.

SAFFRON stigma of a member of the crocus family, available ground or in strands; imparts a yellow-orange colour to food once infused. The quality can vary greatly; the best is the most expensive spice in the world.

SAGE pungent herb with narrow, grey-green leaves; slightly bitter with a slightly musty mint aroma. Refrigerate fresh sage wrapped in a paper towel and sealed in a plastic bag for up to 4 days. Dried sage comes whole, crumbled or ground. It should be stored in a cool, dark place for no more than three months.

SAKE also known as Japanese cooking rice wine and ryori shu. Made from alcohol (about 14%), rice, salt and corn syrup; often used in marinades for meat and fish. In cooking, it is often used to add body and flavour to various tsuyu (soup stock) and sauces, or to make nimono (simmered dishes) and yakimono (grilled dishes).

SALMON see seafood.

SAMBAL OELEK also called ulek or olek; an Indonesian salty paste made from ground chillies and vinegar.

SEAFOOD
blue swimmer crab also known as sand crab, blue manna crab, bluey, sand crab or sandy. Substitute with lobster, balmain or moreton bay bugs.
fish fillet use your favourite firm-fleshed white fish fillet.
mussels must be tightly closed when bought, indicating they are alive. Before cooking, scrub the shells with a strong brush and remove the 'beards'. Some mussels might not open – you do not have to discard these, just open with a knife and cook a little more if you wish. Varieties include black and green-lip.
ocean trout a farmed fish with pink, soft flesh. From the same family as the atlantic salmon; one can be substituted for the other.
octopus usually tenderised before you buy them; both octopus and squid require either long slow cooking (usually for the large molluscs) or quick cooking over high heat (usually for the small molluscs) – anything in between will make the octopus tough and rubbery.
prawns (shrimp) varieties include, school, king, royal red, sydney harbour, tiger. Can be bought uncooked (green) or cooked, with or without shells.
salmon red-pink firm flesh with few bones; moist delicate flavour.
white fish means non-oily fish; includes bream, flathead, whiting, snapper, dhufish, redfish and ling.

SEGMENTING a cooking term to describe cutting citrus fruits in such a way that pieces contain no pith, seed or membrane. The peeled fruit is cut towards the centre inside each membrane, forming wedges.

SEMOLINA coarsely ground flour milled from durum wheat; the flour used in making gnocchi, pasta and couscous.

SESAME SEEDS black and white are the most common of this small oval seed, however there are also red and brown varieties. The seeds are used in cuisines the world over as an ingredient and as a condiment. Roast the seeds in a heavy-based frying pan over low heat.

SHALLOTS see onions.

SHERRY fortified wine consumed as an aperitif or used in cooking. Sherries differ in colour and flavour; sold as fino (light, dry), amontillado (medium sweet, dark) and oloroso (full-bodied, very dark).

SICHUAN PEPPERCORNS also called szechuan or chinese pepper, native to the Sichuan province of China. A mildly hot spice that comes from the prickly ash tree. Although it is not related to the peppercorn family, small, red-brown aromatic sichuan berries look like black peppercorns and have a distinctive peppery-lemon flavour and aroma.

SILVER BEET (SWISS CHARD) also called, incorrectly, spinach; has fleshy stalks and large leaves and can be prepared as for spinach.

SOY SAUCE also called sieu; made from fermented soybeans. Several variations are available in supermarkets and Asian food stores; we use japanese soy sauce unless indicated otherwise.
dark deep brown, almost black in colour; rich, with a thicker consistency than other types. Pungent but not particularly salty; good for marinating.
japanese an all-purpose low-sodium soy sauce made with more wheat content than its Chinese counterparts; fermented in barrels and aged. Possibly the best table soy and the one to choose if you only want one variety.
light fairly thin in consistency and, while paler than the others, the saltiest tasting; used in dishes in which the natural colour of the ingredients is to be maintained. Not to be confused with salt-reduced or low-sodium soy sauces.

SPINACH also called english spinach and incorrectly, silver beet. Baby spinach leaves are best eaten raw in salads; the larger leaves should be added last to soups, stews and stir-fries, and should be cooked until barely wilted.

SPLIT PEAS a variety of yellow or green pea grown specifically for drying. When dried, the peas usually split along a natural seam. Whole and split dried peas are available packaged in supermarkets and in bulk in health-food stores.

STAR ANISE dried star-shaped pod with an astringent aniseed flavour; used to flavour stocks and marinades. Available whole and ground, it is an essential ingredient in five-spice powder.

SUGAR
caster (superfine) finely granulated table sugar.
dark brown a moist, dark brown sugar with a rich, distinctive full flavour from molasses syrup.

demerara small-grained golden-coloured crystal sugar.
icing (confectioners') also known as powdered sugar; pulverised granulated sugar crushed together with a small amount of cornflour (cornstarch).
light brown a very soft, finely granulated sugar that retains molasses for its colour and flavour.
palm also called nam tan pip, jaggery, jawa or gula melaka; made from the sap of the sugar palm tree. Light brown to black in colour and usually sold in rock-hard cakes; use light brown sugar if unavailable.
pure icing (confectioners') also known as powdered sugar.
raw natural brown granulated sugar.
vanilla is available in supermarkets, usually among the spices. Or, you can make your own by putting a couple of vanilla beans in a jar of caster (superfine) sugar.
white (granulated) coarse, granulated table sugar, also known as crystal sugar.
yellow rock is available from Asian supermarkets. It's mainly used in braises and sauces as it gives them a lustre and glaze.

SULTANAS also called golden raisins; dried seedless white grapes.

SUMAC a purple-red, astringent spice ground from berries growing on shrubs that flourish wild around the Mediterranean; adds a tart, lemony flavour to dips and dressings and goes well with barbecued meat. Can be found in Middle Eastern food stores.

SWEDE in the English-speaking world, the hard, slightly yellow root vegetable that slightly resembles a large dried turnip is called a swede in England and Australia, a neep in Scotland and rutabaga in the United States. Because this vegetable thrives in the cold, it has always been popular in Scandinavia, especially in Sweden, hence the name. The swede is a great tasting vegetable with a delicate sweetness and flavour that hints of the freshness of cabbage and turnip.

TAMARI a thick, dark soy sauce made mainly from soya beans, but without the wheat used in most standard soy sauces.

TAMARIND the tamarind tree produces clusters of hairy brown pods, each of which is filled with seeds and a viscous pulp, that are dried and pressed into the blocks of tamarind found in Asian food shops. Gives a sweet-sour, slightly astringent taste to marinades, pastes, sauces and dressings.

TAMARIND CONCENTRATE (or paste) the distillation of tamarind pulp into a condensed, compacted paste. Thick and purple-black, it requires no soaking. Found in Asian food stores.

TARRAGON french tarragon, with its subtle aniseed flavour, complements chicken, eggs and veal, and is perfect in a béarnaise sauce. It is also one of the herbs that make up the French fines herbs. Russian and mexican tarragons are slightly coarser in taste.

THYME a basic herb of French cuisine is widely used in Mediterranean countries to flavour meats and sauces. A member of the mint family, it has tiny grey-green leaves that give off a pungent minty, light-lemon aroma. Dried thyme comes in both leaf and powder form. Dried thyme should be stored in a cool, dark place for no more than three months. Fresh thyme should be stored in the refrigerator, wrapped in a damp paper towel and placed in a sealed bag for no more than a few days.

TOMATOES
bottled pasta sauce a prepared sauce; a blend of tomatoes, herbs and spices.
canned whole peeled tomatoes in natural juices; available crushed, chopped or diced. Use undrained.
cherry also called tiny tim or tom thumb tomatoes; small and round.
paste triple-concentrated tomato puree used to flavour soups, stews and sauces.
puree canned pureed tomatoes (not tomato paste).
roma (egg) also called plum; these are

smallish, oval-shaped tomatoes much used in Italian cooking or salads.
semi-dried partially dried tomato pieces in olive oil; softer and juicier than sun-dried, these are not a preserve thus do not keep as long as sun-dried.
sun-dried tomato pieces that have been dried with salt; this dehydrates the tomato and concentrates the flavour. We use sun-dried tomatoes packaged in oil, unless stated otherwise.
truss small vine-ripened tomatoes with vine still attached.

TREACLE thick, dark syrup not unlike molasses; a by-product of the sugar refining process.

TURMERIC also called kamin; is a rhizome related to galangal and ginger. Must be grated or pounded to release its acrid aroma and pungent flavour. Known for the golden colour it imparts, fresh turmeric can be substituted with the more commonly found dried powder, in the proportion of 1 teaspoon ground turmeric for every 20g (¾ ounce) fresh turmeric. Be aware that fresh turmeric stains your hands and plastic utensils such as chopping boards and spatulas.

VANILLA
bean dried, long, thin pod from a tropical golden orchid; the minuscule black seeds inside the bean impart a luscious flavour in baking and desserts. Place a whole bean in a jar of sugar to make vanilla sugar; a bean can be used three or four times.
extract obtained from vanilla beans infused in water; a non-alcoholic version of essence.
paste made from vanilla beans and contains real seeds. Is highly concentrated: 1 teaspoon replaces a whole vanilla bean. Found in most supermarkets in the baking section.

VEAL
osso buco also called veal shin, usually cut into 3-5cm (1¼-2-inch) thick slices and used in the famous Italian slow-cooked casserole of the same name.

rack row of small chops or cutlets.
scaloppine a piece of lean steak hammered with a meat mallet until almost see-through; cook over high heat for as little time as possible.
schnitzel thinly sliced steak.

VIETNAMESE MINT not a mint at all, but a pungent and peppery narrow-leafed member of the buckwheat family. Not confined to Vietnam, it is also known as cambodian mint, pak pai (Thailand), laksa leaf (Indonesia), daun kesom (Singapore) and rau ram in Vietnam. It is a common ingredient in Thai foods, particularly soups, salads and stir-fries.

VINEGAR
balsamic originally from Modena, Italy, there are now many balsamic vinegars on the market ranging in pungency and quality depending on how, and for how long, they have been aged. Quality can be determined up to a point by price; use the most expensive sparingly.
cider made from fermented apples.
malt made from fermented malt and beech shavings.
rice a colourless vinegar made from fermented rice and flavoured with sugar and salt. Sherry can be substituted.
white made from the spirit of cane sugar.
white balsamic is a clear and lighter version of balsamic vinegar; it has a fresh, sweet, clean taste.

WALNUTS as well as being a good source of fibre and healthy oils, nuts contain a range of vitamins, minerals and other beneficial plant components called phytochemicals. Walnuts contain the beneficial omega-3 fatty acids.

WATERCRESS one of the cress family, a large group of peppery greens used raw in salads, dips and sandwiches, or cooked in soups. Highly perishable, so it must be used as soon as possible after purchase.

WHITE SWEET POTATO is less sweet than kumara; has an earthy flavour and a purple flesh beneath its white skin; is best baked.

WITLOF also known as belgian endive; related to and confused with chicory. A versatile vegetable, it tastes as good cooked as it does eaten raw. Grown in darkness like white asparagus to prevent it becoming green; looks somewhat like a tightly furled, cream to very light-green cigar. The leaves can be removed and used to hold a canapé filling; the whole vegetable can be opened up, stuffed then baked or casseroled; and the leaves can be tossed in a salad with other vegetables.

WOMBOK (NAPA CABBAGE) also called chinese cabbage or peking cabbage; elongated in shape with pale green, crinkly leaves, is the most common cabbage in South-East Asia. Can be shredded or chopped and eaten raw or braised, steamed or stir-fried.

WORCESTERSHIRE SAUCE thin, dark-brown spicy sauce developed by the British when in India; used as a seasoning for meat, gravies and cocktails, and as a condiment.

YEAST (dried and fresh), a raising agent used in dough making. Granular (7g sachets) and fresh compressed (20g blocks) yeast can almost always be substituted for the other.

YOGHURT we use plain full-cream yoghurt in our recipes.
Greek-style plain yoghurt strained in a cloth (traditionally muslin) to remove the whey and to give it a creamy consistency.

ZA'ATAR a Middle Eastern herb and spice mixture which varies but always includes thyme, with ground sumac and, usually, toasted sesame seeds. It is sprinkled on yoghurt and flatbreads and can be used as a rub on lamb or chicken when grilled or roasted.

ZUCCHINI also called courgette; small, pale- or dark-green or yellow vegetable of the squash family. Harvested when young, its edible flowers can be stuffed and deep-fried.

CONVERSION CHART

MEASURES

One Australian metric measuring cup holds approximately 250ml; one Australian metric tablespoon holds 20ml; one Australian metric teaspoon holds 5ml.

The difference between one country's measuring cups and another's is within a two- or three-teaspoon variance, and will not affect your cooking results. North America, New Zealand and the United Kingdom use a 15ml tablespoon.

All cup and spoon measurements are level. The most accurate way of measuring dry ingredients is to weigh them. When measuring liquids, use a clear glass or plastic jug with the metric markings.

The imperial measurements used in these recipes are approximate only. Measurements for cake pans are approximate only. Using same-shaped cake pans of a similar size should not affect the outcome of your baking. We measure the inside top of the cake pan to determine sizes.

We use large eggs with an average weight of 60g.

DRY MEASURES

METRIC	IMPERIAL
15g	½oz
30g	1oz
60g	2oz
90g	3oz
125g	4oz (¼lb)
155g	5oz
185g	6oz
220g	7oz
250g	8oz (½lb)
280g	9oz
315g	10oz
345g	11oz
375g	12oz (¾lb)
410g	13oz
440g	14oz
470g	15oz
500g	16oz (1lb)
750g	24oz (1½lb)
1kg	32oz (2lb)

LIQUID MEASURES

METRIC	IMPERIAL
30ml	1 fluid oz
60ml	2 fluid oz
100ml	3 fluid oz
125ml	4 fluid oz
150ml	5 fluid oz
190ml	6 fluid oz
250ml	8 fluid oz
300ml	10 fluid oz
500ml	16 fluid oz
600ml	20 fluid oz
1000ml (1 litre)	1¾ pints

LENGTH MEASURES

METRIC	IMPERIAL
3mm	⅛in
6mm	¼in
1cm	½in
2cm	¾in
2.5cm	1in
5cm	2in
6cm	2½in
8cm	3in
10cm	4in
13cm	5in
15cm	6in
18cm	7in
20cm	8in
22cm	9in
25cm	10in
28cm	11in
30cm	12in (1ft)

OVEN TEMPERATURES

The oven temperatures in this book are for conventional ovens; if you have a fan-forced oven, decrease the temperature by 10-20 degrees.

	°C (CELSIUS)	°F (FAHRENHEIT)
Very slow	120	250
Slow	150	300
Moderately slow	160	325
Moderate	180	350
Moderately hot	200	400
Hot	220	425
Very hot	240	475

INDEX

A

aïoli, capsicum 460
allspice 473
almonds 473
  almond carrot cake 311
  creamy vegetable and
    almond korma 56
  crumble 398
  mandarin and almond pudding 227
andalusian pork 209
apples, pork and prunes 141
artichokes 473
  chicken and artichoke pot roast 94
  chicken with leeks and 346
  lamb stew with artichoke
    and peas 333
  veal with artichokes, olives
    and lemon 291
asian broth with crisp pork belly 138
asian-style braised pork neck 300

B

bacon 473
  chicken with leek and 283
  pasta, bacon and vegetable soup 85
bake blind 473
baking paper 473
baking powder 473
baltic lamb and rice meatballs 195
barley 473
  beef and barley soup 233
  chicken, porcini and barley soup 334
  irish lamb and barley stew 88
  lamb chops with barley, mint
    and cumin 248
basil 473
  chicken stuffed with ricotta, basil
    and prosciutto 451
  toasted ciabatta with basil butter 362
bay leaves 473
beans 473
  baked prawn, asparagus and
    broad bean risotto 157
  bollito misto 259

(*beans* continued)
  braised veal shoulder with
    white beans 418
  broccolini and beans with garlic
    and anchovies 469
  chicken, celeriac and broad
    bean casserole 48
  chilli beans with tomato sauce 220
  chilli beef with cornbread
    dumplings 241
  chilli con carne 19
  chorizo, chilli and bean stew 187
  cuban black bean soup 199
  duck legs with pancetta and
    white beans 307
  garlicky beans with pine nuts 466
  mexican beans with sausages 238
  minted broad bean and ham soup
    255
  pork, chicken and black-eyed
    bean cassoulet 304
  pork neck, orange and white
    bean stew 91
  pork with beans and beer 382
  red bean, pork and rice 142
  slow-cooked lamb and white
    bean soup 242
  slow-cooked lamb shank and
    bean ragù 134
  south african bean curry 245
  tomato braised beans 467
beef 473–4
  beef and barley soup 233
  beef and shiitake mushroom pie 166
  beef and vegetable soup 105
  beef carbonade pies 288
  braised asian-style beef ribs 323
  braised beef brisket 230
  braised beef cheeks in red wine 413
  braised beef in ginger broth 406
  braised oxtail in peanut sauce 237
  braised oxtail with orange
    gremolata 414
  chilli con carne 19
  country-style beef and potato
    casserole 69
  crisp hot and sweet beef with
    noodles 74

(*beef* continued)
  family beef casserole 125
  indian dry beef curry 70
  italian-style chilli beef 191
  massaman beef curry 320
  meatballs with tomato sauce 183
  oxtail stew with red wine and port 188
  provencale beef casserole 66
  ragù alla bolognese 280
  rib roast with roasted beetroot
    and potatoes puree 405
  shredded beef tacos 23
  shredded spanish beef 97
  simple beef and vegetable
    casserole 16
  sirloin roast with herb stuffing 410
  slow-roasted beef and garlic
    with mustard cream 121
  slow-roasted beef shanks 296
  stew with parsley dumplings 117
  stock 470
  vietnamese beef pho 397
  xacutti 361
beetroot 474
  beef rib roast with roasted beetroot
    and potatoes puree 405
bicarbonate of soda 474
biryani-style lamb 43
bisque, creamy crab and tomato 393
bollito misto 259
braised asian-style beef ribs 323
braised oxtail in peanut sauce 237
brandy 474
  syrup 308
bread 474
  toasted ciabatta with basil butter 362
breadcrumbs 474
broccolini 474
  broccolini and beans with garlic
    and anchovies 469
bruise 474
buk choy 474
burghul 474
  tabbouleh 313
butter 474
  toasted ciabatta with basil butter 362
butter chicken 337

buttermilk 474
butterscotch sauce 224

C

cake
  almond carrot 311
  chocolate cinnamon cake with
    cherry and red wine syrup 464
  rich chocolate 353
  walnut and fig with brandy syrup 308
caperberries 474
capers 474
capsicum 474
  aïoli 460
  italian pork and capsicum ragù 48
  mash 175
  ricotta and capsicum bake 456
caramelised onion brown rice 272–3
caraway seeds 474
  fresh peas with caraway and
    parmesan 469
cardamom 474
cashews 474
casserole
  chicken, celeriac and broad bean 48
  country-style beef and potato 69
  creamy chicken and vegetable 97
  family beef 125
  italian veal casserole 125
  lamb casserole with herb
    dumplings 118
  provencale beef 66
  simple beef and vegetable 16
  spanish chicken 137
  spicy tomato and saffron chicken 55
  veal and rosemary 184
cassoulet
  chicken and merguez 295
  pork, chicken and black-eyed bean 304
cauliflower mornay 425
cauliflower soup 203
cavolo nero 475
celeriac 475
  chicken, celeriac and broad
    bean casserole 48

chana masala 206
char siu sauce 475
cheese 475
  cheese-filled zucchini flowers 389
  cheesy mash 174
  chicken stuffed with ricotta, basil
    and prosciutto 451
  cream cheese frosting 311
  eggplant parmigiana 44
  fresh peas with caraway and
    parmesan 469
  parmesan cheese croûtons 102
  ricotta and capsicum bake 456
  sauce 299
  spinach and ricotta lasagne 219
cheesecake, low-fat lemon and
  blackberry 170
cherry and red wine syrup 464
chervil 475
chicken 475
  baked with ratatouille 149
  butter 337
  chicken and artichoke pot roast 94
  chicken and asparagus pilaf 101
  chicken and merguez cassoulet 295
  chicken, celeriac and broad
    bean casserole 48
  chicken, chorizo and okra gumbo 263
  chicken, porcini and barley soup 334
  chicken tagine with dates and
    honey 379
  classic roast chicken 146
  clay pot 150
  coq au vin 386
  cream of chicken soup with
    parmesan cheese croûtons 102
  creamy chicken and vegetable
    casserole 97
  fennel and orange, with 98
  green olive and lemon chicken 343
  italian chicken soup 52
  jerk-spiced chicken drumsticks 36
  leek and bacon, with 283
  leeks and artichokes, with 346
  moroccan chicken with
    couscous stuffing 452
  mulligatawny soup with 210

(chicken continued)
  poached with soy and sesame 20
  pork, chicken and black-eyed
    bean cassoulet 304
  portuguese-style 340
  pot roast with mustard cream
    sauce 154
  quince and chicken tagine 390
  ricotta, basil and prosciutto,
    stuffed with 451
  roasted, with gremolata 447
  spanish chicken casserole 137
  spicy caribbean-style chicken
    stew 267
  spicy tomato and saffron chicken
    casserole 55
  stock 470
  sweet and sour 213
  tikka masala 203
chilli 475–6
  chilli beans with tomato sauce 220
  chilli beef with cornbread
    dumplings 241
  chorizo, chilli and bean stew 187
  italian-style chilli beef 191
  potato and olive-filled banana
    chillies 161
chilli con carne 19
chinese cooking wine 476
chives 476
chocolate 476
  chocolate cinnamon cake with
    cherry and red wine syrup 464
  rich chocolate cake 353
  self-saucing pudding 63
chorizo sausages 476
  chicken, chorizo and okra gumbo 263
  chorizo, chilli and bean stew 187
  pork belly and chorizo stew 94
choy sum 476
cider roasted pork belly 430
cinnamon 476
  chocolate cinnamon cake with
    cherry and red wine syrup 464
  cinnamon yoghurt cream 354
classic pulao 312
classic roast chicken 146

clay pot chicken 150
cloves 476
cocoa powder 476
coconut 476
compote, rhubarb and orange 354
confit of salmon with herb salad 455
coq au vin 386
coriander 476
   spiced coriander, lentil and
     barley soup 379
cornbread dumplings 241
cornflour 476
country-style beef and potato
   casserole 69
couscous 476
   olive and parsley 315
   pistachio 372
   preserved lemon 314
   stuffing 452
cranberries 476
cream 476–7
cream cheese frosting 311
cream of chicken soup with parmesan
   cheese croûtons 102
cream of tartar 476
creamed spinach 467
creamy chicken and vegetable
   casserole 97
creamy semi-dried tomato and
   veal soup 362
creamy turkey stew with mustard 59
creamy vegetable and almond korma 56
crème fraîche 477
crisp hot and sweet beef with
   noodles 74
croissant custard pudding with
   strawberries 60
cuban black bean soup 199
cucumber 477
cumin 477
   lamb chops with barley, mint
     and cumin 248
curry
   indian dry beef curry 70
   lamb and macadamia curry 252
   lamb rendang 130
   lemon grass and pork 51

(curry continued)
   malaysian lamb 358
   massaman beef curry 320
   okra 216
   pork and vegetable vindaloo 260
   rogan josh 375
   sour pork curry 303
   south african bean curry 245
curry leaves 477
curry pastes 477
   chicken tikka masala 203
   creamy vegetable and almond
     korma 56
   lamb korma 196
   masala paste 272–3
   panang lamb curry 330
   red pork curry 326
curry powder 477
   old-fashioned curried sausages 35
custard powder 477

D

dates 477
   chicken tagine with dates and
     honey 379
   date and apricot creamy rice 110
   sticky date and fig pudding 224
deglaze 477
desserts
   almond carrot cake 311
   baked passionfruit tart 169
   chocolate cinnamon cake with
     cherry and red wine syrup 464
   chocolate self-saucing pudding 63
   croissant custard pudding with
     strawberries 60
   date and apricot creamy rice 110
   low-fat lemon and blackberry
     cheesecake 170
   mandarin and almond pudding 227
   orange poached pears 109
   poached pears and quince with
     almond crumble 398
   quince sponge pudding 463
   rhubarb and orange compote 354

(desserts continued)
   rich chocolate cake 353
   steamed ginger pudding 276
   sticky date and fig pudding 224
   walnut and fig cake with
     brandy syrup 308
dhal
   egg and eggplant, with 269
   mixed 382
   pumpkin and eggplant 73
dhansak with caramelised onion
   brown rice 272–3
dill 477
   mayonnaise 455
dried currants 477
drunken duck 385
duck 477
   drunken 385
   legs with pancetta and white
     beans 307
   slow-cooked duck with cabbage
     and fennel 444
   slow-roasted duck with balsamic
     glazed vegetables 448
dukkah 478
dumplings
   cornbread 241
   herb 118
   parsley 117

E

eggplant 478
   dhal with egg and eggplant 269
   parmigiana 44
   pumpkin and eggplant dhal 73
eggs 476
   dhal with egg and eggplant 269
eggwash 478

F

family beef casserole 125
fennel 478
   chicken with fennel and orange 98

(*fennel* continued)
cream of roasted fennel soup
with capsicum aïoli 460
lamb shank, fennel and vegetable
soup 192
slow-cooked duck with cabbage
and fennel 444
fenugreek 478
fettuccine, braised rabbit sauce
with 284
figs 478
pistachio, pancetta and fig-stuffed
lamb 429
sticky date and fig pudding 224
walnut and fig cake with
brandy syrup 308
wild rice salad with spinach
and figs 314
fish sauce 478
fish stock 471
five-spice powder 478
lamb shanks in five spice, tamarind
and ginger 114
flour 478
french onion lamb chops 39
frosting, cream cheese 311

G

gai lan 478
steamed, in oyster sauce 466
galangal 478
garam masala 272–3, 478
garlic confit 251
garlicky beans with pine nuts 466
ghee 478
ginger 478
broth 406
lamb shanks in five spice, tamarind
and ginger 114
steamed ginger pudding 276
steamed ginger rice 440
gnocchi
oregano lamb stew with 82
greasing/oiling pans 478
greek-style lamb with potatoes 346

green olive and lemon chicken 343
gremolata 417, 447
orange 414
preserved lemon 55
gumbo, chicken, chorizo and okra 263

H

ham *see also* pork
minestrone 376
minted broad bean and
ham soup 255
pea and ham soup 40
harira 77
harissa 478
harissa and mint vegetable stew 106
moroccan-style vegetable stew
with harissa 349
hasselback potatoes 172
hazelnuts 478
herb and olive fish fillets on potato 437
herb dumplings 118
herb stuffing 410
hoisin sauce 478
honey 478
chicken tagine with dates
and honey 379
slow-roasted honey and soy
pork neck 433
veal shanks with honey and
lemon 133
horseradish 479
hummus 479

I

indian dry beef curry 70
irish lamb and barley stew 88
italian braised pork 434
italian chicken soup 52
italian pork and capsicum ragù 48
italian-style chilli beef 191
italian veal casserole 125

J

jerk-spiced chicken drumsticks 36

K

kaffir lime 479
kaffir lime leaves 479
kitchen string 479
korma, creamy vegetable and
almond 56
kumara 479
kumara carrot mash 292
mash 174
moroccan lamb with kumara
and raisins 26

L

lamb 479
baltic lamb and rice meatballs 195
biryani-style 43
braised lamb shanks with tzatziki
and tomato salad 128–9
chops with barley, mint and
cumin 248
french onion lamb chops 39
greek-style lamb with potatoes 346
harira 77
irish lamb and barley stew 88
korma 196
lamb and macadamia curry 252
lamb and okra in rich tomato sauce
with garlic confit 251
lamb and quince tagine with
pistachio couscous 372
lamb casserole with herb
dumplings 118
lamb shank, fennel and vegetable
soup 192
lamb shank soup 365
lebanese lamb and potato bake 122
leg of lamb on lemon-scented
potatoes 437

(*lamb* continued)
malaysian lamb curry 358
maple syrup glazed lamb shanks 81
meat sauce (pastitsio) 299
moroccan lamb with kumara
and raisins 26
moroccan-spiced lamb shoulder 426
navarin of 369
neck chop and lentil stew with
kumara carrot mash 292
oregano lamb stew with gnocchi 82
panang lamb curry 330
pastitsio 299
pistachio, pancetta and
fig-stuffed lamb 429
rendang 130
rogan josh 375
shanks in five spice, tamarind
and ginger 114
shredded lamb and pumpkin soup 32
slow-cooked lamb and white
bean soup 242
slow-cooked lamb shank and
bean ragù 134
stew with artichoke and peas 333
sticky quince roasted lamb 402
stoba 275
tomato-braised lamb shanks 269
traditional roast dinner 425
lasagne, spinach and ricotta 219
lebanese lamb and potato bake 122
leeks 479
chicken with leek and bacon 283
chicken with leeks and
artichokes 346
potato and leek soup 234
lemon grass 479
lemon grass and pork curry 51
lentils 479
dhal with egg and eggplant 269
harira 77
lamb neck chop and lentil stew
with kumara carrot mash 292
mixed dhal 382
petite sale aux lentilles (salted pork
with lentils) 206
pumpkin and eggplant dhal 73

(*lentils* continued)
spiced 312
spiced coriander, lentil and
barley soup 379
spicy lentil soup 32
liqueur, orange-flavoured 479
low-fat lemon and blackberry
cheesecake 170

M

macadamias 479
lamb and macadamia curry 252
macerated strawberries 60
malaysian lamb curry 358
mandarin and almond pudding 227
mango 479
mango and lime mayonnaise 459
maple-flavoured syrup 479
maple syrup 479
maple syrup glazed lamb shanks 81
maple syrup pork belly with
pecans 366
orange and maple glazed
baby carrots 468
marjoram 479
marsala 479
masala paste 272–3
massaman beef curry 320
mayonnaise, whole-egg 479
meatballs, baltic lamb and rice 195
meatballs with tomato sauce 183
meatloaf, prosciutto-wrapped
pork and veal 145
merguez sausages 480
chicken and merguez cassoulet 295
mexican beans with sausages 238
mexican pull-apart pork 180
minestrone 376
mint 480
harissa and mint vegetable stew 106
lamb chops with barley, mint
and cumin 248
minted broad bean and
ham soup 255
mirin 480

mixed salad leaves 480
mixed spice 480
molasses 480
moroccan chicken with couscous
stuffing 452
moroccan lamb with kumara and
raisins 26
moroccan seasoning 480
moroccan-spiced lamb shoulder 426
moroccan-style vegetable stew
with harissa 349
mortar and pestle 480
mouli 480
mulligatawny soup with chicken 210
mushrooms 480
beef and shiitake mushroom pie 166
chicken, porcini and barley soup 334
pork, mushroom and
marsala stew 256
ragù 422
risotto 350
muslin 480
mustard 480
chicken pot roast with mustard
cream sauce 154
cream 121
creamy turkey stew with mustard 59
mustard-crusted rack of veal 421

N

navarin of lamb 369
noodles 480
crisp hot and sweet beef with 74
vietnamese beef pho 397
nutmeg 481

O

oil 481
okra 481
chicken, chorizo and okra gumbo 263
curry 216
lamb and okra in rich tomato sauce
with garlic confit 251

old-fashioned curried sausages 35
olive and parsley couscous 315
onions 481
    caramelised onion brown rice 272–3
orange and maple glazed
    baby carrots 468
orange flower water 479
orange gremolata 414
orange poached pears 109
oregano 481
    oregano lamb stew with gnocchi 82
osso buco 417
oxtail
    braised oxtail in peanut sauce 237
    braised, with orange gremolata 414
    oxtail stew with red wine
        and port 188
oyster sauce 481
    steamed gai lan in 466

P

panang lamb curry 330
pancetta 481
    duck legs with pancetta and
        white beans 307
    pistachio, pancetta and
        fig-stuffed lamb 429
paprika 481
parmesan cheese croûtons 102
parsley 481
    dumplings 117
parsnip 481
    roasted caramelised 468
passionfruit filling 169
pasta 481
    braised rabbit sauce with
        fettuccine 284
    pasta, bacon and vegetable soup 85
    pastitsio 299
    spinach and ricotta lasagne 219
pastitsio 299
pastry sheets 481
patty-pan squash 481
peanuts 481
    braised oxtail in peanut sauce 237

pears
    orange poached 109
    poached pears and quince with
        almond crumble 398
    pork neck with cider and pear 329
peas 481–2
    fresh, with caraway and
        parmesan 469
    lamb stew with artichoke and 333
    mash 175
    pea and ham soup 40
    spanish rice and 315
pecans 482
    maple syrup pork belly
        with pecans 366
pepitas 482
petite sale aux lentilles (salted pork
    with lentils) 206
pie/s
    beef and shiitake mushroom 166
    beef carbonade 288
pilaf, chicken and asparagus 101
pine nuts 482
    garlicky beans with pine nuts 466
pistachios 482
    couscous 372
    pistachio, pancetta and
        fig-stuffed lamb 429
poach 482
polenta 482
    soft 313
pomegranate 482
poppy seeds 482
pork 482
    andalusian 209
    apples, pork and prunes 141
    asian broth with crisp pork belly 138
    asian-style braised pork neck 300
    barbecued american-style
        pork ribs 47
    beans and beer, with 382
    cider roasted pork belly 430
    italian braised 434
    italian pork and capsicum ragù 48
    lemon grass and pork curry 51
    maple syrup pork belly
        with pecans 366

(pork continued)
    mexican pull-apart pork 180
    neck with cider and pear 329
    pork and green olive stew 326
    pork and vegetable vindaloo 260
    pork belly and chorizo stew 94
    pork, chicken and black-eyed bean
        cassoulet 304
    pork, mushroom and marsala
        stew 256
    pork neck, orange and white
        bean stew 91
    prosciutto-wrapped pork and
        veal meatloaf 145
    red bean, pork and rice 142
    red pork curry 326
    slow-roasted honey and soy
        pork neck 433
    sour pork curry 303
    sticky asian glaze, with 78
    twice-cooked asian pork belly
        with steamed ginger rice 440
portuguese cladeirada 29
portuguese-style chicken 340
pot roast, chicken and artichoke 94
potatoes 482
    beef rib roast with roasted beetroot
        and potatoes puree 405
    capsicum mash 175
    cheesy mash 174
    country-style beef and potato
        casserole 69
    greek-style lamb with 346
    hasselback 172
    herb and olive fish fillets on
        potato 437
    lamb and potato stew with
        spinach 29
    lebanese lamb and potato bake 122
    leg of lamb on lemon-scented
        potatoes 437
    pea mash 175
    potato and leek soup 234
    potato and olive-filled banana
        chillies 161
    potato crush 173
    potatoes anna 173

(*potatoes* continued)
roast 81, 172
tuna potato bake 158
preserved lemon rind 482
couscous 314
gremolata 55
prosciutto 482
chicken stuffed with ricotta, basil
and prosciutto 451
prosciutto-wrapped pork and
veal meatloaf 145
provencale beef casserole 66
pudding
quince sponge 463
steamed ginger 276
sticky date and fig 224
pulao, classic 312
pumpkin and eggplant dhal 73

Q

quince 482
lamb and quince tagine with
pistachio couscous 372
poached pears and quince with
almond crumble 398
quince and chicken tagine 390
sticky quince roasted lamb 402
quince paste 482

R

rabbit
braised rabbit sauce with
fettuccine 284
stew 91
radicchio 482
ragù
alla bolognese 280
italian pork and capsicum 48
mushroom 422
slow-cooked lamb shank
and bean 134
raisins 480
lamb and potato stew with spinach 29

(*raisins* continued)
moroccan lamb with kumara
and raisins 26
raita 482
ras el hanout 482
ratatouille
baked chicken with 149
roasted root vegetable 165
red pork curry 326
rhubarb 482
rhubarb and orange compote 354
rice 482–3 *see also* risotto
baltic lamb and rice meatballs 195
caramelised onion brown rice 272–3
chicken and asparagus pilaf 101
classic pulao 312
date and apricot creamy rice 110
red bean, pork and rice 142
spanish rice and peas 315
steamed ginger 440
rich chocolate cake 353
ricotta and capsicum bake 456
risotto *see also* rice
baked prawn, asparagus and
broad bean 157
mushroom 350
roast potatoes 81, 172
roasted root vegetable ratatouille 165
roasting/toasting 483
rocket 483
rogan josh 375
romesco sauce, seafood in 343
rosemary 483
veal and rosemary casserole 184

S

saffron 483
spicy tomato and saffron chicken
casserole 55
sage 483
veal with balsamic sage sauce 323
sake 483
salad
braised lamb shanks with tzatziki
and tomato salad 128–9

(*salad* continued)
confit of salmon with herb
salad 455
wild rice salad with spinach
and figs 314
salted pork with lentils (petite sale
aux lentilles) 206
sambal oelek 483
sauce
butterscotch 224
cheese 299
tomato 161
sausages
bollito misto 259
mexican beans with 238
old-fashioned curried sausages 35
petite sale aux lentilles (salted pork
with lentils) 206
seafood 483
baked prawn, asparagus and
broad bean risotto 157
confit of salmon with herb salad 455
creamy crab and tomato bisque 393
fish stock 471
herb and olive fish fillets
on potato 437
portuguese cladeirada 29
roasted salmon with mango and
lime mayonnaise 459
romesco sauce, in 343
smoky octopus stew with red wine
and olives 394
tuna potato bake 158
segmenting 483
self-saucing pudding, chocolate 63
semolina 483
sesame seeds 483
sherry 483
shredded beef tacos 23
shredded spanish beef 97
sichuan peppercorns 481
silver beet 484
simple beef and vegetable casserole 16
slow-cooked duck with cabbage
and fennel 444
slow-cooked lamb shank and
bean ragù 134

slow-roasted beef and garlic with mustard cream 121
slow-roasted beef shanks 296
slow-roasted duck with balsamic glazed vegetables 448
slow-roasted honey and soy pork neck 433
slow-roasted turkey with wild rice seasoning 443
smoky chickpea and tomato soup 223
smoky octopus stew with red wine and olives 394
soup
  beef and barley 233
  beef and vegetable 105
  cauliflower 203
  chicken, porcini and barley 334
  cream of chicken soup with parmesan cheese croûtons 102
  cream of roasted fennel soup with capsicum aïoli 460
  creamy crab and tomato bisque 393
  creamy semi-dried tomato and veal 362
  cuban black bean 199
  italian chicken soup 52
  lamb shank 365
  lamb shank, fennel and vegetable 192
  minestrone 376
  minted broad bean and ham 255
  mulligatawny soup with chicken 210
  pasta, bacon and vegetable 85
  pea and ham 40
  potato and leek soup 234
  shredded lamb and pumpkin 32
  slow-cooked lamb and white bean 242
  smoky chickpea and tomato 223
  spiced coriander, lentil and barley 379
  spicy lentil 32
  spring vegetable broth with cheese-filled zucchini flowers 389
south african bean curry 245
soy sauce 481
  poached chicken with soy and sesame 20

(*soy sauce* continued)
  slow-roasted honey and soy pork neck 433
spanish chicken casserole 137
spanish rice and peas 315
spice rub 434
spiced coriander, lentil and barley soup 379
spiced lentils 312
spicy caribbean-style chicken stew 267
spicy lentil soup 32
spicy tomato and saffron chicken casserole 55
spinach 484
  creamed 467
  lamb and potato stew with 29
  spinach and ricotta lasagne 219
  wild rice salad with spinach and figs 314
split peas 484
  pea and ham soup 40
  pumpkin and eggplant dhal 73
sponge topping 463
spring vegetable broth with cheese-filled zucchini flowers 389
star anise 484
stew
  beef stew with parsley dumplings 117
  chorizo, chilli and bean 187
  creamy turkey stew with mustard 59
  harissa and mint vegetable 106
  irish lamb and barley 88
  lamb and potato stew with spinach 29
  lamb neck chop and lentil stew with kumara carrot mash 292
  lamb stew with artichoke and peas 333
  moroccan-style vegetable stew with harissa 349
  oregano lamb stew with gnocchi 82
  oxtail stew with red wine and port 188
  pork and green olive 326
  pork belly and chorizo 94
  pork, mushroom and marsala 256
  pork neck, orange and white bean 91

(*stew* continued)
  rabbit 91
  smoky octopus stew with red wine and olives 394
  spicy caribbean-style chicken 267
sticky date and fig pudding 224
sticky quince roasted lamb 402
stoba, lamb 275
stocks
  beef 470
  chicken 470
  fish 471
  vegetable 471
strawberries, macerated 60
sugar 484
sultanas 484
sumac 484
swede 484
sweet and sour chicken 213
syrup 276
  brandy 308
  cherry and red wine 464

T

tabbouleh 313
tacos, shredded beef 23
tagine
  chicken tagine with dates and honey 379
  lamb and quince tagine with pistachio couscous 372
  quince and chicken 390
tamari 484
tamarind 484
tamarind concentrate 484
  lamb shanks in five spice, tamarind and ginger 114
tarragon 484
tart, baked passionfruit 169
toasted ciabatta with basil butter 362
tomatoes 484–5
  braised lamb shanks with tzatziki and tomato salad 128–9
  chilli beans with tomato sauce 220
  creamy crab and tomato bisque 393

(*tomatoes* continued)
  creamy semi-dried tomato and
    veal soup 362
  lamb and okra in rich tomato sauce
    with garlic confit 251
  sauce 161
  smoky chickpea and tomato soup 223
  spicy tomato and saffron
    chicken casserole 55
  tomato braised beans 467
  tomato-braised lamb shanks 269
  vegetable pithiviers with
    tomato sauce 162
traditional roast dinner 425
treacle 485
tuna potato bake 158
turkey
  creamy turkey stew with mustard 59
  slow-roasted turkey with wild rice
    seasoning 443
turmeric 485
twice-cooked asian pork belly with
  steamed ginger rice 440
tzatziki 128

V

vanilla 485
veal 485
  artichokes, olives and lemon,
    with 291
  balsamic sage sauce, with 323
  braised veal shoulder with
    white beans 418
  creamy semi-dried tomato and
    veal soup 362
  italian veal casserole 125
  mustard-crusted rack of 421
  osso buco 417
  prosciutto-wrapped pork and
    veal meatloaf 145
  shanks with honey and lemon 133
  shin on mushroom ragù 422
  veal and rosemary casserole 184
vegetable pithiviers with
  tomato sauce 162

vegetable stock 471
vietnamese beef pho 397
vietnamese mint 485
vindaloo, pork and vegetable 260
vinegar 485
  slow-roasted duck with balsamic
    glazed vegetables 448
  veal with balsamic sage sauce 323

W

walnuts 485
  walnut and fig cake with
    brandy syrup 308
watercress 485
white sweet potato 485
wild rice salad with spinach and figs 314
wild rice seasoning 443
witlof 485
wombok 485
worcestershire sauce 485

X

xacutti 361

Y

yeast 485
yoghurt 485
  cinnamon yoghurt cream 354
  tzatziki 128–9

Z

za'atar 485
zucchini 485
  cheese-filled zucchini flowers 389

First published in 2013 by Bauer Media Books, Sydney
Reprinted in 2014.
Bauer Media Books are published by Bauer Media Limited.

MEDIA GROUP

BAUER MEDIA BOOKS
Publisher Sally Wright
Editorial & food director Pamela Clark
Director of sales, marketing & rights Brian Cearnes
Creative director & designer Hieu Chi Nguyen
Senior editor Stephanie Kistner
Food concept director Sophia Young
Food editor Emma Braz
Writers Rose Fittler, Stephanie Kistner, Hieu Chi Nguyen
Marketing manager Bridget Cody
Senior business analyst Rebecca Varela
Business analyst Ashley Metcalfe
Operations manager David Scotto
Production controller Corinne Whitsun-Jones

Published by Bauer Media Books, a division of Bauer Media Limited,
54 Park St, Sydney; GPO Box 4088, Sydney, NSW 2001.
phone (02) 9282 8618; fax (02) 9126 3702
www.awwcookbooks.com.au

Cover photographer William Meppem
Cover stylist Vivien Walsh
Cover Osso buco, page 417.

Additional photography Ian Wallace
Additional styling Louise Pickford
Photochef Rebecca Kirk

Printed by C&C Offset Printing, China.

Australia Distributed by Network Services,
phone +61 2 9282 8777; fax +61 2 9264 3278;
networkweb@networkservicescompany.com.au
New Zealand Distributed by Bookreps NZ Ltd,
phone +64 9 419 2635; fax +64 9 419 2634;
www.bookreps.co.nz
South Africa Distributed by PSD Promotions,
phone +27 11 392 6065/6/7; fax +27 11 392 6079/80;
orders@psdprom.co.za

Title: Cook it slow / food director Pamela Clark
ISBN: 978-1-74245-361-3 (pbk.)
Notes: Includes index.
Subjects: Casserole cooking. Electric cooking, Slow.
Other Authors/Contributors: Clark, Pamela.
Also Titled: Australian Women's Weekly.
Dewey Number: 641.5884

© Bauer Media Limited 2013
ABN 18 053 273 546
This publication is copyright. No part of it may be reproduced or transmitted
in any form without the written permission of the publishers.

To order books
phone 136 116 (within Australia) or
order online at www.awwcookbooks.com.au

Send recipe enquiries to:
recipeenquiries@bauer-media.com.au